SONGS &
MUSIC OF THE
REDCOATS

SONGS &
MUSIC OF THE
REDCOATS

A History of the War Music of
the British Army 1642—1902

Lewis Winstock

LEO COOPER   LONDON

First published in Great Britain 1970
by Leo Cooper Ltd
47 Museum Street, London W.C.1
Copyright © 1970 Lewis Winstock

ISBN 0 85052-003-7

Printed in Great Britain by
Lowe & Brydone (Printers) Ltd., London

To my Mother

Contents

Musical Examples

Introduction

WAR MUSIC: THE POOR RELATION
OF A RICH MILITARY HERITAGE

S ONGS AND MUSIC OF THE REDCOATS is a history of the war music of the British Army from the mid-seventeenth century to the end of the Boer War in 1902. The first date has been chosen simply because few reliable records of war music exist earlier than the Civil War – the second, because the years after 1902 are already soundly documented*. Surprisingly perhaps, the present work is the first to attempt a continuous history of the music that has been part of Britain's wars.

It should be made clear in the beginning that by 'war music' is meant the songs and music that were an integral part of military events – that were played on the march, in camp, sometimes even in combat. Our concern is with the songs sung by the soldiers themselves, and with the instrumental music that was actually played in war – by fifes and drums, and by bands**. But there are other objectives. The role of music in war – why there was singing or playing at all, or why particular tunes were played on particular occasions – is studied, as well as the ways in which British war music influenced, and was influenced by, the music of our friends and our enemies. Finally, the book examines the attitudes of great figures in our military history to war music.

---

*In such works as THE LONG TRAIL, J.P. Brophy and E. Partridge.
**A study of signalling music – e.g., the blowing and beating of a charge, or reveille – is not included here.

Categorically and emphatically, this is not a history of regimental marches except in so far as a few of them have direct associations with war. Still less is it a history of music that is military only by courtesy of having been scored for military bands. Nor does it concern itself with the form of military bands — how and when they began and developed, or who composed for them or conducted them. It disregards the songs *about* wars, battles, commanders and soldiers which lie thick in ballad collections masquerading as songs *of* war.

SONGS AND MUSIC OF THE REDCOATS has been written from the standpoint of the fighting men themselves. It tries to recreate their music as they knew it, so that a reincarnated "Tom Lobster" could unfailingly beat time to the marches and whistle the choruses printed here. Other works have studied the music of sailors, miners, cowboys, navvies, and lumberjacks, recording their rhythms of work and leisure, and these books have been regarded (rightly) as contributions to the field of folk music. This book is, by the same logic, a work on folk music; it shows what a certain class of labouring man chose to sing and play while involved in the very real work of war. (The days when folk music meant exclusively anonymous compositions handed down by oral tradition have long passed).

Folk music, established procedure insists, is best collected "in the field". Ideally, this means that some hoary fisherman or miner is primed with a few ales in the comforts of a pub and then, under the gentle guidance of the collector, sings all for the tape recorder. And indeed, this is a pleasant enough technique. But the singers of Blenheim and Badajoz are long dead and their oral tradition lost and buried with them. As the singers were not available for interview (except in a few cases noted below), their words have been read instead of heard.

Memoirs and diaries of soldiers (and civilians) have been the richest source of material. These ear-witness accounts have been supplemented by contemporary papers and pamphlets, by a few MS songbooks compiled by soldiers, and by conversations with veterans whose military careers fell within the period of this book. There has also been a wary reliance on tradition. Tradition, once defined as the oral transmission of knowledge or belief from one generation to another, now implies as often as not, some ill-conceived notion foisted on later generations by slapdash scholars, or by amiable romantics to whom the wish was father to the fact. If just two traditional tales surrounding war music are examined, it will be readily seen why tradition has been treated with suspicion.

There is the tradition, for example, that *Sir Manley Power*, the quick march of the old 57th Regiment, the West Middlesex, was a tune found by an officer of that name in a French camp during the Napoleonic Wars. But *Sir Manley Power* is so clearly a variant of the English air *Soldier, soldier, won't you marry me?* that we are forced to assume that either the French found the tune in an English camp first before Sir Manley recaptured it, or that this particular "tradition" is nonsense. Yet another bewhiskered tale proposes that *We've lived and loved together* passed into the repertoire of the 11th Regiment, the Devonshires, on an occasion in the Peninsular War when they played it in the presence of a passing French regiment whom, charitably, they did not choose to fight at that time. But no officer of the regiment ever seems to have taken the story seriously, and research has not revealed the origins of this "tradition". It should long ago have been mercifully smothered in a blanket of silence ; there are enough noble and well-founded traditions in the Army for the fables to be rejected without a tear.

Ballad collections, as stated on p. ii, have rated very low as source material, for the appearance there of a song even fifty times guarantees only that it was a favourite with civilians at home. A song or march has required supporting approval from a soldier's own pen, or at least from a civilian other than the publisher of the ballad book, to earn a place in this collection, although some of the resulting omissions and conclusions may surprise and disappoint readers. It may also seem to readers that the dates recorded for the first appearance of a song or march as *war music*, are much later than more tradition-directed studies have indicated. This is because it has not been taken for granted that a song written at the beginning of the 18th century and a favourite in the Napoleonic Wars 90 years later was necessarily adopted by the troops in the intervening years. The probability that such was the case is in fact high, but so many such probabilities seem to have been shamelessly abused in the few existing studies of military and war music, that a more conservative approach has been adopted here.

If the approach of SONGS AND MUSIC OF THE REDCOATS is conservative in one way, it is generous in another. Footnotes are liberal, and this is deliberate. Dates, facts, and circumstances for this book have often been extraordinarily difficult to come by, since too high a proportion of military historians, and musicologists, have been notoriously lax about documenting sources. As a result, despite the co-operation of the British Museum, the London Library, the National Army Museum, the Institute of War Studies, and the Royal United Service Institution, certain works mentioned by earlier writers have never been found. Who, for example, was that Pigot who around 1843 wrote (or compiled) SONGS FOR SOLDIERS, and when did Jackson write CURIOSITIES OF WAR, and why wasn't either awarded a Christian name for his achievements? Because it has so often been difficult to get at original sources, care has been taken in the present work to footnote every fact about British Army music — footnoted from the earliest accessible source, not from the secondary reference that may have led us to it. With sources at last in the open, facts may be checked and theories examined by anyone who is interested. In the treatment of primary material, two small liberties have been taken; punctuation has been modernised, and "souldiers going to the antient warres" have been made to do so in contemporary spelling.

That there has not yet been a definitive study of British war music is a strange hiatus in military history — an omission lamented as long ago as 1934 by Sir John Fortescue in THE LAST POST.[1] "It is rather shameful that we should pass from *Lilliburlero* to *Tipperary*, from Marlborough to Haig by the solitary stepping stone of *Over the hills and far away*." By Fortescue's standards it is a strange piece — less a scholarly study than an exercise in thinking aloud. On the one hand he regrets that no quantity of English military music survives and that there are no historians willing to approach the subject, and on the other, promptly deters any possible candidates for the job with a discouraging list of qualifications. The historian required by Fortescue was to be a thoroughly accomplished musician able to read a modern orchestral score and Elizabethan MS with equal facility, a theorist and preferably a performer on all wind instruments and the drums, and a scholar of the general and regimental history of the Army. Not incidentally, he was also to be blessed with copious leisure. The only scholar in the field who approximated Sir John's qualifications was the late Dr. Henry G. Farmer who wrote MEMOIRS OF THE ROYAL ARTILLERY BAND (1904), THE RISE OF MILITARY MUSIC (1912),

MILITARY MUSIC (1950) and many excellent articles, particularly in the JOURNAL OF THE SOCIETY FOR ARMY HISTORICAL RESEARCH. His work has often been invaluable in pointing the way to material for this book, but it is fair to say that his interests lay predominantly with the band and its instruments, rather than with music in the context of war.

There is little other literature in the field. Some general works on military customs and traditions have glanced at the subject in passing, but they fell short of the standards of scholarship set by Dr. Farmer, and contain little that is new. Even the considerable number of books on the bagpipe, describing its role in war, suffer the usual problem of inadequate documentation and it is difficult to distinguish between fact and tradition (or the fiction that passes as tradition). Only Major Ian MacKay Scobie's PIPERS AND PIPE MUSIC IN A HIGHLAND REGIMENT (1924) is adequate in this respect but unfortunately it is restricted to one corps, the Seaforth Highlanders. Further, the one work written on regimental marches does not yield much material. In 1896, Walter Wood wrote an article for the PALL MALL GAZETTE entitled THE ROMANCE OF REGIMENTAL MARCHES and was soundly attacked for his careless scholarship. But in 1932 Mr. Wood, undeterred, or perhaps assuming that his critics had died off, published a book with the same title. Its contents showed that like the Bourbons he had learned nothing and forgotten nothing, and Dr. Farmer called his work with some charity, "more romance than history".[2] To this day no-one has attempted to remedy its shortcomings with a more definitive work and thus, the only published work on regimental marches gives no illumination to our subject.

That so little material exists in accessible form (with the exception of the bagpipes) can to a large extent be blamed on the Army itself. This is not to suggest that no-one cared — witness the pages of the JSAHR — but that little seems to have been done by those with the position and authority to have achieved most. It would be a macabre experiment to try to measure who has done more (or less) to preserve the old war music — the Army's central authority or the individual corps. Counsel for the War Office might point out that as long ago as 1835 the Horse Guards, realizing that fine old British marches were being supplanted by foreign imports of no recognizable merit, made a praiseworthy effort to check the trend. And indeed, they did forbid Grenadier and Fusilier regiments to play imported airs on ceremonial occasions. So far so good. But rather than encouraging alternative marches distinctive to each unit, they then forced upon the whole lot *The Grenadiers March*[3]. Counsel might also point out that in the 1880's the War Office required that quick-steps should be registered, and all regiments were instructed to file their marches at the War Office along with relevant historical data. Unfortunately, few colonels had an historical conscience, and although the music came in, there was not much in the way of accompanying historical fact. Whitehall might well have pressed for more background—colonels no longer enjoyed the same degree of autonomy they had thirty years earlier — but seems to have contented itself with the original gesture. There was some sifting and weeding of the material but the outcome was unimaginative. "Official recognition was given not to those marches that with a little delving, could have been revived as the traditional marches but simply to those in use at the time, which revealed a motley assortment," wrote Dr. Farmer, adding with justifiable contempt: "these were approved and published on an auspicious day — 1st April, 1883".[4]

Before the codification of 1883 it had been distressingly easy for fine old tunes to be discarded. A band sergeant who was with the 4th Regiment for more than thirty years and who enlisted in 1836 said that nearly every new colonel, new adjutant, or new bandmaster adopted a different march-past.[5] This craze for novelty saw many fine old marches like the 55th's *Bronze horse*, the 86th's *Ballycarrick slashers*, and the 99th's *Kinloch of Kinloch*, unceremoniously dumped on the rubbish heap.[6] Once these marches were played no more, they were spoken of less and less, until their historic associations were finally forgotten and lost forever.

The correspondence columns in the BRITISH BANDSMAN and BRITISH MUSICIAN of the time showed that some soldiers were alarmed by the offhand manner in which these tunes were discarded, but the correspondents were powerless to check it. Many of the colonels were not so much indifferent to the old music as positively hostile to it; simply by failing to register some tunes, they accepted the registration of 1883 as a fine opportunity to sink undesirable marches without trace. And indeed, there was a definite tendency to pretend towards the end of the century, that Army music had been improved (see p. 274) by this disappearance of unrefined material from a barbarous past. Although this lamentable attitude has long since changed, it is remarkable how few regimental histories published today contain information about the regimental music. At best, the regiment's contemporary marches are all that one finds, with little if any additional information about their date of adoption or history.

If it was difficult to preserve old marches, which had at least some sort of official recognition, it was infinitely harder to keep regimental songs alive, although a great number existed, and some are given in this book, in various degrees of entirety. In 1871, A. Wyatt Edgell published A COLLECTION OF SOLDIERS' SONGS, but the collection is less significant than the foreword: "When I began to collect military songs I hoped to obtain at least one song from each regiment that would record its service and history, but in this I have failed signally. The collection I have here to offer, derived from different sources, is so imperfect, that I should hesitate to publish it did I not hope that it may induce everyone whose favourite song is omitted to send it to me for insertion in a future edition."

A fruitless hope – no second edition ever appeared. Unfortunately for the present work, the songs Wyatt Edgell collected were mostly *about* soldiers, with only a minority the genuine articles that were sung *by* soldiers. An even sadder experience befell Miss Laura Alexandrine Smith of Baker Street, at a time when the protests about vanishing army music hung heavily in the air. Encouraged by the publication in 1886 of a volume of sailors' songs entitled MUSIC OF THE WATERS, she tried in the 1890's to compile a companion volume of soldiers' songs, requesting contributions through the columns of NOTES AND QUERIES. The replies she received were few and discouraging – the poor lady deserved a better reception for her worthwhile venture – and the projected book never saw the light of day. In 1896, John Farmer in his collection, SCARLET AND BLUE OR SONGS FOR SOLDIERS AND SAILORS, was able to include only thirteen "regimental songs . . . collected throughout the service." But as no less than seven of these songs were composed by a mysterious "K.R.", it does not seem likely that they were genuine army songs. More probably, K.R. was a busy lyricist trying to induce soldiers to sing his verses, and there is no evidence to suggest that they did. In 1889 F. J. Crowest, a prominent writer on music, made an impassioned plea for literature on army music which "as a phase in the country's art . . . deserves some record at the hands of the historian and musical writer,"[7] but like everyone else who approached the subject he received negligible encouragement from those who should have been most concerned – the soldiers themselves. Even the Royal Military School of Music at Kneller Hall, Twickenham, has never been able to supply a positive lead. Founded in 1857, Kneller Hall has trained generations of superbly efficient bandsmen, but its function has remained exactly what its name implies – a school, a place of technical education. No government largesse has provided adequate finances for it to become a library, an archive, or a research centre in army music. Any modest achievements in these areas have been a labour of love by individuals on its staff. If the home of British military music was unable to assume a strong, informed leadership, the likelihood that colonels, bandmasters, or regiments would do so was remote.

A final word should be added here about the philosophy behind this edition. SONGS AND MUSIC OF THE REDCOATS is the result of an open-ended research programme. The work is not yet completed. Virtually everything written by and about soldiers may be relevant to this study, but (although over 600 printed volumes have been consulted) there has been opportunity to see too few MSS, and only too limited a use could be made of the countless regimental magazines that have been published. There are bound to be omissions and shortcomings in the following pages. Not only this, but much of the information is unavoidably fragmentary – words for which no music could be found, titles for which there were neither words nor music, couplets where one would have hoped for verses.

The author, therefore, hopes that suggestions and contributions will be made by readers of this volume. It is to be desired that a second edition will see facts added, amplified, and if necessary, amended. Perhaps this sounds like the conscious echo of poor Wyatt Edgell, whose enthusiasm and optimism received such slight reward, but it would be a pity if SONGS AND MUSIC OF THE REDCOATS failed to provoke any constructive response. But whatever its fate, this first attempt to write a continuous history of the music that has been part of Britain's wars remains a long overdue undertaking.

1. Sir J. Fortescue, *The Last Post*, ed. P. Guedalla, (1934).
2. *Grove's Dictionary of Music* (1954) V, p.567.
3. War Office General Orders, 19th August, 1835.
4. *Grove's*, V, p.566.
5. *British Musician* (September, 1896), p.205.
6. *Ibid*, p. 205.
7. *National Review* (May, 1889).

Chapter 1

THE CIVIL WARS 1642–1655

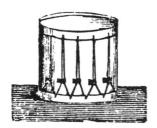

ALTHOUGH our study properly begins with the Civil Wars, the history of war music in England could be said to start in 1066. In that year, before the general fighting at Hastings, a Norman named Taillefer, more blessed with high spirits than common sense, rode out from the ranks and entertained his comrades by juggling his lance and singing from *La chanson de Roland*. Perhaps his act was bad – history does not say – but when some humourless Englishmen tried to end his cabaret he lived up to his name – "Iron cutter" – by killing two of them before he himself was slain.[1]

Apart from having songs like the *Song of Roland* to rouse their spirits in the field the Normans also had a place for music in the ceremony of war. When William I died his troublesome half-brother Odo, Bishop of Bayeux, contested the succession of the Conqueror's son Rufus, and only after considerable effort was Odo evicted from Rochester Castle. Because the castle had not actually been stormed Odo asked that the royal trumpeters should not sound a fanfare as his garrison marched out – "the custom when an enemy is conquered or a fortress is taken by assault." But Rufus, exploding into one of the fierce rages for which all his family were famous, swore that no such concession would be made, not even for one thousand marks in gold. And so, at the appointed time, Odo and his rebels evacuated the castle with royal trumpets blaring triumphantly in their ears.[2]

Unfortunately, although illuminating incidents like this do appear in medieval chronicles, they are few and far between and no continuous history of war music in the Middle Ages is feasible. An average of one sketchy reference for each reign with no indication of what the music sounded like would quickly make tedious reading – rather like a history of art with no illustrations.

The only logical starting point for a sustained history of war music in fact, must be the Civil Wars. The conflict between Crown and Parliament which began in 1642 and petered out with Penruddock's Rising of 1655, is the first to be described extensively and in depth by contemporaries. Engagements were reported in detail as fast as they took place – not only major battles like Edgehill, Marston Moor and Naseby, but also countless skirmishes fought out all over the country by local partisans.

These accounts were published as broadsheets, and the writers were often eye-witnesses or even participants, so that the "true and perfect relation" headlines borne by many of these dingy little sheets were not idle boasts; that is, in so far as an account of a battle by a writer involved on one side or the other can ever be quite true. To give some idea of the volume of source material which exists, the major collection of Civil War pamphlets – the Thomason Tracts in the British Museum – comprises over 17,000 items for the years 1642–1655, of which around half refer to military events. Quite apart from these pamphlets, many participants in the long-drawn struggle kept diaries or wrote memoirs when the fighting was over.

It is not unreasonable to suppose that the Civil Wars had a rich musical flavour, at least on the Royalist side. Charles I, after all, was supported by some outstanding ballad writers (notably Martin Parker and John Taylor), and a number of promising titles, such as *Prince Rupert's March* and *When the king enjoys his own again*, do exist. Moreover, the cavaliers were traditionally a jolly crew, come weal or woe. But this vast collection of tracts, so rich in human-interest stories that they might be expected to reflect something of the music of the cavaliers, regrettably provides spiceless fare.

Nevertheless, one incident, which is perhaps typical of many that went unmarked, runs true to the swashbuckling form expected of the cavaliers. In 1645 the cavalry of Sir William Waller, a tenacious Parliament veteran of the German wars, executed a successful raid on Devizes in Wiltshire. They caught the Royalists unprepared and in a blistering charge slashed and pistolled their way through the streets at will. When the raid was over a group of indignant cavaliers gathered in the quarters of a Welsh captain named John Gwyn to see what should be done. Gwyn was a real-life Fluellen, brave and effervescent, and respected as a soldier for his efforts to hold Tenby in Pembrokeshire against long odds. After two hours heated discussion the cavaliers decided to save face with an unofficial counter attack and twenty seven of them rode over the downs to Marlborough ten miles away, to smash Waller's rearguard camped unsuspectingly on the outskirts of the town. It was agreed that after swords had been drawn not a word was to be spoken but they were to fall on, one and all, singing "a brisk lively tune". True to plan, they charged in at noon on market day, singing lustily, and to the great delight of the countryfolk drove the astounded Parliament men through the streets before returning unscathed to Devizes with a haul of prisoners, horses, and weapons.[3] The "brisk lively tune" which so braced their hearts was similar to the Scottish air *Up in the morning early*, and if this was the thought it conveyed in 1645 its message to the roundheads is quite obvious.

I

Tune from John Gwyn's *Memoirs*

MUSIC   Traditional
SOURCE   J. Gwyn – Military Memoirs

Other references to Royalist music are meagre. This does not mean that they were without music for a pamphlet printed at Tavistock in 1645 describing a Royalist retreat says that they "fled without beat of drum or sound of trumpet" implying that their movements were usually accompanied by martial sounds.[4] A Royalist writer also mentions "trumpets prattling their marches" before Donnington Castle in Oxfordshire.[5] But these are the sole direct references to the King's music that have been found in pamphlet literature.

The Puritan cause is considerably better served, and the most emphatic feature of Parliamentary music is a fondness for psalm singing. In Thomas Shadwell's THE VOLUNTEERS (1693) the old cavalier Major General Blunt recalls how the Puritans "used to sing a psalm, fall on, and beat us to the devil",[6] a portrait that many survivors of the wars would easily recognize. A number of contemporary pamphlets assert that the roundheads were incorrigible psalm singers, both in defence and on the attack. In 1642 James Stanley, Earl of Derby, who thought that any Parliament activity in Lancashire was a direct affront to his personal dignity, advanced against Manchester, and although his Cheshire levies deserted, considering it no part of their obligation to follow the noble Earl out of their own county, he still had sufficient troops to invest the town. For eleven wet autumn weeks Derby hung on, while the Puritan defenders kept up their morale by daily prayer meetings and psalm sessions on street corners, rather in the fashion of the present-day Salvation Army.[7] There was also a good deal of religious singing in taverns and inns, "where it might not put in the head formerly".[8] The grammar of this phrase leaves something to be desired, but the message is plainly that such haunts usually pulsated to more secular rhythms, so presumably during the siege the taverns were the billets of god-fearing soldiers. Before Parliament troops under Sir Thomas Fairfax stormed Leeds in January 1643 they were led by Jonathan Schofield, minister of Crofton chapel at Halifax, in the 68th Psalm, *"Let God arise and His enemies shall be scattered"*.[9] At the second Battle of Newbury in October 1644 they actually advanced to the sound of psalms,[10] although with little success, for the forces of the Earl of Essex, Sir William Waller and Oliver Cromwell himself failed to rout a smaller Royalist force, although they fought on after dark. The roundheads' appeal to the God of Battles had been more successful the previous June at Marston Moor; there, after a preliminary bombardment, they chanted psalms in the cornfields,[11] and when the day was assured they sang again in circumstances vividly described by John Vicars, one of the best Parliament pamphleteers.

Marston Moor, was an unusual battle, inasmuch as it did not start until 7.30 in the evening, when Cromwell precipitated an action that took Prince Rupert and, more predictably, the Earl of Newcastle quite by surprise. It was also odd because Cromwell's Ironsides, who began the day on the Parliament left wing facing north, ended it – after scattering Rupert's opposing horse and completing a semi-circular clockwise tour of the field – facing south in the position originally held by the Royalist George Goring. Goring's riders meanwhile, who had chased their first opponents off the field, trickled back to find Cromwell on their ground. It was now their turn to face north, but only briefly, for they were soon in headlong flight back the way they had come. In this confusing and fluid situation, with night falling and the air heavy with the smoke of black powder, a band of Royalist fugitives inadvertently blundered into Cromwell's position "where some of the regiments of horse . . . were religiously singing of psalms". Not until that moment did the Royalists realize their mistake, "for they only knew them . . . to be the Parliament soldiers by their singing of psalms". And Vicars ends piously : "a blessed badge and cognisance indeed".[12]

Probably the most famous of all psalm singing in these wars – it fired the imagination of both Thomas Carlyle and John Buchan – occurred at Dunbar in 1650. Cromwell had allowed the Scottish General Leslie to trap him on a narrow coastal plain ; the only escape was to embark on a fleet lying offshore and retreat to England. But Leslie abandoned his strong position – intending to prevent this small-scale Dunkirk – and Cromwell, who had "much hope in the Lord" now declared that He had delivered the Scots into his hands. A dawn attack – as unexpected as the evening advance at Marston Moor – wrecked the fine Scots army, and as they fled Cromwell halted his Ironsides for the 117th psalm ;

Oh give you praise to the Lord.
All nations that be.

On first sight it might seem that piety had vanquished common sense, and a good opportunity to push home a relentless pursuit had been squandered, but the key to the story lies in one sentence : "By the time they had done their party was increasing and advancing".[13] It was Cromwell, of course, who reputedly told his men to put their trust in God but to keep their powder dry, and at Dunbar he is seen following his own advice. Helmets were doffed and thanks dutifully offered to Jehovah, Lord God of Battles, but the pause also provided a convenient opportunity for blown horses to gather second wind, for stragglers to come up, and for the Lieutenant General to have a quick think about the next move. In his very first battle at Edgehill, eight years before, Cromwell had learned the military imperative of keeping his cavalry together after a successful charge. On that occasion he had seen Rupert's failure to keep his cavalry intact dissipate a valuable tactical advantage ; Marston Moor might have gone a different way if Goring's horse had not streamed away in joyous and pointless pursuit of the broken Parliament right. Psalm singing, as practised at Dunbar, was not only good religion; it was also sound tactics.

Apart from psalms the Parliamentarians had other sorts of religious songs, one of which is mentioned in a context that is not without dry humour. In August 1642 the roundheads descended on Canterbury in a fury of anti-episcopal zeal, bent on an orgy of vandalism against the Cathedral. As a rule they wrecked church organs out of hand on these forays, but at Canterbury they stopped short and someone began to play *The zealous soldier*, but so hamfistedly that the instrument never sounded right again.[14]

1st verse

For God and for His cause I'll count it gain
To lose my life. Oh can one happier die,
Than for to fall in battle to maintain
God's worship, truth, extirpate Popery?
I fight not for to venge myself nor yet
For coin, but God's true worship up to set.

10th verse

Sing to the Lord a psalm of praise and thanks,
And to His holy temple let us bring
An heart unspotted; let's an echo raise
Which our loud voices may to nations ring,
Far distant from us, chanting loudly thus,
Praise be the Lord that hath assisted us.[15]

It is worth mentioning that one of England's foremost composers of hymns, George Wither, was a staunch Parliament supporter who laid aside his pen to raise a troop of horse and subsequently become governor of Farnham Castle in Hampshire. It seems probable that his men would have flattered their captain by singing his verses but no direct references to this were found.

The psalm and hymn singing of the soldiers can be easily understood if it is remembered that many of them were fighting from genuine religious conviction. The 17th century was a time when most men were believers to whom devotions came naturally. In addition, the example of the Protestant armies in Germany during the Thirty Years War exerted a strong influence on every possible department of the British military scene. Tactics were borrowed from Gustavus Adolphus, stakes used against cavalry became "Swedish feathers", and a particularly unpleasant brutality was administering "Swedish punch". This imitation extended to religious services. In the army of Gustavus they had been held morning and night, their hour signalled "by sound of trumpet playing the tune of some psalm, unto which the other trumpets shall likewise answer in the tune of a psalm, and so shall the drums of every regiment".[16] (The roundheads never seem to have attempted instrumental accompaniment to their singing). And before the battle of Lutzen the Swedish king and his troops sang three hymns, including Luther's *A mighty fortress is our God.*

Despite their reputation for piety not all the Parliament soldiers can be lumped together as gloomy Puritans, and anecdotes show that they knew and liked secular music. The first of these concerns the distinguished Oxford antiquary and historian Anthony à Wood who, as a young man of 22, disguised himself as a country fiddler and with some kindred spirits played at Faringdon Fair in Berkshire and other nearby towns. On their way home from one such expedition the gentlemen-minstrels were overtaken by a band of soldiers and commanded to halt. Had this been Germany in the Thirty Years War, or most other European countries for that matter, the fate of the musicians is easy enough to imagine. If they were very lucky they would have been robbed and beaten ; if they were moderately fortunate they would have been robbed, beaten, and stripped naked ; if they were unlucky they would have been summarily butchered. In England, however, the soldiers merely "forced them to play in the open field and left them without giving them a penny". Mr. à Wood seems to have considered this so appalling an atrocity that he could never bear to talk about it afterwards.[17] A second story is set in Scotland soon after Dunbar, when General George Monk and his army were holding the country for Parliament. A Scotswoman, hailed before the dreary elders of her Presbyterian kirk on a charge of rowdyism, pleaded not guilty, and laid the blame on the roundhead soldiers. They had neither raped, robbed, not rioted on her premises but they "brought over a piper with them and did dance".[18] Finally, there is the case of the organ wreckers at Exeter who played unspecified tunes on the organ pipes they had stolen, and jeered at the choirboys : "We have spoiled your trade. You must go and sing *Hot pudding pies*".[19] Clearly they meant that there would be no more accompanied church music, but whether *Hot pudding pies* was a street cry and pie-vending was all that the future held for the ex-choristers, or whether it was the name of a popular song that the roundheads knew is a mystery.

So far, the music of the Civil Wars has not been strictly military but it is safe to say that two fine marches were heard regularly throughout the period, although no contemporary writer says so directly. The first of these was the traditional *English March* which held a special place in the heart of that precise little monarch, Charles I. In 1632 he issued a warrant that left no doubt of this. "Whereas the ancient custom of nations hath ever been to use one certain and constant form of march in the wars, whereby to be distinguished one from another. And the march of this our nation so famous in all the honourable achievement and glorious wars of this our kingdom in foreign parts (being by the approbation of strangers themselves confessed and acknowledged the best of all marches) was through negligence and carelessness of drummers, and by long discontinuance so altered and changed from the ancient gravity and majesty thereof, as it was in danger utterly to have been lost and forgotten. It pleased our late dear brother Prince Henry to revive and rectify the same by ordaining an establishment of one certain measure, which was beaten in his presence at Greenwich, anno 1610. In confirmation whereof we are graciously pleased, at the instance and humble suite of our right trusty and right well-beloved cousin and councillor Edward Viscount Wimbledon to set down and ordain this present establishment hereunder expressed. Willing and commanding all drummers within our kingdom of England and principality of Wales exactly and precisely to observe the same, as well in this our kingdom, as abroad in the service of any foreign prince or state without any addition or alternative whatsoever. To the end that so ancient, famous and commendable a custom may be preserved as a pattern and precedent to all posterity".[20]

As Charles was so positive in his approval of this march it would be a rash cavalier captain who neglected to beat it in time of war.

2

The English March

MUSIC Traditional
SOURCE Sir J. Hawkins – History of Music

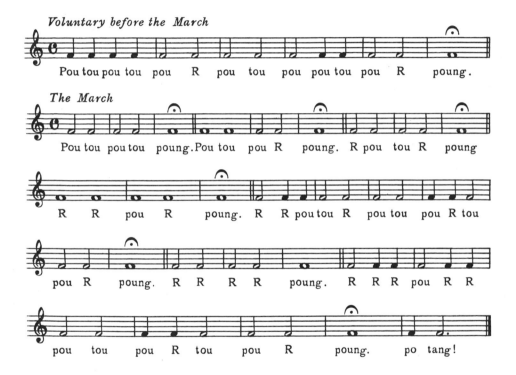

The statement about the fame of the march "in all the honourable achievement and glorious wars . . . in foreign parts" may not be mere bombast. There is a story (although it appears in print only in 1684) that at the end of the 16th century the French Marshal Biron had criticised the march for being slow, and had been sharply reminded by Sir Roger Williams that slow or not it had been heard through the length and breadth of France.[21] Admittedly, the conversation between Biron and Williams may never have taken place at all, or if it did, Sir Roger's history may have been exaggerated but on the other hand, it may just be possible that *The English March* does go back to the Hundred Years War.

The other march that was heard in the Civil Wars was *The Scots March* – probably played indiscriminately by the armies that aided the Parliament cause in 1644 and those which fought for the Royalists at Preston, Dunbar, and Worcester, because it was very much a national and not a partisan tune. It was this march that bothered Samuel Pepys on June 30th, 1667: "Here in the streets I did hear *The Scots March* beat before the soldiers which is very odd". Whether it was the musical form of the march or its use in London that disturbed the querulous Pepys is neither clear nor important, for either way he was listening to a great martial tune. There is an unsubstantiated tradition, that the march was composed in 1527 during the siege of Tantallon Castle when James V of Scotland subdued his rebel subject Archibald Douglas, and the cadence is supposed to express the sound "ding doun Tantallon".[22] What is beyond all doubt is that this was the march of the Scots Brigade which did such fine work for the Protestant cause during the Thirty Years War, first in the service of Denmark and then under Gustavus Adolphus. One of the most famous occasions when it was played was at Leipzig in 1631, when Robert Monro sounded it in the dust and smoke of battle so that his position should be known to both friend and enemy.[23]

The mere sound of this ominous march could frighten off an enemy not anxious to try conclusions with the fierce Scots, and for this reason the Swedish Chancellor Oxenstierna had it sounded by the Dutch regiments in 1632, "thinking thereby to affright the enemy". The plot misfired on this occasion and the Dutch "being charged . . . made a base retreat".[24]

The identity of *The Scots March* has been established by Dr. H. G. Farmer who demonstrated, after a scholarly struggle nearly as bitter as Lutzen or Leipzig, that it was neither *Dumbarton's drums* nor *The lowlands of Holland* but almost certainly *The Scots March* which appears in Elizabeth Rogers' Virginal Book.[25]

B*

3
The Scots March

MUSIC   Traditional
SOURCE   Elizabeth Rogers Virginal Book

1. E. A. Freeman, *The History of the Norman Conquest of England* (1869), III, p.478.
2. Ordericus Vitalis, *The Ecclesiastical History of England and Normandy* (1854), II, p.441.
3. J. Gwyn, *Military Memoirs of the Great Civil War*, ed. Sir Walter Scott (1822), p.65.
4. Thomason Tracts, E.84. (36).
5. R. Symonds, *Diary of the Marches Kept by the Royal Army during the Great Civil War* (1859), p.149.
6. Thomas Shadwell, *The Volunteers* (1693), III, i.
7. G. Ormerod, *Tracts Relating to Military Proceedings in Lancashire during the Great Civil War* (1844), p.56.
8. *Ibid*, p.120.
9. Thomason Tracts, E.88. (23).
10. Sir E. Walker, *Historical Discourses upon Several Occasions* (1705), p.113.
11. Sir H. Slingsby, *Diary* (1836), p.112.
12. J. Vicars, *Jehova Jireh* (1646), Part III, p.281.
13. J. Hodgson, *Memoirs* (1806), p.148.
14. Thomason Tracts, E.52. (10).
15. Thomason Tracts, 669.f.10. (50).
16. *The Swedish Discipline* (1632), Part II, p.14.
17. C. Burney, *A General History of Music* (1789), III, p.425.
18. Sir J. G. Dalyell, *Musical Memoirs of Scotland* (1849), p.32.
19. Thomason Tracts, E.52. (10).
20. Sir J. Hawkins, *A General History of the Science and Practice of Music* (1853), I, p.229.
21. R. Burton, *Admirable Curiosities, Rarities, and Wonders in England, Scotland and Ireland* (1684), p.7.
22. F. Grose, *Antiquities of Scotland* (1789), I, p.80.
23. R. Monro, *Expedition* (1637), Part II, p.66.
24. *Ibid*, Part II, p.113.
25. *JSAHR*, XXV (1947), pp.76–82.

Chapter 2

LILLIBURLERO AND THE WAR OF
THE SPANISH SUCCESSION
1688–1713

ALTHOUGH the music of the Civil Wars has a certain historical interest, and although it casts light on the psychological make-up of the combatants, its interest to us is primarily antiquarian, for there is no continuity between it and the subsequent development of English war music. *The English March* — which is as much a part of our military heritage as the red cross of St. George — will sound no more. English soldiers would not again spontaneously express their feelings through religious music until 1899–1902. The music of the Civil Wars is less the overture to a great opera than a self-contained curtain raiser by a different composer. Not until the end of the 17th century does the continuous performance begin.

It does so to the music of *Lilliburlero*, which became popular again in World War Two as the signature tune of a nightly BBC programme called *Into Battle* and as the unofficial march of the commando units. Today it is firmly re-established in the Army's repertoire as the march of the Royal Electrical & Mechanical Engineers, which is cause for satisfaction, since this magnificent piece of music lends itself with equal facility to a full military band, fifes and drums, or to a harpsichord, while its venerable history and associations have made it worthy of preservation.

4
Lilliburlero

WORDS Lord Thomas Wharton
MUSIC Traditional
SOURCE W. Chappell – Popular Music of the Olden Time

With a swing

Lilliburlero first attained popularity in 1688 because the strange "stage Irish" words that were set to it both reflected and inspired the growing hostility towards James II.

Ho, brother Teague, dost hear de decree?
Lilliburlero, bullen a la.
Dat we shall have a new deputy,
Lilliburlero, bullen a la.
Lero, lero, lilliburlero,
Lilliburlero, bullen a la.
Lero, lero, lilliburlero,
Lilliburlero, bullen a la.

Ho, by my shoul, it is de Talbot,
Lilliburlero, bullen a la.
And he will cut all de English throat,
Lilliburlero, bullen a la, etc.

Though, by my shoul, de English do prate,
Lilliburlero, bullen a la.
De law's on dare side, and Creish knows what,
Lilliburlero, bullen a la, etc.

But if dispense do come from de Pope
Lilliburlero, bullen a la.
We'll hang Magna Charta and dem in a rope.
Lilliburlero, bullen a la, etc.

And de good Talbot is made a lord,
Lilliburlero, bullen a la.
And he with brave lads is coming abroad.
Lilliburlero, bullen a la, etc.

Who all in France have taken a sware
Lilliburlero, bullen a la.
Dat dey will have no Protestant heir.
Lilliburlero, bullen a la, etc.

O, but why does he stay behind?
Lilliburlero, bullen a la.
Ho, by my shoul, 'tis a Protestant wind.
Lilliburlero, bullen a la, etc.

Now Tyrconnel is come ashore,
Lilliburlero, bullen a la.
And we shall have commissions gillore.
Lilliburlero, bullen a la, etc.

And he dat will not go to mass
Lilliburlero, bullen a la.
Shall turn out and look like an ass.
Lilliburlero, bullen a la, etc.

Now, now, de heretics all go down,
Lilliburlero, bullen a la.
By Creish and St. Patrick, de nation's our
Lilliburlero, bullen a la, etc.   [own.

As James' throne tottered and the House of Stuart faced the last of the crises that periodically bedevilled it, the way in which Mr. Henry Purcell's pretty music had been put to political use made a good talking point. There is not the least doubt that in the hectic months before and after the Protestant Wind blew William of Orange into Torbay, *Lilliburlero* played an important part in moulding public opinion. Its fame and its impact, and its status as a soldiers' song, were described by Gilbert Burnet, the politically active Bishop of Rochester. "A foolish ballad was made at that time treating the Papists, and chiefly the Irish, in a very ridiculous manner which has a burden said to be Irish words — lero, lero, lilliburlero — that made an impression on the army that cannot be well imagined by those who saw it not. The whole army, and at last all people in city and country, were singing it perpetually. And perhaps never had so slight a thing so great an effect".[1]

There was no reason to suppose he was exaggerating, for in 1715 the preface of A PILL TO PURGE STATE MELANCHOLY claimed that it "so perfectly struck in with the humour of the people that we feel some of the consequence of it to this very day . . . That ballad was highly instrumental in singing out a bad monarch". There are a number of references to *Lilliburlero's* popularity in that time of crisis. Macaulay says that the very sentries on duty at the royal palace whistled it,[2] and when Lord Lovelace and his Whig partisans rode into Oxford in the dying days of James' reign his drummers beat it.[3] It was sung in a London theatre by a group of officers led by Colonel Harry Wharton, the composer's brother, and when a number of Irish officers seemed inclined to stop the proceedings, Wharton's band rose in their seats as keen to fight as to sing.[4] Still later, in 1698, when James was a refugee at the court of St. Germain, moping over his three lost kingdoms, the City waits were cheerily performing it at the Lord Mayor's procession.[5]

But despite all this, a more critical scrutiny suggests that the effective life of *Lilliburlero* as a soldiers' song – until its revival in our own time – was remarkably short. Burnet says it was the army's song in 1688, and Laurence Sterne's Uncle Toby was eternally whistling it, but although Sterne was a soldier's son and doubtless met other veterans of the wars, a novel is not the best historical evidence on which to base a case. Strange though it may appear, there is not a single piece of conclusive evidence to prove that *Lilliburlero* was played or sung by the army in the 18th and 19th centuries, although it was played during William III's Irish War of 1689–1691, and very probably at the Battle of the Boyne. According to the ballad of that name,

> . . . . the hautboys played,
> Drums they did beat and rattle.
> And *Lilliburlero* was the tune
> We played going down to battle.

Folk songs are notorious for providing garbled facts, but a good case has been made out to show that the *Battle of the Boyne* was written by one of the Enniskillen men who fought on the left wing of William's polyglot army, and its information is basically reliable.[6] *Lilliburlero* was also played during a daring Williamite raid on Dublin Harbour on April 10, 1690, when a vessel loaded with confiscated Protestant goods was cut out. It must have been a very confused action indeed. "In the fight two men and two pipers made their escape, who, pursued by a horseman, were relieved by a boat, who shot the horse under him and caused him to wade and then played up and down the river *Lallibolero* [sic]."[7] On the other occasion when *Lilliburlero* sounds in William's war it is being played by the Irish war pipes. In 1690 the Irish sacked Kilbrogan and the town was pillaged to the music of three pipers. One of them, perched on the communion table, played *When the king enjoys his own again,* another *The humors of Bandon,* and the third *Lilliburlero.*[8] The last two are Whig tunes, and where could the Irish have learned them if not from the Williamites?

But once the Jacobite Irish had been beaten the song fades into disuse. Admittedly, the fact that a tune is not mentioned is not conclusive proof that it was not used for, as this book often laments, references can be woefully sparse. Nevertheless, it seems barely possible that the once-famed *Lilliburlero* should be consistently neglected by writers for two centuries if it were being sung or played. The reason why memoirs of the 18th and 19th centuries omit comment on *Lilliburlero* is not because the authors forgot it but quite genuinely because they did not hear it.

A Chelsea pensioner whose military career went back to the Sudan and who had known men who fought in the Indian Mutiny described *Lilliburlero* as "a bad tune for the Catholic lads", and so of course it was, especially after its melody was used for the Orange song *The Protestant Boys.* It seems probable that as long ago as 1700 there was a tacit acknowledgement that while *Lilliburlero* had been a highly suitable tune to instil in the public a fear of an Irish Catholic army manipulated by an English Catholic king, it would give gratuitous and dangerous offence to the many "Catholic lads" who wore the English red, and it was discreetly dropped. For even as some of James' last adherents in the British Isles – the defenders of Limerick – were bound for exile in France under their gallant leader Patrick Sarsfield, others were immediately entering William's service, either from economic necessity or from sheer love of a fight. And this pattern continued throughout the Age of the Red Coat – there was a liberal sprinkling of Irishmen in almost any "English" regiment.

But at the time the popularity of *Lilliburlero* was slipping, another famous military tune was emerging to ring out though the War of the Spanish Succession. This was *The Grenadiers March,* and it must be said straight away that any problems posed about the origin, use, and disappearance of *Lilliburlero* are child's play compared with the tangle surrounding this second title. Grenadiers were originally a French innovation, but by 1678 the British Army had them on the basis of one company to each regiment. They were men of exceptional physique and distinctive attire; they received special training in throwing the new-fangled grenades, marched at the head of the regiment, and were the right flank unit when it stood in line. Sometimes, for special assignments, the grenadiers of several companies would be temporarily combined in one battalion. An entry in John Evelyn's diary for 29th June, 1678, describes the initial impression they made when they paraded on Hounslow Heath. "Now were brought into service a new sort of soldiers called grenadiers who were dexterous in flinging hand grenades, every one having a pouch full. They had furred caps with coped crowns like Janizaries, which made them look very fierce, and some had long hoods hanging down as we picture fools. The clothing being likewise piebald, yellow and red". These troops, half Turk and half court jester, caught the popular imagination as the commandos did in World War Two. By 1680 when Dumbarton's Regiment was on active service in Tangier, (part of Catherine of Braganza's dowry to Charles II) their deeds were already being celebrated in a thirteen verse ballad, *The Granadeer's rant*, or *Hey, the brave granadeers, ho!*

> Captain Hume is bound to sea,
> Hey boys, ho boys,
> Captain Hume is bound to sea ho,
> Captain Hume is bound to sea,
> And his brave company,
> Hey, the brave granadeers, ho![9]

By 1685 they had their own distinctive march, which is rather more distinguished than the miserable doggerel just quoted.

5
Grenadiers March 1685

MUSIC Traditional
SOURCE Nathaniel Thompson –
A Choice Collection of 180 Loyal Songs

Quick and rhythmic

In fact there must have been two *Grenadiers Marches*, because at the time of Monmouth's Rebellion a loyalist ballad appeared on the streets, also set to the air of *The Grenadiers March*, but obviously not suited to the tune above.

1st verse

Come my lads, let's march away,
Let drums beat and pipes play.
I think it a twelvemonth every day,
Till the rebels are confounded.

3rd verse

We'll drown Argyle in the raging sea,
Bring rampant Monmouth to his knee
And cuckold Grey to the triple tree,
With a number of lay elders.[10]

Which of these two marches (the one whose music is given, or the "lost" one) was to endure as *The Grenadiers March* cannot be known. The complexity of the situation is further increased by references that appear in George Farquhar's THE RECRUITING OFFICER, which opened in Drury Lane on April 8, 1706. From this it becomes apparent that *The Grenadiers March* was already commonly recognized and firmly established with the public, otherwise the audience would have been thoroughly mystified by the way in which Farquhar dwells lovingly upon it. As it was, satisfied but not surfeited with victories over the French and their allies, they must have roared with patriotic fervour as the playwright explained how the March was an "overture to a battle . . . performed with wonderful success at the great operas of Vigo, Schellenberg and Blenheim (where) it came off with the applause of all Europe, excepting France; the French found it a little too rough for their delicatesse". Although the music is not quite as soft as that of Bononcini, the Italian composer of the current hit *Camilla*, "it has laid more people asleep than all the *Camillas* in the world". And Farquhar concludes with the assurance that he is adapting some words to *The Grenadiers March* for the next performance, "if the lady who is to sing it should not happen to be sick". Most regrettably there is no indication of the tune for which Farquhar was penning his lyrics. It might have been the stately march on page 28, it might have been the "lost" tune for the anti-Monmouth words, or as a third possibility it might have been the air now called *The British Grenadiers*.

For *The British Grenadiers*, the best known among British marches and war songs, has the most obscure origins of all. The first version whose words are consistently similar to those now sung appeared in a revised version of the burletta pantomime HARLEQUIN EVERYWHERE which re-opened in January 1780 at Covent Garden, after the Americans had been bloodily thrown back from Savannah during the War of Independence.

6

British Grenadiers

WORDS Traditional
MUSIC Traditional
SOURCE Harlequin Everywhere

Some talk of Alexander and some of Hercules,
Of Conon and Lysander and some of Meltiadies [sic.]
But of all the world's brave heroes there's none that can compare,
With a tow row row row row
To the British Grenadiers.

None of those ancient heroes e'er saw a cannon ball,
Or knew the force of powder to slay their foes with all.
But our brave boys do know it and banish all their fears,
With a tow row row, etc.

When'er we are commanded to storm the palisades
Our leaders march with fusees and we with hand grenades.
We throw them from the glacis about our enemies ears,
With a tow row row, etc.

The god of war was pleased and great Bellona smiles,
To see these noble heroes of our British Isles.
And all the gods celestial descending from their spheres,
Beheld with adoration the British Grenadiers.

Then let us crown a bumper and drink a health to those
Who carry caps and pouches, that wear the louped clothes.
May they and their commanders live happy all their years,
With a tow row row, etc.

THE MORNING CHRONICLE AND LONDON ADVERTISER of January 18th
notes the song, "the words and music of which were neither excellent nor
execrable", but although it seems as if the reviewer had never heard it
before and felt bound to comment, it could not possibly have been new.
Firstly, Francis Grose, writing in 1786 says the words came from "the
old grenadier song",[11] which would not have been an appropriate description of something produced just six years previously. Even more conclusively, the "louped clothes" were distinctive of grenadiers some 80
years earlier, grenade-tossing was now out of fashion, and "fusees" were
no longer carried. The only conclusion must be that the song was composed in the final years of the 17th century, that it was preserved orally,
and transmitted to paper for the first time after the victory at Savannah.[12]
It was long thought that the 1780 version was the earliest printed version
of any sort of *The British Grenadiers,* but in the course of research for this
book another was discovered which dates from 1745 and confirms that

the authorized version was well enough known by that date to be parodied. It is six verses long, and since there is no mention of Culloden it must have been written before the Young Pretender had been finally vanquished.

> Some talk of Alexander and some of Achilles,
> Of Coron [sic] and Lisander [sic] and some of Melchides [sic].
> But of all the world's brave heroes,
> There's none that can compare
> With the noble Duke of Cumberland
> And the British Grenadiers.[13]

To return to THE RECRUITING OFFICER it seems unlikely that Farquhar was writing about Alexander and Hercules for his lady with impending 'flu, for although there are many 18th century allusions to the *Grenadiers March* being played there are none to its being sung. The March and the song would therefore appear to have co-existed.

The Grenadiers March was not sacrosanct for, while in the first part of the 18th century it was either the tune of page 28 or the "lost" version, by the time of the American War of Independence it had been superseded by this rather more lively tune.

7
Grenadiers March c. 1776

MUSIC Traditional
SOURCE John Greenwood MS

By the time of the Napoleonic Wars this march was accepted throughout the Army. It is even found in a MS music book begun in 1812 by Edward Russell of the West Monmouthshire militia.[14] In 1815 when the 1st Foot Guards were re-named the Grenadier Guards, they adopted this march to commemorate their role at Waterloo. They still play *The Grenadiers March* as a quickstep and it is heard in slow time at the ceremony of Trooping the Colour.

It is impossible to draw irrefutable conclusions from the available evidence, but the chronological outline of "grenadier music" seems to have been this. In the 1680's there were two *Grenadier Marches*, at least one of which survived, was played in the War of the Spanish Succession (see p. 29) and into the mid-century when it was superseded by another march of the same title. This newer version found popular favour during the American War of Independence, was used in the Napoleonic Wars, and is still played. Also, about 1700, *The British Grenadiers* was written; alternative versions were written in 1745 and 1780, and by the time of the Napoleonic Wars it had become the most popular of all songs and was being played by regimental bands.

There is one tiny footnote to the story of "grenadier music" — nonproductive but fascinating. On November 9, 1755, the GENTLEMAN'S MAGAZINE printed a brief obituary on Thomas Marshall, a drummer. He was 105 years old, 90 years in service, "and was the first that beat *The Grenadiers March*".

Farquhar may have borrowed one established soldier's tune for THE RECRUITING OFFICER, but he undoubtedly popularized another that was to find a ready place in the army music. This was *Over the hills and far away*.

1st verse	Hark, now the drums beat up again,
	For all true soldier gentlemen,
	Then let us 'list and march, I say,
	Over the hills and far away.
	    Over the hills and o'er the main,
	    To Flanders, Portugal and Spain,
	    Queen Anne commands and we'll obey,
	    Over the hills and far away.

2nd verse	All gentlemen that have a mind, To serve the queen that's good and kind, Come 'list and enter into pay, Then o'er the hills and far away. Over the hills and o'er the main, etc.
7th verse	No more from sound of drum retreat, While Marlborough and Galway beat The French and Spaniards every day, When over the hills and far away. Over the hills and o'er the main, etc.
10th verse	The 'prentice Tom he may refuse, To wipe his angry master's shoes, For then he's free to sing and play, Over the hills and far away. Over the hills and o'er the main, etc.
12th verse	We then shall lead more happy lives, By getting rid of brats and wives, That scold on, both night and day, When o'er the hills and far away. Over the hills and o'er the main, etc.

8

Over the the hills and far away

WORDS Traditional
MUSIC Traditional
SOURCE Pills to Purge Melancholy

Although it is eminently reasonable to suppose that the song found instant acceptance no contemporary writer mentions it and the silence persists through the Seven Years War and the American War of Independence. Only with the French Wars of 1793–1815 do soldiers report hearing this song, especially played as a loth-to-depart, one of the tunes traditionally used when a regiment left its cantonments. There is, however, one piece of evidence dating from 1776, that claims Marlborough's soldiers sang the melody.

Despite his victories in the field Marlborough was not proof against intrigues at home, nor against the justifiable viewpoint of his enemies that he wanted the war to continue almost regardless of cost. And so, in 1711, he was dismissed and replaced by the Duke of Ormonde, to the great chagrin of the troops, who not only respected his military ability but also appreciated the care that he showed for them in an age when generals were rarely sparing of their soldiers' lives or mindful of their comforts. If Major Donkin, writing long after the event, is to be believed the redcoats lamented the passing of "Corporal John" in a song to the tune of *Over the hills and far away*.[15]

1st verse	Grenadiers, now change your song And talk no more of battles won. No victory shall grace us now, Since we have lost our Marlborough.
2nd Verse	You who have fought on Blenheim's field And forced the strongest towns to yield. Break all your arms and turn to plough, Since we have lost our Marlborough.[16]

There is yet another song that comes into the loose category of "possibly sung". In 1845 a Sergeant Thomas Morris looking back on the hardships of a soldier's life and its meagre rewards quoted a cynical couplet.

You may fight till you die, do the best that you can
And the captain will reward you with, There lies a brave man.[17]

This song appears in Thomas D'Urfey's PILLS TO PURGE MELANCHOLY and it is probable that Morris was repeating words known to veterans of Blenheim and Ramillies, and passed by them to successive generations of redcoats. The song's wry philosophy is appropriate to the disillusioned hard-cases of any war, an 18th century reverberation of "no promotion this side of the ocean".

1st verse	You madcaps of England who merry would make And for your brave valour would pains undertake, Come over to Flanders and there you shall see, How merry we'll make it, how frolic we'll be. Boys drink, boys drink.
2nd verse	If you have been a citizen broke by mischance And would by your courage your credit advance, Here's stuff to be won by venturing your life, So you leave at home a good friend by your wife. Wear horns, wear horns.

4th verse	As soon as you come to your enemies' land,
	Where fat goose and capon you have at command,
	Sing take them or eat them or let them alone.
	Sing go out and fetch them or else you get none.
	Make shift, make shift.
5th verse	Your sergeants and officers are very kind,
	If that you can flatter and speak to their mind,
	They will free you from duty and all other trouble,
	Your money being gone, your duty comes double.
	Hard case, hard case.
7th verse	At last when you come to your enemies' walls,
	Where many a brave gallant and gentleman falls,
	And when you have done the best that you can,
	Your captain rewards you, there dies a brave man.
	That's all, that's all.

9
Song from *Pills to Purge Melancholy*

WORDS Traditional
MUSIC Traditional
SOURCE Pills to Purge Melancholy

If so far it has only been possible to say that a *Grenadiers March* was played during the War of the Spanish Succession, and that three songs *might* have been sung, it is because the anecdotal accounts of the war are so few. One man who did write his personal viewpoint of these campaigns was John Blackader, colonel of the 26th or Cameronian Regiment. No-one challenges his bravery but it is difficult to know exactly what he was doing in the army, for never was a man so sorely miscast. His true vocation was that of hellfire preacher, in which he would have shone fiercely. Blackader himself was slightly bemused by the square hole in which he was caught. "What do I then in the army, where the scum and dregs of mankind are gathered together?" he asked bitterly. At the best of times his comrades-in-arms were uncongenial, officers included, but he suffered most of all on Sundays. "It is hell to be chained all day, especially a sabbath day, in such an army, hearing such language as devils would speak had they tongues." The wanton conduct and sabbath breaking he so stridently deplores must have amounted in large part to song, and not necessarily unprintably vulgar song at that. It is particularly galling therefore, that the one man who heard most of the soldiers' songs that there were, and obviously gave them plenty of thought, makes no specific mention of the abominations that so sullied his ears.

There was, however, one chronicler of the Netherlands campaigns who was very much the type of debauchee reviled by Colonel Blackader — that is he drank, sang, danced, and unashamedly admitted as much. His name was John Scot, a private in the Scots Brigade paid for by the United Provinces of Holland and a part of Marlborough's army. His chronicle covers the campaigns of 1701–1711 in some 12,000 rhymeless and atrociously mis-spelled lines, but he can be forgiven these literary shortcomings for his lively intelligence, observant eye, insight and honesty. He often comes tantalisingly close to the music of the army but never quite as close as one would wish. At Bergen-op-Zoom,

> We mounted our guards like brave soldier lads
> And we took us a drink and a song.[18]

The rot had set in, at least by Blackader's standards, and near Brussels,

> We drink, we dance, we career.[19]

He was not blind to all good acts nor wholly beyond redemption for when Liège fell in 1702 he noted that Marlborough's friend and colleague, Prince Eugene of Savoy,

> Went to St. Paul's Kirk
> And the O Te Deum he sweetly did sing
> And a Pater Nos [sic] in the mirk.[20]

Private Scot is too self-effacing to say exactly what *he* (and his fellow tipplers) sang by way of celebration, but he recalls that at Malplaquet,

> *The Grenadiers March* we several times beat.[21]

He also gives a most lively account of one of those colonels who couldn't leave well enough alone (the kind mentioned in chapter 1) and who meddled endlessly with the regiment's music. This officer was Brigadier Douglas whose ancestor not only had fought by the side of Robert Bruce but, after the king's death, had been charged with conveying the royal heart to Palestine. As a reminder of this the regimental drums were emblazoned with "the royal heart and crown". When Douglas took over command of Scot's regiment,

> The drums he caused them beat
> A new march and tattoo.[22]

That was just the start, for next he dismissed many of the drummers, took new men, and had them trained to play to his liking on a fresh set of drums. When he was wounded and became increasingly crotchety, "most peremptor in all his orders", the tattoo was changed yet again.

> And every day they were learning to play
> A deal of new beatings for shows.[23]

Some of these frantic and harassed musicians must have yearned for life in a regiment like Blackader's where there would have been a minimum of such goings-on.

The drum beating at Malplaquet mentioned by Private Scot was not unusual, for in this war both the English and French used military music not only for relaying orders but also to animate their forces. In 1708 when a large force of grenadiers was sent with artillery to Pont d'Espières to dislodge the French they were accompanied with "hooboyes",[24] which can be nothing but oboes, although a task force with music is alien to our ideas of how war should be waged. At Ramillies a French officer had his oboes play "to entertain us a while" until the trembling musicians melted away,[25] and at Oudenarde the French drums and pipes were active until a brisk and discourteous fusillade terminated their performance.[26] Music could also be used as a ruse. Just as the Dutch had played *The Scots March* during the Thirty Years War, so some English troops once played *The French March* in the hope of being left alone. This happened in 1707 at the Battle of Almanza where the Earl of Galway was defeated by the Duke of Berwick, a bastard of James II. Galway with 5,000 British troops, 3,000 Dutch, Germans and French Huguenots and 8,000 battle-shy Portuguese put up a game but vain resistance against a Franco-Spanish force some 25,000 strong. Inside two hours he suffered 4,000 casualties and lost 3,000 prisoners. According to Captain Henry Hawley, some of the British retreated "beating *The French March* very near several of the enemy's brigades till we came pretty near one of our batteries".[27]

Marlborough's personal attitude to music in wartime cannot be gauged, although when the shooting stopped he apparently felt that the less spent on bands the better. In his last years he was restored to favour, and according to tradition that may well be authentic he accompanied George I on an inspection of the dragoons. The king peered around and then enquired what had become of the regimental oboes. Marlborough smiled dourly — he has been called the only truly great man who loved money for its own sake — and struck his pockets until the golden guineas jingled. "Here they are, your majesty. Don't you hear them?".[28] Tradition, alas, fails to describe the effect of this crisp repartee on the stolid Hanoverian.

1. G. Burnet, *History of his own Time* (1823), III, p.139.
2. Lord Macaulay, *The History of England from the Accession of James II* (1914), III, p.1176.
3. *Ibid*, p.1180.
4. J. Oldmixon, *The History of England during the Reigns of the Royal House of Stuart* (1730), p.758.
5. Ned Ward, *The London Spy* (1955), p.27.
6. *Ulster Journal of Archaeology* (1854), p.10.
7. Ormonde MSS, New Series, VIII (1920), p.381.
8. R. M. Sibbett, *Orangeism in Ireland and Throughout the Empire* (1914), I, p.107.
9. *Roxburghe Ballads*, II, No. 582.
10. British Museum Pamphlets, 807.g.5. (47).
11. F. Grose, *Military Antiquities* (1786), I, p.180.
12. *JSAHR*, VI (1927), pp.23–30.
13. British Museum Pamphlets, 11621.b.11 (8).
14. National Army Museum, Camberley.
15. R. Donkin, *Military Collections and Remarks* (1777), p.67.
16. *A Pill to Purge State Melancholy* (1715), p.141.
17. T. Morris, *Recollections of Military Service* (1845), p.136.
18. J. Ferguson, *The Scots Brigade in the Service of the United Netherlands, 1572–1782* (1901), III, p.345.
19. *Ibid*, p.399.
20. *Ibid*, p.445.
21. *Ibid*, p.497.
22. *Ibid*, pp.518–520.
23. *Ibid*, pp.518–520.
24. J. M. Deane, *A Journal of the Campaign in 1708* (1846), p.23.
25. M. de la Colonie, *The Chronicle of an Old Campaigner* (1904), p.307.
26. M. Bishop, *The Life and Adventures of Mathew Bishop* (1744), p.160.
27. *JSAHR*, XXV (1947), p.29.
28. Grose, *Military Antiquities*, II, p.249.

Chapter 3

THE JACOBITE RISINGS
1715 AND 1745

IN April 1713 the Treaty of Utrecht formally ended the War of the
Spanish Succession, and the disbanding of the British Army which
had started with the peace preliminaries was accelerated. But when
Queen Anne died in August 1714 many Whigs felt that the mass de-
mobilisation had been premature, for the spectre of a Stuart restoration
loomed unpleasantly large. Their fears were somewhat allayed when those
Tories who would have most welcomed this turn of events proved
dilatory, and Elector George of Hanover arrived safely in England to
become George I.

Nevertheless, in the north of England and in Scotland, some of the
more active Jacobites took up arms, and local, ineffectual rebellions flared
briefly – so briefly, in fact, that there was little real opportunity for the
British Army to add to its now considerable battle honours. A small force
of northern Jacobites who had failed to achieve anything in their own
country entered Scotland to link up with their Lowland fellows and a few
Highlanders, and then drifted south to unceremonious defeat at Preston
on September 6.

The Jacobite insurrection most likely to succeed, on the face of it,
was that in the Highlands led by the Earl of Mar, known for his vacilla-
tions as "Bobbing John". At Sheriffmuir, also on September 6, he
clashed inconclusively with a smaller army of Scots loyalists under John
Campbell, Duke of Argyll, and then scurried north. Only when the
Highland army had begun to disperse did the Old Pretender – the man

for whom they had been invited to rise, fight, and die – land in Scotland. James II was criticized for his rapid departure from Ireland after the Battle of the Boyne, but the behaviour of his son James Edward, who reached Scotland on December 22 and left on February 4, is even more remarkable, assuming that he even wanted the crown of his father.

If the rising of 1715 was inglorious it was also, for the purposes of this book, practically mute. It is poetic justice that the one known fact about its music derives not from the English redcoats (whose role in suppressing it was almost incidental), but from the loyal clansmen who blunted Bobbing John's rebellion – the single outbreak that might have become dangerous. As they marched into Perth and Dundee their three divisions were led by pipers, the vanguard playing *The Campbells are coming*, the main body *Wilt thou play me fair, highland laddie?* and the rear, *Stay and take the breeks with thee*. The first tune was unmistakeably Whig, but the others must have been primarily Jacobite, for the Stuart supporters in Dundee perked up at the sound, not realising at first that these airs were played "evidently in derision".[1] So with this brief skirl of pipes, Argyll's dark plaids swing through the town, and silence falls on the 1715 uprising.

The rising of 1745 is considerably better documented, and its most memorable contribution to the music of the British Army is that it inspired *Johnny Cope*, the accompaniment to many a famous victory when Scots and English fought side by side, and still played by Scottish regiments as their reveille.

> Hey, Johnny Cope, are ye waking yet,
> Or are ye sleeping, I would wit?
> Oh, haste ye, get up, for the drums do beat,
> And it's fie Cope, rise in the morning.

Poor Sir John has been cruelly maligned by this song. As the Royalist commander in Scotland when Prince Charles Edward landed, his first tentative manœuvres did not suggest that he was a first-class military thinker, but other generals have begun worse, achieved less, and been treated more lightly by posterity. When he eventually deployed his army to face the Highlanders at Prestonpans, close to Cromwell's field of Dunbar, his disposition could scarcely be faulted. When the Highlanders marched around his position he was well and truly "waking", and ready to meet them on a new front. It was no fault of his that the clans attacked "with a swiftness not to be conceived" which quite paralysed his dragoons, nor that the Scots' savage demeanour soon had his infantry "crouching and creeping gently backwards". Cope did whatever a general could do to rally shaken troops, short of using the flat of his sword. He rode among them, pleading and exhorting with a shrewd combination of flattery, patriotism, and appeal to their military instincts. "For shame, gentlemen, behave like Britons! Give them another fire and you'll make them run". But the appeal fell on deaf ears, and if Cope himself eventually left the field at the head of a squadron of horse he should not be too sternly criticized. It was better to lead his cavalry off in a semblance of military order than to allow their utter disintegration. But Johnny Cope was not taken unawares (except by the flabbiness of his troops), he was not a coward, and he did not, as the ballad says, carry the news of his own defeat to Berwick. Nevertheless, the unfortunate man became the butt of words set to a thus-far undistinguished tune, and the words gave the tune an importance it will retain as long as Scots have their bagpipes.

IO

Johnny Cope

WORDS   Mr. Skirven
MUSIC   Traditional
SOURCE   The Scots Musical Museum

Before Prestonpans the prince had danced at the house of Lude, near Blair, to a significant tune of his own choice, *This is not my ain house,*[2] and after the battle his "ain house", the palace of St. James in London, must have seemed no more than a short walk away. But as he advanced into England his advisers noticed that the population was sometimes indifferent and often hostile, and only at Manchester was he joined by any recruits. These were in any case riff-raff and unemployed, scarcely deserving the title of the Manchester Regiment that was bestowed upon them. At Derby, just 125 miles from London, the prince reluctantly accepted the advice of cooler heads and turned back towards Scotland, where he could count on some popular support and where supplies and reinforcements from France might more easily reach him.

When the Jacobites reached Manchester they found the pendulum had swung back again and they were met by open hostility. But despite the ugly mood of the mob, several officers found time to ascend the organ loft of a church and play *When the King enjoy his own again*.[3] Also, according to a traditional story that may be less authentic, the Jacobites played *Farewell Manchester* as they marched from the sullen town.[4]

Between Shap and Penrith the Jacobite rearguard, encumbered by artillery and ammunition carts that were supposed to be further up the line of march, had an unwelcome surprise when a "prodigious number of trumpets and kettle drums" echoing through the hills warned that a powerful Royalist force was about to fall upon them. In fact, the noise was made by a mere 300 light horse, carrying all the instruments that could be assembled.[5] It was hoped that the Jacobite rear might be bluffed into a time-consuming deployment for battle, thus allowing the main English force to catch up, but Lord George Murray who commanded the rearguard was too old a hand to be caught this way. The light horse were brushed aside and the march continued.

This unsuccessful ruse was dreamed up by William Augustus, Duke of Cumberland who had been brought back from the continent with a number of battle-hardened British regiments to bolster his father's throne. He is now so firmly established as an ogre in British history that it is difficult to remember he was the same age as his cousin the Young Pretender, 25, and that earlier that year he had won universal admiration for his courage at Fontenoy, sharing with common soldiers the heaviest fire of the French army for hours on end. It is fascinating to speculate on his reaction when he first heard the Scots pipes across the hills, for there could have been no more poignant reminder of Fontenoy where his Anglo-Hanoverians had finally been pushed from the field by the Irish

Brigade. The pipes had played, on that occasion, one of the best-known of all Jacobite airs, *The white cockade*.[6] If, as is likely, that was one of the tunes Cumberland now heard from the Scots it seems more in keeping with his character that he tapped his foot than gnashed his teeth. No British general before or since has been more alive to music than this tubby young man with dark, popping eyes. When it came to a good tune he never stood upon his dignity. As he was about to leave Edinburgh in pursuit of the Pretender he said to the company that was wishing him god-speed, "Come, let us have a song before parting"; and without inhibition launched into,

> Will ye play me fair,
> Highland laddie, highland laddie.[7]

(This tune from the '15 seems to have been played when Cumberland's army forded the Spey,[8] surprised that the Jacobites made no attempt to prevent the crossing, and perhaps hinting that an attack while they were vulnerably placed in mid-stream would be unchivalrous). When the Highlanders had been crushed at Culloden the Duke returned to London as the nation's darling. The severity which he had shown in the aftermath of battle, and which would return to bedevil him as the years brought disappointment and physical afflictions, was absent, and no pleasantry was too extravagant for the conqueror of Culloden. He could afford to dance with the Jacobite Lady Anne Mackintosh, who had been brought to London, partnering her to a Whig tune that became popular after Sheriffmuir, *Up and waur them a', Willie*, and as the victor he could be chivalrous and show his sense of humour by accepting her invitation to dance to *her* choice – *The Old Stuart's back again*.[9] Perhaps because Cumberland liked *Will ye play me fair* there was a belief even in his own time that it had been written for him;[10] it was not, and neither – despite contrary claims – was Handel's *See, the conquering hero comes*, although it is easy to understand how this second belief arose. *See, the conquering hero comes* is now part of *Judas Maccabaeus*, written in 1746 to celebrate the victory of Culloden, but it was not originally in that oratorio. It was composed for *Joshua* (1748) but was put into later performances of the more popular *Judas Maccabaeus*. The army soon adopted it, but it had nothing to do with Cumberland and Culloden.

I I

See, the conquering hero comes

MUSIC　G. F. Handel

Johnny Cope was not the only song to become famous as a result of the Jacobite risings. By 1764 some distinctly improbable tunes had been introduced into the Guards regiments, and the LONDON CHRONICLE of May 19–22 reported, probably tongue in cheek, that "it is no uncommon thing to see a file of English redcoats beating time to *Over the water to Charlie*"

12

Over the water to Charlie

MUSIC Traditional
SOURCE John Greenwood MS

Although after the '45 almost everything that was part of the martial tradition of the clans – their weapons, tartans, and distinctive garb – was proscribed in the Highlands, all these were still to be found in the Scots regiments. The Crown was unwilling to lose the services of such doughty fighters as the Highlanders, but it was realized that if the Scots could not fight surrounded by their familiar trappings they were unlikely to enlist at all. And so pipes continued to skirl even within earshot of Cumberland. Just two years after Culloden, while campaigning in the Low Countries, the piper of the 21st Scots Fusiliers was piping his regiment along until the Duke, suddenly finding the music "disagreeable" forbade it. (He was liable to these odd fits of pique, and once wanted the Scots Guards renamed the English Guards and restricted to playing English airs).[11] For some days thereafter the Fusiliers were conspicuously dull on the march, and Cumberland realized it. "The Butcher" of tradition would have called a halt while some of the more sluggish marchers were flogged at the halberds, *pour encourager les autres*, but Cumberland changed both his mind and his order, and the pipes were soon playing again. "This seemed to work upon our men as a dram would have done that cold morning, with this difference, that its effect was more durable than that of the gin".[12]

In the anti-Gaelic frenzy that followed the rising it seems that even *The Scots March* (which was a Lowland air, although the Jacobites played it at Falkirk) came under the general proscription, and much disliked the order was.

> Very irksome to their spirit
> The dinging down of Tantallon.[13]

No-one, however, seems to have taken this particular veto too seriously.

> But Tantallon was ne'er beat down.
> The Scots kept by their old march,
> In spite of all their foes could urge.[14]

The '45 was not suppressed exclusively by redcoats and loyal Scots; troops were brought over from the continent – among them 6,000 bluecoated Hessians. Their music was greatly appreciated, in the way that every aspect of German war music has always aroused the admiration of British soldiers. The casual dismissal of the bagpipe by Sir James Turner is well-known – "good enough music for them who love it, but sure it is not so good as the Almain whistle" (i.e. the fife)[15] – and this comment on Hessian fifes and drums deserves to be noted.

> The finest music you e'er did hear,
> Would make one dance who could not stir.
> Their whistles and drums in chorus join,
> To cheer one's heart they played so fine.[16]

The fife had not been used in the British Army since the end of the 17th century, but it was restored shortly after 1745. Details are obscure, but Cumberland is thought to have been responsible, 1747 is the conjectured date, and the happy event may have occurred at Maestricht in Holland.[17] But no-one has yet suggested that it was the fine playing of the blue-coats that tipped the scales in favour of the fife's comeback.

1. Dalyell, p.23.
2. R. Forbes, *Jacobite Memoirs of the Rebellion of 1745*, ed. R. Chambers (1834), p.26.
3. B. W. Kelly, *The Conqueror of Culloden* (1903), p.48.
4. W. Chappell, *Popular Music of the Olden Time* (1859), II, p.682.
5. J. C. O'Callaghan, *History of the Irish Brigades* (1870), p.404.
6. O'Callaghan, p.356.
7. J. Marchant, *The History of the Present Rebellion* (1746), p.329.
8. D. Graham, *An Impartial History [. . .] of the Late Rebellion* (1774), p.87.
9. R. Chambers, *History of the Rebellion of 1745–6* (1869), p.301.
10. Marchant, p.329.
11. Kelley, p.89.
12. *JSAHR*, XXVIII (1950), p.10.
13. Graham, p.115.
14. *Ibid*, p.115.
15. Sir J. Turner, *Pallas Armata* (1683), p.219.
16. Graham, p.75.
17. *JSAHR*, XXIII (1945), p.71.

Chapter 4

THE SEVEN YEARS WAR
1756–1763

THE Seven Years War was another stage in the long struggle with France, fought in several theatres already made familiar by the War of the Spanish Succession. Some of the music that one would have expected to emerge (because it is known to have existed) fails to do so – there is no *Lilliburlero*, no *Over the hills*, and no *British Grenadiers* (although the popularity of *The Grenadiers March* continues) – but two heroes of the war, the Marquis of Granby and General James Wolfe are celebrated in music.

John Manners, the Marquis, still smiles down from inn-signs, and very properly for he was a good man at the bottle. His critics even attributed his popularity with the allies' European commander, Prince Ferdinand of Brunswick, to this conviviality, but toper or not, he was brave, energetic, intelligent and – like Marlborough – very alive to the welfare of his troops. He distinguished himself at Gravenstein, Wilhelmstahl, Homburg and Cassel, but his chief fame is to have led one of the great cavalry charges of British history. On July 31, 1760, at Warburg, with his wig off and his bald head glistening in the sunshine, he led 22 squadrons against the French, first driving their horse from the field and then routing their infantry. *Away to the Marquis of Granby* was soon being hawked in the streets and not surprisingly it took the fancy of the troops. As the Guards marched from the Tower of London to embark for Germany 1,000 men sang it all the way to the Borough, where they paused for wine, punch, and beer provided by local patriots, before resuming their march and their chorus.[1] The song survived the war, for Granby's entrance into a theatre in 1765 brought the house down, the audience interrupting the play and calling for the orchestra to salute the gallant Marquis with his tune.[2]

13
The Marquis of Granby

MUSIC Traditional
SOURCE J. Greenwood MS

Two songs are associated with Wolfe and the capture of Quebec in 1759, and although they are both better known than *The Marquis*, they lack the contemporary endorsement that it can boast. The first of these is *Why, soldiers, why?* also called *How stands the glass around?* During the Napoleonic Wars it was named *Wolfe's song* because he was thought to have sung it the night before the Battle of Quebec. This song was featured in THE PATRON (1729) so Wolfe may well have known it, but the story of his solo looks improbable for two reasons. The tradition stems from W. B. de Krifft's sonata, *The siege of Quebec*, (c. 1790–1800) but there has never been any likelihood that he made an effort to authenticate the airs he inserted in his sonata, and secondly, de Krifft never claimed that Wolfe personally sang the song. It is simply described in the sonata as "a favourite song of General Wolfe's, and sung the evening before the engagement wherein he was killed". Although the legend of the solo can be disregarded, *Wolfe's song* remains important in the story of war music because of its undoubted popularity in the Napoleonic Wars.

How stands the glass around?
For shame, ye take no care, my boys!
How stands the glass around?
Let mirth and wine abound.
The trumpets sound!
The colours they are flying, boys,
To fight, kill or wound.
May we still be found,
Content with our hard fare, my boys,
On the cold, cold ground.

Why, soldiers, why,
Should we be melancholy, boys?
Why, soldiers, why?
Whose business 'tis to die!
What, sighing? Fie!
Damn fear, drink on, be jolly boys!
'Tis he you or I.
Cold, hot, wet or dry,
We're always bound to follow, boys.
And scorn to fly.

'Tis but in vain,
(I mean not to upbraid you, boys),
'Tis but in vain
For soldiers to complain.
Should next campaign
Send us to Him who made us, boys,
We're free from pain.
But should we remain,
A bottle and kind landlady
Cures all again.

14
Why, soldiers, why?

WORDS Traditional
MUSIC Traditional
SOURCE W. Chappell – Popular Music of the Olden Time

Rather slowly and firmly

The second song from the Quebec campaign has unusual undertones. It is called *Hot stuff*, and it was rediscovered by Francis Parkman when he was writing his 19th century epics on the Anglo-French struggle for North America, although he could not bring himself to disclose the last verse to the public.

Come, each death-doing dog who dares venture his neck,
Come, follow the hero that goes to Quebec.
Jump aboard of the transports and loose every sail,
Pay your debts at the tavern by giving leg-bail.
And ye that love fighting shall soon have enough,
Wolfe commands us, my boys; we shall give them Hot Stuff.

Up the River St. Lawrence our troops shall advance,
To *The Grenadiers March* we will teach them to dance.
Cape Breton we've taken and next we will try
At their capital to give them another black eye.
Vaudreuil, 'tis in vain you pretend to look gruff
Those are coming who know how to give you Hot Stuff.

With powder in his periwig and snuff in his nose,
Monsieur will run down our descent to oppose.
And the Indians will come, but the Light Infantry
Will soon oblige them to betake to a tree.
From such rascals as these may we fear a rebuff?
Advance, grenadiers, and let fly your Hot Stuff.

When the Forty-seventh regiment is dashing ashore,
While bullets are whistling and cannon do roar,
Says Montcalm: "Those are Shirley's – I know the lapels."
"You lie," says Ned Botwood, "we belong to Lascelles."
Though our clothing is changed yet we scorn a powder-puff
So at you, ye b———, here's give you Hot Stuff".

With Monckton and Townshend, those brave brigadiers,
I think we shall soon have the town 'bout their ears
And when we have done with the mortars and guns,
"If you please, Madam Abbess, a word with your nuns."
Each soldier shall enter the convent in buff,
And then never fear we will give them Hot Stuff.

Hot stuff was first printed in RIVINGTON'S NEW YORK GAZETTEER of May 5, 1774, as "a song by Ned Botwood, sergeant of Grenadiers in the 47th Regiment, composed before they embarked for Quebec. Tune: Lilies of France". The information is added that Botwood was killed "sword in hand" on July 31, 1759, the date of the Battle of Montmorenci, an unsuccessful frontal assault on the eastern approaches to Quebec. His belated obituary was thus printed in RIVINGTON'S 15 years after his death. No-one had previously thought it worthwhile to record the death of Botwood, nor had his song received previous recognition, so the date of its publication – May 5, 1774 – could be highly significant. The political situation between the American colonists and the British government was deteriorating rapidly and the coming conflict was already foreshadowed. *Hot stuff* could have been printed with an eye to this political situation. Mr. Rivington was an American loyalist and he may have intended Botwood's verses to recall the old happy days when unity of colonists and redcoats had brought victory to both. Alternatively, the song could have served as a reminder to the homespun patriots of North America that Botwood and his fellows had beaten sterner foes than the insurgents appeared to be. The twentieth century has bestowed a reputation for fame upon *Hot stuff* that it may or may not deserve. Certainly, *Lilies of France* is a good tune though difficult to sing, and it inspired other sets of words besides *Hot stuff*, but there are no grounds for the claim by the author of THE LOYAL NORTH LANCASHIRE REGIMENT that it was "popular among British troops", nor for the fact that it has become stock in trade for historical novelists. Its fame rests solely on the one issue of RIVINGTON'S GAZETTEER.

15
Hot stuff

WORDS   E. Botwood
MUSIC   "Lilies of France" – Traditional

Rather strangely, the circumstances of Botwood's death fall squarely within the terms of this book, for he may be described as a victim of *The Grenadiers March*. Wolfe's plan at the Montmorenci River was for picked troops to land on the water's edge at low tide and to seize one of the

French redoubts, provoking Montcalm into a counter-attack that might escalate to a full-scale action. Thirteen companies of Grenadiers – about 800 men – were put ashore, closely supported by 200 Royal Americans, with the 15th Regiment and Fraser's Highlanders as the third wave. Exactly what went wrong is not clear, but the Grenadiers ran amok, storming forward unaligned and unsupported. They were, said Captain John Knox, "impatient to acquire glory" but another eyewitness says that it was *The Grenadiers March* which whipped them into this disastrous white heat,[3] and it was certainly played as they rushed up the slippery incline into a murderous French fire and eventual rout.[4] Wolfe was understandably bitter about these "impetuous, irregular and unsoldierlike proceedings" which cost him nearly 500 men, or half the assault force. Botwood, dead or dying, was presumably scalped along with the other casualties, by Montcalm's Indians.

The Grenadiers March was regularly played at this time. No sooner had the Seven Years War ended than the American frontier was ablaze with an Indian rising engineered by the great Ottawa war chief Pontiac, and those garrisons which were not massacred were beseiged. On June 17, 1763, Captain Lewis Ourry wrote from Fort Bedford in Pennsylvania : "I long to see my native scouts come in with intelligence, but I long more to hear *The Grenadiers March*".[5] *The Grenadiers March* was also played under rather comic circumstances, thousands of miles from Fort Bedford. On April 8, 1759, the British and their sepoy troops stormed Masulipatam in southern India, but once the fort was breached one of those irrational panics arose which can seize even the best trained soldiers. A magazine housing relatively inoffensive powder kegs was taken for a mine, and the British troops fled headlong leaving their commander in the courtyard with his sepoy drummers beating vainly to induce the fugitives back to their colours.[6]

Returning to Quebec, there is a story about music in battle which has often been quoted to show the importance of the bagpipes to the morale of Highland soldiers. General Wolfe, the tale goes, had forbidden the pipers to play that day and during the battle he complained bitterly to an officer that Fraser's Regiment was in flight. "Sir," replied the aggrieved Scot, "you did very wrong in forbidding the pipes to play this morning ; nothing encourages the Highlanders so much in the day of action. Even now they would be of use". Wolfe, with an equally acid tongue, said the pipes might "blow like the devil" if they could bring the men back, and sure enough on hearing "a favourite martial air" – a beloved stock phrase of the old writers – they reformed and returned to the fray.[7] This is good sterling tradition; it is marred only by the fact that the Frasers never so much as faltered at Quebec!

Although it falls just outside the period of the Seven Years War one regimental song of the 1760s must be mentioned here because it relates to Canada. In 1767 the 10th Regiment, stationed in Ireland, was ordered to North America where there were already rumblings of disaffection from the American colonists. They sailed for Quebec on June 3 and even if allowance is made for hyperbole their voyage must have been epic. The performances of the young officers – and the not-so-young – were still being celebrated many years later.

> On the third day in June of the year '67
> The Tenth in three transports sailed out of Cork Haven.
> All jovial and hearty like soldiers so valiant,
> And Commodore Holmes was top and top-gallant.
>
> Sing fal de ral la la, fal de ral lal de ral,
> La trallal la, lal trallal lal de ra!
>
> The Tenth, jolly fellows, were Basset and Vertis,
> Fitzgerald, and Thompson, and Lecky, and Bathurst,
> Montgomery their chaplain, Thwaites, Edwards, and Haly,
> Crampton and Parsons, Shute, Shaw, Green, and Kelly.
> Sing fal de ral la la, etc.
>
> But of all jolly fellows, the first to be reckoned
> Was Marmaduke Savage, of the Fifty-Second;
> For he of the bottle was such a brisk shover,
> That before they left land they were near half seas over.
> Sing fal de ral la la, etc.
>
> Fitzgerald was hearty, and Kelly was rosy,
> And Thompson was rocky, and Vertis was boozy;
> And all were as merry as ducks in a shower,
> And thus they sailed on nine knots by the hour.
> Sing fal de ral la la, etc.
>
> The sea ran so high, sir, that not an old stager
> Could come upon deck for three days, but the Major;
> And he looked so round, as he sat with his wraps on,
> That the sailors mistook him oft times for the capstan.
> Sing fal de ral la la, etc.

The Major commanded on board the Caernarvon,
A ship twice as big as the town of Dungarvon,
Which carried their women, and baggage so weighty,
Of officers seventeen, and men three times eighty.
Sing fal de ral la la, etc.

But such was the courage of fresh-water sailors,
Next day they all look'd like a parcel of tailors;
And though the king's birth-day, the glass was neglected,
And Crampton and Parsons, for once were dejected.
Sing fal de ral la la, etc.

Now, still the same sadness made each day as one day,
And only for prayer-day, they'd never known Sunday;
But Montgomery, their chaplain, just like a good vicar,
Took care of their meat, and their souls, and their liquor.
Sing fal de ral la la, etc.

But such was their loyalty, such was their boozing,
That in nine weeks, of wine they drank eighty-one dozen –
Of rum, shrub, and brandy, just fifty-six gallons,
And ninety-eight dozen of porter, to balance!
Sing fal de ral la la, etc.

Now, quite out of wine, and almost of provision,
They came to Port Levi in doleful condition;
But the sight of Quebec soon with courage renewed them
And the spirit of Wolfe, as they landed, reviewed them.
Sing fal de ral la la, etc.[8]

16

10th Regiment song

WORDS Traditional
MUSIC "Corporal Casey" – Traditional

No one could say conclusively which march has been played on the most occasions by the British Army, but a good contender for this distinction would surely be *The girl I left behind me*, the most famous of all loth-to-departs. It is another of those pieces called to our attention by the prolific anecdotal writings on the Napoleonic Wars, but it is generally accepted that it was written (and played?) during the Seven Years War.

1st verse

> I'm lonesome since I crossed the hill,
> And o'er the moor and valley,
> Such grievous thoughts my heart do fill,
> Since parting with my Sally.
> I seek no more the fine or gay,
> For each does but remind me,
> How swift the hours did pass away,
> With the girl I've left behind me.

2nd verse

> Oh, ne'er shall I forget the night
> The stars were bright above me,
> And gently lent their silvery light,
> When first she vowed to love me.
> But now I'm bound to Brighton Camp
> Kind heaven, then, pray guide me,
> And send me safely back again
> To the girl I've left behind me.[9]

The key line, which makes possible precise dating of the song, is the one referring to Brighton Camp, for when a French invasion was expected in 1758 nine camps were built along the south coast. But after victories by Admirals Boscawen and Hawke in 1759, the invasion threat lifted and the bases became obsolete. No-one was bound for Brighton camp any longer, so the song was almost certainly written in 1758.[8]

1. *The British Magazine* (July, 1760).
2. *Lloyd's Evening Post* (11 November, 1765).
3. S. M. Pargellis, *Military Affairs in Northern America 1748–1765* (1936), p.434.
4. *New York Mercury* (31 December, 1759).
5. L. W. G. Butler, *The Annals of the K.R.R.C.* (1913), I, p.335.
6. Sir J. W. Fortescue, *History of the British Army* (1899), II, p.451.
7. Sir J. Carr, *Caledonian Sketches* (1809), p.180.
8. H. Ward, *Recollections of an Old Soldier* (1849), p.151.
9. Chappell, II, p.708.

17
The girl I left behind me

WORDS Traditional
MUSIC Traditional
SOURCE W. Chappell – Popular Music of the Olden Times

Chapter 5

THE AMERICAN WAR OF INDEPENDENCE 1775–1783 AND THE WAR OF 1812

THE American War of Independence was virtually a Civil War. Most of the rebels had either been born in Britain or were the sons and grandsons of English, Scots, Welsh or Irish emigrants. The insurrectionists shared the legal, ethical, cultural, and linguistic heritage of Britain, barely modified by transplantation across the seas. Many American-born colonists, moreover, felt that the Crown had a good case and were prepared to defend it by force of arms. Even the German mercenaries hired by His Majesty were not wholly strangers in a strange land, for there were Germans in New York, Pennsylvania, and other states, fighting both for and against the rebels.

This common heritage is reflected by satirical ballads and political songs published at the time, in which both sides drew on the same sources of inspiration. In two obvious instances, for example, the British sang *The British Grenadiers* while their enemies sang the same tune as *Free America*. The redcoats came to attention for *God save the King*, while the rebels cheered *God save great Washington*. It should be possible to elaborate this theme from the wealth of American writings on the war, for many colonists were inveterate diarists whose journals have been published by learned societies in various States, but their British heredity seems to have influenced the diarists' style. "It rained. Marched ten miles", is a typical entry – and not much is said about music.

Not until 1856 did anyone make a serious effort to collate the music of the war. His name was Frank Moore and his SONGS AND BALLADS OF THE AMERICAN REVOLUTION is a useful anthology, but like British writers he does not differentiate between music sung in the war, and music published during it. When he says that *Heart of Oak* was popular with the British in 1775–1783 and again in 1812[1] he is almost certainly quoting reliable hearsay, but he cites no authority for this claim. Even more frustratingly Moore states that "some few songs have been received from the recollections of a few surviving soldiers who heard and sang them amid the trials of camp and field", but he does not specify which songs were the result of this precious personal communication. As with the music of wars before and since, one is left to grope towards conclusions.

Quite the most famous song of the war – indeed, one of the most famous tunes in history – was *Yankee Doodle*, but it is not always realized perhaps for how long this was a redcoats' tune. It is generally accepted that the words were written by Dr. Richard Shuckburgh around 1755 in derision of the odd-looking colonials who had come to help the British regulars fight the French, and the redcoats continued to use it in contempt. After all, the great Wolfe had called Americans "the worst soldiers in the world" and his successor Murray believed "the native American is a very effeminate thing, very unfit for and impatient of war". The British commanders were surprised, therefore, when on April 18–19, 1775, troops under Colonel Francis Smith sent to seize American arms stored at Concord, just 20 miles from Boston, were so stoutly resisted as to need rescue by Lord Percy's reinforcements. But Brigadier Lord Percy, who had not yet met the American sharpshooters, thought it high fun to have his music play the jeering *Yankee Doodle* as his 900 men swung through Roxbury; he good-naturedly asked a young American bystander what there was to laugh about. "To think that soon you will dance to *Chevy Chase*," answered the boy, referring to the very old ballad about Otterbourne where Percy's great ancestor was defeated and captured.[2] Even the running fight between Concord and Lexington, in which the rebels dealt out far more punishment than they received, failed to convince the British commanders of the determination and mettle of the American soldier, so the opportunity for a massed frontal assault on the American position overlooking Boston was positively relished.

The resulting Battle of Bunker Hill is one of the few battles in which both sides played the same tune. (See p. 107 for a similar happening at Famars). In 1826 an old man named Robert Steele played, at a Bunker Hill re-union, the same airs that he had drummed at the fight, and *Yankee Doodle* was among them.[3] An American fifer from nearby Cambridge, called Parks, who had served with Gardner's Regiment, said that *Yankee Doodle* was "first employed at that time, being introduced by the British to ridicule the Americans".[4] In 1853, 93-year old Benjamin Smith of Needham, Massachusetts, said that the popular rebel tunes of the period were the *Road to Boston* and *The President's March,* until their musicians learned *Yankee Doodle* and *The white cockade* "from hearing the British play them in the distance".[5] The fact that *Yankee Doodle* was an essentially redcoat tune was established as early as 1787 when it was recorded that "the English army at Bunker Hill marched to the insulting tune of *Yankee Doodle,* but from that period it became the air of triumph".[6] This was not surprising, for although the British drove the rebels from their positions, they lost over 1,000 men to the Americans' 400. The British may have continued to use the tune, but there is no evidence to contradict John Trumbull's contemporary assertion that,

> . . . every rebel fife in play,
> To *Yankee Doodle* turned its lay.[7]

Despite setbacks such as the losses at Bunker Hill, and the evacuation of Boston (which of course the Americans entered to the strains of *Yankee Doodle!*),[8] the British were still confident of victory, and in the security of London a grand strategy was devised. Reduced to its simplest terms, one army under Sir John Burgoyne was to move south from Canada to Albany in New York State, where it would be met by the troops of General Lord Howe, advancing northward up the Hudson from New York. The effect, when the two armies linked up, would be to cut the colonies in half, severing the leadership of New England from the resources and rich manpower of the Mid-Atlantic and Southern Colonies. Once firmly astride the insurgents' lines of communication, the Crown could easily win the war of attrition that would necessarily follow. Moreover, a "side-show" was also arranged — an advance from west to east along the Mohawk River, which joined the Hudson near Albany. In June 1777 Burgoyne was at the head of Lake Champlain with 7,000 regulars, including 3,000 Brunswickers under an outstandingly good officer, Major-General von Riedesel. Like German soldiers anywhere they demanded and delighted in war music. They had been pleased by the numerous songs composed about von Riedesel in Trois Rivières, Quebec, although they did not much care for the French-Canadian style of singing – "the bawling of chansons from stentorian lungs".[9] But once on the march this alien music was forgotten, and they reverted to type. "The men were in great spirits and sang and longed for victory," wrote von Riedesel's wife, who accompanied her husband on campaign.[10] When they met the Americans at Hibberton (or Hubbardtown) their English comrades were surprised to see the Germans sing psalms before going into action;[11] further, to bluff the Americans that he was in great strength, von Riedesel had his bands play the troops into combat. "Under their brave leader Captain von Geyso they advanced upon the enemy, with fixed bayonets and to the sound of music,"[12] although the American marksmen must have done terrible execution among the musicians. The combination of psalm singing and rousing music did the trick and the battle was won, but its significance was minimal. Howe had not marched north, but had ventured west towards Philadelphia and although he won battles – (at Brandywine Creek his men, too, advanced playing *The Grenadiers March*[13]) he had failed in his primary mission – to support Burgoyne. "Gentleman Johnny" Burgoyne found his depleted force, with just over 3,000 troops fit for duty, surrounded and hopelessly outnumbered and on October 17, at Saratoga, was forced to surrender. The honours of war granted by the Americans did little to cheer his men. "Though we beat *The Grenadiers March* which not long before was so animating yet then it seemed by its last feeble effort as if almost ashamed to be heard on such an occasion."[14] The Americans enlivened the scene with *Yankee Doodle*. In the words of a local clergyman,

> As they began to march, as soon,
> The conquerors all agree.
> To sound the *Yankee Doodle* tune,
> Upon the highest key.[15]

Some of the German bandsmen who had withstood the vicious fire at Hibberton so bravely saw in Burgoyne's capitulation an opportunity to better what was doubtless a pretty hard lot. Somehow they contrived to evade their officers and stay on in New England, becoming from 1783–1790 Frederick Granger's Band, the pride of Boston.[16] No one can really blame them for making the change, and they were certainly not as traitorous as the band of the 62nd Regiment who the following year deserted their bandmaster and travelled to Boston to play for an American regiment.[17]

Although Saratoga was a diplomatic as well as a military disaster (it encouraged the French, Spanish and Dutch to join against the hard-pressed British) it still did not strike the high command of either side that the war was entering a particularly critical stage. Indeed Sir Henry Clinton, Howe's second-in-command, could still afford to spend a good deal of time relaxing, and at a splendid ball he called for the band to play the well-known war song, *Britons, strike home!* The American girl to whom he had been talking sweetly suggested that his tongue had slipped. "The commander in chief has made a mistake. He meant to say, Britons, go home!"[18] This particular song had been written by Henry Purcell for *Bonduca* in 1695, and although it appears dramatic by modern standards the soldiers liked it.

> Britons, strike home!
> Revenge, revenge, your country's wrongs.
> Fight, fight, and record,
> Fight, fight, and record,
> Yourselves in Druid songs.

A certain Corporal Ephraim Tristram Bates confessed he rallied his martial spirits by singing it,[19] and it was also played in 1743 at Dettingen in rather quaint circumstances. As the French infantry gave way before the charge of the Life Guards, the trumpeter of the Earl of Craufurd's troop gave an impromptu rendering of *Britons, strike home*, and the Earl, with old-fashioned courtesy, wheeled his horse to thank the imaginative musician.[20]

18
Britons, strike home

MUSIC   H. Purcell

The message of *Britons, strike home* was not entirely wishful thinking on Clinton's part, for so far as actual fighting was concerned his men, at least, were holding their own against the rebels. The redcoats were no longer the over-burdened pipe-clayed puppets of Bunker Hill, neatly lining up to be shot. The Light Infantry companies could now play the Americans at their own game, the loyalists, of course, fought in the rebels' style, and the Highland regiments were as feared, fierce, and unorthodox as their fathers who had scattered Cope at Prestonpans. Happily, a little survives from the music of all three.

The Light Infantry were disgruntled because they felt they had not "hitherto received their merited tribute from the muses", although the British soldier was generally able to compose his own doggerel (or better) when the mood took him. Anxious to please, a Philadelphia paper printed a song about the Light Infantry exploits (which was so vulgar that it probably delighted them) but this roughness seems to have caused a few blushes, and an American loyalist wrote new verses to the air of *Black sloven*, which were published in THE ROYAL GAZETTE.[21] This is obviously a song intended for soldiers and there is no direct evidence that they chose to sing it. It is included, however, because there seems every probability that it was sung when the officers were entertained by the female loyalists of New York even if it found less favour in stag company.

> For battle prepared in their country's just cause,
> Their king to avenge and support all his laws,
> As fierce as the tiger, as swift as the roe
> The British Light Infantry rush on their foe.
>
> Though rebels un-numbered oppose their career
> Their hearts are undaunted, they're strangers to fear,
> No obstacles hinder, relentless they go
> And death and destruction attend every blow.
>
> The alarm of the drum and the cannon's loud roar,
> The musket's quick flash but inflames them the more.
> No dangers dismay for they fear no control,
> But glory and conquest inspires every soul.
>
> Whenever the foe stands arranged in their sight,
> With ardour impatient they pant for the fight.
> Rout, havoc, confusion—they spread through the field
> And rebellion and treason are forced to yield.

19
Light Infantry song

WORDS Traditional
MUSIC "Black Sloven" – Traditional
SOURCE Universal Magazine Feb. 1771

It has been said that at some periods of the war there were more Americans fighting for the British than against them, and if the advice of these loyalists had been more frequently heeded, and if they had been treated with more consideration by the British, the war might have had a different conclusion. In the southern states particularly, the war between the loyalists and the rebels was savage, with quarter rarely asked or given, but there is no hint of this savagery in the cheery words that follow. Sung to the air *Langolee*, they were composed by Barney Thompson, piper to the Volunteers of Ireland, for the St. Patrick's Day celebrations of March 17, 1780.

> Success to the shamrock and all those who wear it,
> Be honour their portion wherever they go.
> May riches attend them and stores of good claret,
> For how to employ them, sure, none better know.
> Every foe surveys them with terror,
> But every silk petticoat wishes them nearer,
> So Yankee keep off or you'll soon learn your error,
> For Paddy shall prostrate lay every foe.[22]

20

Volunteers of Ireland song

MUSIC "Langolee" – Traditional
SOURCE Bland and Weller –
Entire New and Compleat Instructions for the Fife

On that day in March 1780 Barney Thompson's loyalist audience could have felt optimistic enough. Although the French had come into the war and their expeditionary force had reached America, "the damned mounseers" were again taking their traditional drubbing from the redcoats. The previous autumn the Comte d'Estaing with his American allies had invested Savannah in Georgia, and for days the besiegers listened to Scots pipes wailing from the defences, "this music of the Scottish mountains . . . most sad and most remarkable".[23] On the night of October 9, joint Franco-American troops prepared for a surprise attack, but this "lugubrious harmony" demoralized the storming columns before

they fairly began. It showed that the attack was no surprise, and as
d'Estaing wrote, "that they wanted us to know their best troops were
waiting for us".[24] So indeed they were and the discomforted French and
Americans lost 900 men. Like the British, the Americans have their
"tradition-mongers", and ale-house historians sometimes claim that this
assault was met by the British playing *Come to the maypole, merry farmers
all*; but if there was a tune of that name, it has never been found, and no
contemporary historian of the siege tells the story.

When the allies broke up the siege of Savannah the American commander, General Benjamin Lincoln (no relation to the President), with-
drew to South Carolina and Sir Henry Clinton left New York to engage
him in the southern theatre. By April 1, Lincoln was trapped in
Charleston and on May 12, after a forty-five day siege, he surrendered
6,000 men, 400 guns and three ships. Lincoln's capitulation provides
the starting point for one of the most famous and perplexing incidents in
the history of war music. The seventh article of capitulation that Lincoln
proposed on May 8, 1780, was quite unexceptional since it embodied a
time-honoured privilege, "the garrison . . . to march out with shouldered
arms, drums beating and colours flying". But the next day Clinton amended
this : "the drums are not to beat a British march, or colours to be un-
cased". Note that it is Clinton who first mentions a British march, although there is no reason to suppose that the Americans would have
dreamed of playing one. Nonetheless, on the same day, Lincoln rushed
back his alterations to Clinton's amendment. "Number seven. This
article to stand as first proposed ; the drums beating a British march".[25]
In fact Lincoln was not demanding the article "as first proposed" for
only Clinton's specific denial of the rebels' right to play a British tune
now led them to claim it. Clinton remained unmoved, and when Lincoln
finally surrendered the town his music played *The Turk's March*[26] (which
may or may not have been Mozart's composition), while the incoming
British played *God save the King*.[27] There is no obvious reason why
Clinton insisted, out of the blue, that the Americans should not play
British music. The most likely supposition is that the redcoats were still
playing *Yankee Doodle* with uncomplimentary refinements and elabora-
tions, and Clinton did not intend to hear British martial airs executed by
the defeated Americans with derisory brayings.

But this childish quibbling was no more than the prelude to a far more dramatic event. In 1781 the course of the war changed, and with Clinton's return to New York the British command in the south devolved upon General Cornwallis. After a bright beginning, his fortunes turned sour, and on October 19 he surrendered at Yorktown with 8,000 men to a combined Franco-American army. Two distinguished American historians have written of this event, "The British stacked arms while their band played *The world turned upside down*"[28] and a comparably eminent Briton confirms "the tradition" that the British Army "marched to the melancholy tune of *The world turned upside down*".

> If ponies rode men and grass ate cows,
> And cats were chased into holes by the
> mouse . . .
> If summer were spring and the other way
> round,
> Then all the world would be upside down.[29]

But this story, which has appealed to imaginations on both sides of the Atlantic and has been quoted in authoritative texts, is best treated with some hesitation. First, the importance at Yorktown of *The world turned upside down* was not even mentioned until 1828, when the story was published in Alexander Garden's second series of ANECDOTES OF THE AMERICAN REVOLUTION.[30] He said that he obtained it in 1822 from Major William Jackson of Philadelphia, who – in turn – had received it either orally or by letter from Lieutenant-Colonel John Laurens, one of the officers involved in the negotiations leading up to the surrender at Yorktown. Laurens left no written records and was inconveniently killed in 1782, so it is only certain that Jackson told Garden something that he'd learned, somehow or other, 40 years before. The third article of capitulation stipulated "shouldered arms, colours cased, and drums beating a British or German march" and according to Laurens' story as told by Jackson the Americans' reprisal for the terms imposed on General Lincoln inspired the redcoats to play *The world turned upside down*.

There is no doubt that this particular article was a great talking point among the Americans. Washington's artillerist, General Henry Knox, informed his wife that the British would not be permitted to play *Yankee Doodle*, and he wrote to John Jay: "They were prohibited playing a French or American tune".[31] The NEW JERSEY GAZETTE of November 7, 1781, was just one of the papers that thought its readers would be interested in this detail. But no contemporary mentions exactly what the British and their German allies *did* play.

The provenance of *The world turned upside down* is only a trifle less elusive than that of *Come to the maypole, merry farmers all* (p. 79). As long ago as 1890 a correspondent from Washington D.C. wrote to NOTES AND QUERIES: "I have sought during five years this song in several collections of old ballads and among much old music, and have sent by two importers of music in New York to England for it, all without avail",[32] nor does it seem that he had much satisfaction from NOTES AND QUERIES. It is definite only that in 1781 there was no well-known British air with that title although the phrase "the world turned upside down" had found its way into various ballads through the centuries, and one set of words with that title were put to Mathew Parker's old cavalier air, *When the king enjoys his own again*.

> I took delight in jovial life 'till fate on me did frown.
> Until alas, I got a wife, and the world turned upside down.[33]

In short, though the words were most appropriate for an event in which the king's ex-subjects were showing such *lèse-majesté* there is no evidence to show that this air, with its original message, was well-known in 1781. The words given above date from 1646 and it is improbable that they would have remained in common use until 1781. Another theory has suggested that the tune played was the old air *Derry down*, for in 1766 a song sympathetic to the colonists had been written to this melody and called *The world turned upside down*, or, *The old woman taught wisdom*. But this title does not appear in the words of the ballad and it seems to have been published only in THE GENTLEMAN'S MAGAZINE[34] and nowhere else. In any case, it would have been unthinkable for British soldiers to play a melody which had even the slightest favourable association with the victorious rebels.

The origin of the words quoted by Professor Mackesy, and the tune that goes with them, is uncertain. In the course of research for this book, the words and their tune were sung on a BBC programme and information about their origin was requested. It was hoped that the melody might be well known in some part of the British Isles and that the words could be proved to date from the 18th century. From virtually every corner of the country letters arrived showing that the words were based closely on a nonsense poem called *Topsy-turvy world* written in the 19th century by William Brighty Rands. As for the tune, it was not conclusively identified by anyone.

One other fact suggests that *The world turned upside down* was not of central importance at Yorktown. It is simply that the Anglo-German forces did not have a massed band, but musicians from 15 separate units, and since the capitulation ceremony involved something like 23,000 men and lasted several hours, it is almost certain that a whole range of music was heard, not just one tune.

There is one other observation about this ritual of playing other people's marches. There was nothing unusual in doing it as a bluff, as was seen at Almanza and in the Thirty Years War, (p. 19) or in doing it in derision. Long before the British began playing *Yankee Doodle*, the Dutch fleet which sailed up the Medway in 1667, burned the English men o' war lying there, and towed off the *Royal Charles*, played *Joan's placket is torn* from the decks of the captured vessel.[35] But no 18th century book of military procedure which describes the routine for capitulation, not even Thomas Simes's encyclopaedic MILITARY MEDLEY of 1768, suggests that a worthy loser might expect to play his conqueror's march. It seems almost certain that the quibbling at Charleston and Yorktown stemmed originally from the British trick of playing *Yankee Doodle* with a raspberry.

Although this particular problem is never likely to be solved, there are a number of contemporary comments about the music of the various armies on that fateful day at Yorktown. One American soldier said that the British music was "slow and solemn"[36] another that "the drums beat as if they did not care how",[37] and Aedanus Burke was, against his intentions, moved. "One hour ago I was one of the many spectators who saw the British Army march prisoners of war out of the garrison of York... They marched through both armies in a slow pace and to the sound of music, not military marches but of certain airs which had in them . . . a strain of melancholy".[38] Aedanus Burke was a Galway Irishman who fought for the Americans and his failure to mention the names of these haunting airs provides circumstantial evidence of a sort. Burke, from a country where they still looked back with regret to the Stuarts, is more likely to have recognised *When the king enjoys his own again* than an English listener, if it had been played, and to have made comment.

Secondly, there is another "tradition" that when the Irish surrendered a city – as Limerick in 1691 – they played one particular sad tune, and this was the tune which the British Army borrowed in 1781. No real Irish authority so far encountered believes this tradition, and Burke does not seem to have recognized any Irish lament.

Quite apart from the sad strains of the British troops, who always took capitulation very unsportingly, there were other bands playing at York-town. Johann Konrad Doehla, an Ansbach sergeant, mentions bands – presumably German ones – and he has a word for the French who "played delightfully",[39] while an American also spoke of "the lovely French music". Both the Americans and the French played *Yankee Doodle*, the Americans as their right,[40] and the French to discomfort the British, for according to the Marquis of Lafayette, as the British marched out between the parallel lines of French and Americans they turned their heads to the French and ignored the ex-colonials. "A little piqued at this piece of affectation he thought he would try the effect of music upon them, and ordered his band to strike up *Yankee Doodle*. The British turned their heads at the sound of the tune"[41] – presumably marching "eyes front" and thus denying both victorious armies the courtesy of a salute.

While the Americans were fighting for their independence, the French, Spaniards, and Dutch (who had all been encouraged to join in after Saratoga) were fighting for whatever territorial aggrandizement they could acquire on the side. The main attention of the Army was, of course focused on North America, but these encroachments by European powers also had to be opposed. Although not, strictly speaking, part of the War of Independence, these derivative campaigns do make contributions to the music of the redcoats. The Spaniards were particularly hopeful of regaining Gibraltar, which the British had seized in 1704, and with French assistance they besieged it for four years. The opening British salvoes, fired on September 12, 1779, were heralded by the citadel's eccentric and heroic defender, General Eliott, with *Britons, strike home!*[42] – a tribute to the song's popularity – and when the siege was finally raised the band of the 12th Regiment played *See, the conquering hero comes*.[43] In the interim a soldier nick-named Jack Careless, either an itinerant lunatic or the stuff of which V.C.s are made, was found wandering the streets during a heavy bombardment singing as though his heart

D*

would burst,

> A soldier's life is a merry life,
> From care and trouble free

"Damn me, if I don't like fighting", was the only excuse he had to offer.[44]

While the Spaniards were vainly trying to regain Gibraltar, the French were making equally futile efforts to recapture ground they had lost to Britain in earlier wars, particularly in India where Robert Clive had bested their own empire-builder, Joseph Dupleix. Opposing the French in this struggle were European regiments of the East India Company, sepoys paid from the same bottomless purse, and regiments of the regular British army, including the 72nd Seaforth Highlanders with their soul-stirring pipes.

The Comte d'Estaing, gazing morosely at the walls of Savannah in America and depressed by "the lugubrious harmony" of bagpipes, calculated they were intended to discourage his men, but he would have been surprised to see the animating effect of the pipes on Highland troops campaigning under the exhausting Indian sun. At the day-long action of Cuddalore (1783) which began at 4 a.m. the 72nd were raised to a final conclusive attack in the later afternoon by the challenge of the pipes.[45] Before Madras, also 1783, after a gruelling day's march which left the rest of the army collapsed on the ground, the Seaforths' pipers struck up and the Scots danced bounding reels, to the utter amazement of their comrades.[46]

Apart from soldiers' own memoirs and newspapers, one other source for the American War of Independence was discovered – a MS music book[47] compiled by a British soldier during the war. It became the property of John Greenwood, fife major in the 15th Massachusetts Regiment, veteran of Bunker Hill, Quebec, Trenton, and the American marine service by the time he was 23, and who was eventually to win a more portentous fame as the "Father of Scientific Dentistry in America". He left the army after the battle of Trenton, very lousy, but in possession of the song book which he obtained, it is said, from a redcoat fifer – dead or alive we do not know – and from which, in the words of his son "he got great store". The book is particularly interesting because it must be a true guide to what the band played and what the soldiers danced to, for it is essentially a mixed personal collection – not an official list of items the British fifer had to practise. Many of the tunes are completely unmilitary – minuets, hornpipes, and the like – but some have a martial flavour. They include *Over the water to Charlie*, *A song of Major Andrea* [sic], the ill-fated hero of the Benedict Arnold Affair, and a series of marches: *Roslyn Castle*, *Dickson's March*, *The Marquis of Granby*, *The York Fusiliers*, *A Highland March*, (which turns out to be *The garb of old Gaul*), *A favourite Irish March*, (which is *The harp that once through Tara's halls*). *Boston March*, *The Warwickshire lads*, *Dorsetshire March*, *Jockey to the fair*, and *The Grenadiers March* noted on p. 34.

Manuscript books such as these can prove extremely useful in dating particular tunes and for assessing what musically-inclined (if possibly atypical redcoats) liked to play. They are, unfortunately, all too rare. Only two of these books are known to exist in England, both at the National Army Museum, Camberley. One is an unpretentious little collection, begun by Edward Russell of the West Monmouthshire Militia in 1812. It includes *The Prussian March*, *The Duke of York's Troop*, *The roast beef of old England*, *The white cockade*, and *The Grenadiers March*. The other book, compiled by Sergeant F. Newman of the 97th Regiment in the 1850s, is far more ambitious. It contains several hundred pieces, and ranges from waltzes and polkas to fashionable marches like *Rory O' More*, and takes in traditional soldier tunes such as *The plains of Waterloo*, *Barrosa plains*, and *How happy the soldier*. Another MS book is in the Sutro Library, San Francisco and once belonged to William Brown of the 6th (Inniskilling) Dragoons, who compiled it in 1797. Brown was a trumpeter who eventually became bandmaster and his little book, like the one Greenwood acquired, is strictly a labour of love. The notation is for the violin and the book can only have been intended to help this musically inclined trooper while away his leisure hours; his tastes were even less military than those of Greenwood's compiler, and only *The Duke of York's March*, *The Coldstream March*, and, as befits a good Ulsterman, *Boyne Water* come into our category. A fifth book of this sort is also in North America, and although not strictly a soldier's compilation it has to be mentioned here. It is in the museum of the 22nd Regiment at La Citadelle, Quebec, and was put together around 1853 by a certain James Thompson Junior, deputy commissary general for Lower Canada. His father had been a sergeant in those Fraser Highlanders who did *not* run at Quebec (see page 64). Thompson Senior had stayed on in Canada, and was appointed Overseer of Works for the Royal Engineers in Quebec. He was still actively overseeing at the age of 95, and died just two years short of his century. James Junior seems to have been well steeped in military tradition and his book contains some temptingly titled items — a number of regimental marches, "a favourite march of my father's", a bellicose ballad or two, and a regimental song of the 71st Regiment called *The knight from Palestine*. Regrettably, neither text nor music of any of these tunes could be obtained.

Before saying farewell to North America a paragraph has to be added on the war of 1812, and no more than a paragraph is possible. In the words of a 19th century writer : "The anecdotal history of this second war with [sic] North America is not very copious. In fact few persons have cared to write the story of a campaign which did not shed refulgence upon our arms."[48] It is known that when Canadian loyalists marched out of Fredericton in New Brunswick bound for threatened Quebec they tried to keep their spirits up with *The girl I left behind me*, but the march seemed so desperate that "it was impossible not to feel in a certain degree low spirited as our bugles struck up the merry air".[49] There is also the story of the subaltern who, before the British attacked New Orleans, wanted to find out more about American military music. When the Yankees sounded reveille two hours before dawn, two or three "tolerably full military bands began to play" and the writer, inching past his own pickets in the dark, crawled to within easy earshot of the American lines. Whether he judged the expedition worth while is not quite clear. "The Yankees are not famous for their good taste in anything, but one or two of the waltzes struck me as being peculiarly beautiful". He was a rash young man, this subaltern, to work in so close to Andrew Jackson's keen-eared and straight-shooting pickets, especially since he had to endure, between the "peculiarly beautiful" waltzes, *Yankee Doodle* "at least six times".[50]

1. F. Moore, *Songs and Ballads of the American Revolution* (1856), p.47.

2. W. Gordon, *The History of the United States of America* (1788), I, p.481.

3. S. Swett, *History of the Bunker Hill Battle* (1827), p.25.

4. *Ibid*, p.25.

5. *Boston Historical Magazine* (July, 1859), p.220.

6. F. J. de Chastellux, *Travels in North America* (1787), I, p.52.

7. W. L. Stone, *Ballads and Poems Relating to the Burgoyne Campaign* (1893), p.15.

8. D. Dudley, *Diary* (1876), p.60.

9. W. L. Stone, *Letters of Brunswick and Hessian Officers during the American Revolution* (1891), pp. 71–72.

10. F. C. L. von Riedesel, *Letters and Memoirs* (1827), p.167.

11. R. Lamb, *Memoir of his Own Life* (1811), p.174.

12. W. L. Stone, *Memoirs of Major General Riedesel* (1868), I, p.115.

13. *Oxfordshire Light Infantry Chronicle* (1897), p.130.

14. W. Digby, *Some Account of the American War* (1887), p.320.

15. W. L. Stone, *Burgoyne Campaign*, p.59.

16. *Bostonian Society Proceedings* (January, 1949), p.42.

17. T. Anburey, *Travels Through the Interior Parts of America* (1789), II, p.228

18. A. Garden, *Anecdotes of the Revolutionary War* (1822), p.412.

19. E. T. Bates, *The Life and Memoirs of Mr. Ephraim Tristram Bates* (1756), p.66.

20. *Memoirs of the Life of John, Earl of Craufurd* (1769), p.274.

21. Moore, p.204.

22. *Rivington's Gazette* (18 March, 1780).

23. A. A. Lawrence, *Storm over Savannah* (1951), p.103.

24. *Ibid*, p.103.

25. W. Moultrie, *Memoirs of the American Revolution* (1802), II, pp. 88–101.

26. B. A. Uhlendorf, *The Siege of Charleston* (1938), p.293.

27. *Ibid*, p.293.

28. A. Nevins and H. S. Commager, *America: The Story of a Free People* (1954), p.91.

29. P. Mackesy, *The War for America, 1775–1783* (1964), p.427.

30. A Garden, *Anecdotes of the American Revolution* (1828), p.17.

31. F. S. Drake, *Life and Correspondence of H. Knox* (1873), pp.70–72.

32. *NQ*, Seventh Series, IX, p.408.

33. Thomason Tracts, 669.f.10 (47).

34. *Gentleman's Magazine* (1766), pp.140–141.

35. S. Pepys, *Diary* (22nd June, 1667).

36. J. Thacher, *Military Journal* (1823), pp.345–346.

37. W. H. Denny, *Military Journal of Major E. Denny* (1860), p.248.

38. E. C. Burnett, *Letters of Members of the Continental Congress* (1921–36), VI, p.249.

39. F. Kapp, *The Life of Frederick William von Steuben* (1859), pp.461–462.

40. *Boston Independent Ledger* (12 November, 1781).

41. Harvard University Library, Jared Sparks MS 32, p.248.

42. J. Drinkwater, *Siege of Gibraltar* (1785), p.2.

43. *Ibid*, p.352.

44. S. Ancell, *Circumstantial Journal of the Siege of Gibraltar* (1783), p.133.

45. I. H. M. Scobie, *Pipers and Pipe Music in a Highland Regiment* (1924), p.8.

46. *Ibid*, p.8.

47. Archives of New York Historical Society.

48. J. H. Stocqueler, *The British Soldier* (1857), p.135.

49. USM (1831), Part III, p.180.

50. [Anon], *A Subaltern in America* (1833), p.244.

Chapter 6

THE FRENCH WARS 1793–1815

T HE Revolutionary and Napoleonic Wars persisted, with one short break of fourteen months, from 1793 to 1815. The redcoats of these wars were less reluctant than previous generations of soldiers to recount their deeds, and there is no lack of material from which to build up a musical history of the period. This welcome prolixity is due in the first instance to simple mathematics ; the British Army was larger than ever before, and fighting for a longer continuous period, so the law of averages dictated that there would be more men wanting to write about themselves. In 1748 there had been 74,000 regular troops, a lesser number in the Seven Years War, and a maximum of 110,000 during the American War of Independence. By 1807, however, there were almost 200,000 redcoats dispersed around the world, and in 1813 Wellington commanded 52,000 British regulars in the Peninsula alone.

But it was the quality of these men, as much as the quantity, that explains their writing. Few men enlisted under Marlborough or Wolfe from any deep-seated conviction ; but the struggle against Jacobin France and subsequently Napoleonic imperialism became a life-or-death struggle for Britain. The same ideological impulses that involved a later generation in the Spanish Civil War leavened the usual rag-tag of the ranks with a core of intelligent, lettered men, who had enlisted because they felt a strong obligation – to defend their country, – as Cromwell said, "Men who made some conscience of what they did". Being men of a more elevated class than was usual for common soldiers they had both the ability and the desire to express themselves. Men such as these – shopkeepers, artisans, yeomen – expected to rise according to their abilities, but in the British Army commissions were generally the prerogative of "gentlemen". This explains why "the common soldier" of 1793–1815 often writes so well; he was far from unlettered or unimaginative, and it is thanks to the wretched caste system of the British Army that so many lucid accounts of life in the ranks were written. Added to the memoir writing of the rank and file were the usual number of officers who published their reminiscences.

It was not only the quality and quantity of potential soldier-authors, moreover, that created the wealth of anecdotal military literature; it was also due in large part to the tastes of the reading public. People knew more about these French Wars than they had known of any conflict since the Civil War. The British public were not directly affected as were non-combatants of warring nations on the Continent, and the blockade imposed by Napoleon's Berlin Decrees of 1806, being more theoretical than real, caused little hardship. But signs of the war were everywhere; the streets were thronged by regiments *en route* for embarkation, by wounded men, and by prisoners shuffling to the hulks. There were regular reports in the newspapers, and in particular, there was prosperity. The many items needed to keep great armies in the field were fabricated throughout the land, and with Britain's navy ruling the seas, and French overseas trade strangled, the rich American market was virtually monopolized by British goods. So while the war was on the nation basked in a glow of prosperity and pride, and was receptive to the first hand accounts of its warriors.

When the war was over there was no slackening in the output of books by veterans. They wrote to get something out of their system, to supplement their income if they were half-pay officers, or if they were ordinary soldiers again restricted by the social and economic structure of Britain, to retain their pride. As for the public, they saw less glory in the early years of accelerating industrialization than in the golden age of national unity and war, and they welcomed reminders of Britain's past glories, and bought the soldiers' books as a form of light relief.

Because of all these circumstances there exist, apart from strictly strategic accounts of campaigns and countless MSS, over 100 works of lighter weight – anecdotal, informal, and personal. The material varies immensely in style and in value to the military historian but it has yielded up a myriad of fragments about war music.

One of the most interesting things to emerge was the importance of music as an inducement to enlisting ; a broadside ballad puts it in a nutshell.

> When first I heard the drum and fife
> Strike up a march so neatly oh!
> I thought I never in my life
> Heard music sound so sweetly oh!

This sentiment was not new in the French Wars. A 17th century writer summed it up this way : "neither for mine own part have I heard more sweet and solemn music than that which the drum and flute hath afforded".[1] For a veteran of the American War of Independence, "the rattling of a British fife and drum is the sweetest of music".[2] Now, any number of soldiers of the Napoleonic era joined the chorus. "Enthusiasm seized me and I felt as if the soldier's life was the only station for which nature had designed me," wrote one, thinking of the time he first heard a military band.[3] Another, who became a fifer himself, describes how in the 1790's Edinburgh was in the throes of a continual martial pageant, boasting three volunteer regiments plus artillery and yeoman cavalry, and "several regiments of little boys in the New Town who had flags, drums, swords, belts, and military caps". Quite inflamed, he took the king's shilling and grasped the fife, although he later admitted that "the sequel of my history will show that I had enough of it before all was finished".[4] He was not the only redcoat who lived to regret the snare of the syren drum which ostensibly, "leads him to pleasure as well as to fight". The band of the Royal Horse Artillery playing *Over the hills and far away* in 1797 "kindled a flame in my bosom which nothing but death can extinguish", claimed one warrior, but then – remembering the war he endured was one part ecstasy, one part horror, and ninety-eight parts boredom – he added : "I have now long since had my full share of the reality of the Scotch melody".[5]

Music also proved valuable in maintaining the spirits of the Johnny Raws who took the shilling under the influence of the spirit-stirring drum, the recruiting sergeant's outrageous patter, or, not too rarely, an excess of drink. A lieutenant of the 31st Regiment shepherding some hundred wild Irish from Portsmouth to their base at Ashford in Kent kept them together by playing their native airs on his flute. Although, as he confessed, "I was no great proficient," the Irish were as enchanted as the children of Hamelin.[6] Sometimes the recruits would sing themselves along. One motley crew – a truly Falstaffian band which included a lawyer, an actor, a poet, and assorted sweeps, tinkers, and tailors – marched behind their officer singing and one of them presented him with a commemorative verse.

> To Painswick brave Harley led the way,
> His great commands the troops did obey.
> From him till death they ne'er did stray,
> Sing *Garryowen*, and clear the way![7]

Music also played its part on the home front, and the innumerable volunteer corps which were raised to counter the threat of invasion inevitably had their own music and their specially composed or adopted marches. Before Nelson's victory at Trafalgar in 1805, there was always a lurking threat of a French assault, so that "every town was a sort of garrison". Along with the tramp of feet on the parade ground and the crash of grounded musket could be heard "in one place . . . the tattoo of some youth learning to play the drum, at another place some march or national air being practised upon the fife".[8] This music was not a makeweight, a substitute for soldiering, but an integral part of the real thing. When a false alarm alerted the Scottish border in 1804 the riding and rallying took place to the accompaniment of traditional music. Sir Walter Scott tells how "the different corps on arriving at the alarm posts announced themselves by their music, playing the tunes peculiar to their own districts, many of which had been gathering signals for centuries". The Liddesdale men entered Kelso with a challenge booming down from the great days of their moss-trooper ancestors.

> Oh wha dare meddle wi' me?
> And wha dare meddle wi' me?
> My name is little Jack Elliott,
> And wha dare meddle wi' me?[9]

At Selkirk, Lord Home – whose family had often been entangled in the feuding past – called on the volunteers he commanded to sing an old song whose refrain "up with the souters of Selkirk and down with the Earl of Home" never failed to put them in a fighting mood. The souters, or burgesses, were taken aback, for the song contrasted their own doughty work at the Battle of Flodden in 1513 with the less glorious part played by the House of Home. Despite Lord Home's obvious good nature they all professed ignorance of the words, until the nobleman, tiring of their excessive delicacy, sang a solo. Next day the Selkirk men had the good grace, and humour, to enrol Home as a souter.[10]

21

The souters o' Selkirk

WORDS Traditional
MUSIC Traditional
SOURCE The Scots Musical Museum

Overseas, "in Flanders, Portugal and Spain", instrumental music had a number of accepted, although not officially specified, functions. The long and wearisome marches – typical of the Peninsular War – were lightened by cheery quicksteps and "those who were tired and jaded sprang up, endued as it were with additional life and vigour".[11] One writer describes a dusty column trudging wearily into the Portuguese town of Thomar on March 17, 1811, responding magically to *St. Patrick's Day*. "The most tired and dejected were, for a time, enlivened by the strains of this favourite quickstep".[12]

Bands, or fifes and drums, also took part in parades when towns were captured or battles were won. One of the earliest British successes in the Revolutionary war (when the initiative was generally in French hands) was the capture on July 28, 1793, of Valenciennes. It was optimistically regarded as practically a suburb of Paris and the war seemed as good as finished. The British marched up to take possession of the gate with "the band of the 14th Regiment playing and the drums beating the *British Grenadiers* march. On the drawbridge they played *God save the King*, the march in *Scipio*, and other pieces".[13] When San Sebastian fell, years later in 1813, no one thought the war was won this time, but a victory was a victory and the Fifth Division made a grand entry playing *See, the conquering hero comes*.[14] After Wellington (or more properly at that time, Wellesley) had defeated Junot at Vimeiro, north of Lisbon in 1808, his senior Sir Hew Dalrymple had the massed bands play the national anthem,[15] and after Waterloo the infantry bands in Paris again played *God save the King*, outside the gates of the Tuileries Palace.[16]

Regimental bands as well as fifes, drums and pipes, also provided music on solemn occasions. In 1811 as the funeral cortège of the Marquis of Romana, a Spanish general, passed through Cartaxo the band of the 79th saluted it with *To the land of the leal*.[17] After a toast to the memory of Sir John Moore, who died in the hour of victory at Corunna, the muffled drums beat out *Peace to the fallen brave*.[18] On Sundays, if a church service was possible, the band served as a substitute for the church organ,[19] while the flag-draped drums became altars, and the drummer boys perhaps were pressed into service as a choir. On at least one occasion a new and zealous chaplain mistook the purpose of the drums and before they had been covered, leaped upon one, and began to preach. The sermon was naturally spoiled by the reverberations of the instrument, and the noise of stifled belly-laughs as the redcoats anticipated the disappearance of the minister through his makeshift pulpit.[20] If the church used the army's apparatus, there was also one British soldier who used the church for military purposes. Sir Brent Spencer who commanded the First Division in the Peninsula had an intense pathological aversion to drums, and whenever it was possible his troops were summoned to parade by tolling bells.[21]

One of the less enviable tasks also allotted to drummers was flogging their comrades found guilty of infringing regulations, but even when not so directly and unpleasantly engaged, musicians were often involved in punitive ceremonies. *The Dead March in Saul* was played before military executions, and the *Rogues March* was beaten when undesirable characters, military and civil, were drummed from camps and cantonments, sometimes with a halter about their necks,[22] sometimes helped on their way by a farewell ritual kick from the regiment's youngest drummer.[23] Yet anyone hearing the sprightly rhythm of the *Rogues March* might well assume it to be the property of some crack regiment.

2 2

The Rogues March

MUSIC   Traditional
SOURCE   Bland and Weller –
Entire New and Compleat Instructions for the Fife

Its date of origin is uncertain. The earliest version that could be found
appeared in ENTIRE NEW AND COMPLEAT INSTRUCTIONS FOR THE FIFE, by
Bland and Weller and may be dated between 1793 and 1800. As early
as June 1736, however, the COURANT AND MERCURY notes that nine young

whores, "very naked and meagre beings", were flogged through the streets of Edinburgh as the drums beat *Cuckolds come dig*,[24] which may have been the *Rogues March* original title. On the other hand, an order of 1746 commands that the *Pioniers [sic] March* be used for ceremonies of degradation,[25] and by the time NEW AND COMPLEAT INSTRUCTIONS was published the *Pioneers* and the *Rogues* were different airs. But the ceremony itself seems to have died out as mysteriously as it appeared. Veterans of the Sudan and the South African War had never seen a man drummed out, although several of them recollected old soldiers who had witnessed the ritual. The *Rogues March* found its way into the American Army and was used in the Civil War with embellishments that do not seem to have occurred to the redcoats; sometimes the victims had half their heads shaved, sometimes they were tarred and feathered, or dragged behind a mule, and if they were pilferers, they might be deprived of all their clothes and be forced from the camp wearing nothing but a barrel.

The old-time redcoats, who boasted of the number of lashings they had received, found that the *Rogues March* was as amenable to doggerel lyrics as any other air, and in the mid-19th century they used to sing —

> Fifty I got for selling my coat,
> Fifty for selling my blanket.
> If ever I 'list for a soldier again,
> The devil shall be my sergeant.[26]

Quite the most thorny problem concerning the music of the French Wars is the extent to which it was played in battle for although there is plenty of comment much of it is obscure or contradictory. Dr. Henry G. Farmer in BANDS IN THE NAPOLEONIC WARS[27] makes out a seemingly strong case for the presence of bands on the battlefield. He quotes two stories from "James A. Browne, the Artillery historian" about Talavera (where two bands played from the shelter of a ravine) and Busaco (where Wellington "sent forward the bands to play the national anthem, and instantly the men seemed to fight with fresh vigour"). Unfortunately, the one book by Browne that could contain these stories, ENGLAND'S ARTILLERYMEN (1865), does not do so. If Dr. Farmer had access to unpublished MSS belonging to Browne one assumes he would have cited them in discussing such a controversial subject. Further, in the same article Dr. Farmer claimed that "when face to face with the French during the Peninsular War our bands would play French melodies in derision, such as the *Marche des Marseillois* [sic] and *Ça Ira*, which would be played in turn with *Rule Britannia* and the *British Grenadiers*".

To state categorically that on any issue involving war music Dr. Farmer is wrong would be dangerous, for his erudition was immense, but none of the works by Peninsular veterans consulted for SONGS AND MUSIC OF THE REDCOATS mention this particular habit. Moreover, Napoleon specifically forbade the playing of *Ça Ira* – a good air for anarchists perhaps but loathsome to a despot who substituted the hierarchy destroyed by the Revolution with one of his own. Consequently, it seems improbable that this air was heard by the British in the Peninsula. Dr. Farmer also recounts another delightful but again undocumented story. "Perhaps the most unusual use to which a regimental band was ever put happened during the Netherlands campaign of 1799 when the Duke of York, who commanded the British Army, ordered his bands to strike up martial airs . . . to drown the sounds of the French musketry which were frightening the notorious Elizabeth, Lady Holland". While Dr. Farmer was a scholar of enormous reputation, it is best to take his statement about the role of music in battle cautiously.

Memoirs of the wars are quite positive that before a battle bandsmen were detailed to act as medical orderlies. Sometimes, if a regiment was below strength or a particularly hot fight was foreseen, the bandsmen might be ordered to take a musket and join the ranks, and occasionally it seems that some of the musicians played while others fought. Thomas Hewitt, writing about the battle of Talavera, describes the 48th Regiment advancing with colours flying and band playing but he adds – inconsistently, unless it is accepted that the band was divided –"we had a dreadful hand-to-hand engagement for even the band had to fight in the ranks this day".[28]

At the storming of Ciudad Rodrigo in April 1812 the 43rd Regiment approached the breach *preceded* by their band, playing *The downfall of Paris* but this sight created such a stir among those who witnessed it that it was obviously extremely rare.[29] On occasion the bands played just before an action (and safely out of range) ; as the storming columns formed up to advance against the walls of Badajoz the band of the 88th Connaught Rangers played haunting Irish melodies and an untimely depression settled over the troops as they listened to the beautiful but melancholy *Savourneen deelish*,[30] ("dearest darling").

23
Savourneen deelish

WORDS   Traditional
MUSIC   Traditional

Sentimentally

Oh the mo - ment was sad when my Love and I __ part - ed, Sa-

vour - neen __ dee - lish, __ Eile - en __ oge! As I

kiss'd off her tears I was nigh __ brok-en heart - ed, Sa-

vour - neen __ dee - lish, __ Eile - en __ oge!

Wan was her cheek which hung on my shoul-der, damp was her hand no

mar-ble was cold-er, I felt that I ne-ver a - gain should be-hold __ her, Sa-

vour - neen __ dee - lish, __ Eile - en __ oge!

Oh the moment was sad, when my love and I parted,
Savourneen deelish, Eileen oge!
As I kissed off her tears I was near broken hearted
Savourneen deelish, Eileen oge!
Wan was her cheek, which hung on my shoulder,
Damp was her hand, no marble was colder
I felt that I never again should behold her.
Savourneen deelish, Eileen oge!

When the word of command put our men into motion
Savourneen deelish, Eileen oge!
I buckled my knapsack to cross the wide ocean,
Savourneen deelish, Eileen oge!
Brisk were our troops, all roaring like thunder,
Pleased with the voyage, impatient for plunder.
My bosom with grief was almost torn asunder
Savourneen deelish, Eileen oge!

Long I fought for my country, far, far, from my true love
Savourneen deelish, Eileen oge!
All my pay and my booty I hoarded for you, love.
Savourneen deelish, Eileen oge!
Peace was proclaimed, escaped from the slaughter,
Landed at home, my sweet girl I sought her,
But sorrow, alas, to her cold grave had brought her,
Savourneen deelish, Eileen oge!

As the Connaughts surveyed the bristling walls of Badajoz many of them must have thought that they, rather than Savourneen deelish, were the more fragile, and events proved them right.

The situation was reversed on the last day of 1811 when the French stormed the breach at Tarifa. They were fought off by the 87th Regiment, whose band stationed in the immediate rear played *Garryowen* and, as the attackers were routed, *St. Patrick's Day*.[31] According to another account, however, the music was a solo provided by a scapegrace Irish bugler with the apocryphal sounding name of Paddy Shannon.[32] At the battle of Famars in 1793 the band of the 14th Regiment was certainly well up with the combat troops,[33] and the story is told of Lord Cathcart at Geldermalsen (1795) crying, as the 28th Regiment came under fire: "Where is your band, sir? Now is the time for it to play".[34]

But two writers contemptuously dismiss the suggestion that music was an adjunct of battle. "The story one used to hear in one's boyhood of the bands of the regiments playing during the raging of a battle to drown the cries of the wounded is a myth".[35] Although this gentleman had many contacts among the Peninsular veterans he had not fought himself, and the evidence of a man who actually fought is therefore more valuable. Lieutenant-Colonel Wilkie asserts that a band was accustomed to play for the entertainment of the nuns in a convent near Salamanca and at length one of "the ancient virgins" asked for the tune that was played when they went into battle. "It would have been idle to persuade them that people had other things to think of", and the ferocious old lady was placated by the drums rattling reveille,[36] *Run, boys, run* as the troops called it.[37] These Iberian nuns tended to be eccentric in their musical tastes. Officers visiting a convent near Coimbra in Portugal were first treated to a beautiful organ voluntary, followed by the *Marseillaise*. "It was probably in compliment to us as military men and as the only march known to the invisible performers," suggested one of the visitors.[38]

Wellington's orders displayed his keen eye for minute detail and it seems strange that he issued none on the use of bands in battle – or anywhere else. It can only be assumed that what musicians did and where was left to the discretion of individual divisional or regimental commanders.

Even the part played by drummers in action is not wholly clear. The famous 19th century painting by Lady Elizabeth Butler showing the drums and fifes of the 57th (West Middlesex) Regiment at Albuera, bloody but erect, owes more to imagination than probability. From passing references it appears unlikely that the drummers accompanied the charging troops, although this was certainly the custom in the French Army. Redcoats were well acquainted with close-ups of young lads beating the *pas de charge* – which they ungallantly called *Old trousers*[39] – and the French paid dearly for this recklessness. A soldier who fought at Waterloo mentions that "the number of drums found on the field was particularly great as the French drummers continue to roll during the charge and are consequently much exposed".[40]

The three most consistently popular marches of the French Wars were *The British Grenadiers*, *Garryowen*, and *The downfall of Paris;* (the first two could also be sung). *The British Grenadiers* is mentioned repeatedly; it was heard – for example – after the victory of Fuentes d'Onoro – "a little like dunghill cock crowing, but the men like it", explained their general.[41] It was played too as the Army crossed the Garonne in April, 1814.[42]

Garryowen was written about 1770–1780 in praise of the moneyed young hooligans who ran riot in Limerick.

24
Garryowen

WORDS Traditional
MUSIC Traditional

Let Bac-chus's sons be not dis-may'd, But join with me each jo-vi-al blade; Come booze and sing, and lend me your aid, To help me with the cho-rus, In-stead of spa, we'll drink down ale, And pay the reck'-ning

on the nail, No man for debt shall go_ to jail, From Gar - ry o-wen in

glo - ry.

Let Bacchus' sons be not dismayed,
But join with me each jovial blade,
Come, booze and sing and lend me aid,
To help me with the chorus.

> Instead of spa we'll drink down ale,
> And pay the reckoning on the nail,
> For debt no man shall go to jail,
> From Garryowen in glory.

We are the boys who take delight in
Smashing the Limerick lamps when lighting
Through the streets like sporters fighting,
And tearing all before us.
> Instead of spa we'll drink down ale, etc.

We'll break windows, we'll break doors,
The watch knock down by threes and fours,
Then let the doctors work their cures,
And tinker up our bruises.
> Instead of spa we'll drink down ale, etc.

We'll beat the bailiffs out of fun,
We'll make the mayors and sheriffs run,
We are the boys no man dare dun,
If he regards a whole skin.
> Instead of spa we'll drink down ale, etc.

Our hearts so stout have got us fame,
For soon 'tis known from whence we came,
Where'er we go they dread the name,
Of Garryowen in glory.
> Instead of spa we'll drink down ale, etc.

This tune later gained great popularity in the United States, especially after General George Armstrong Custer's 7th Cavalry adopted it. It has been said that the 7th acquired the song through Captain Miles Keogh, an Irishman and a former member of the Papal Guard, but it seems unlikely that this can be ascribed to a particular person, since *Garryowen* appeared in a number of Civil War songsters, and was therefore presumably well known to any number of American soldiers in 1861–1865 – dates preceding Keogh's association with the 7th.

As for *The downfall of Paris*, it is now forgotten by this title, although in its day it may have surpassed even *The British Grenadiers* in popularity. It was played when the 22nd Regiment marched into Fort George in Guernsey in 1797,[43] when the British Army sallied out of Rueda in 1812 hoping but failing to entice the French to stay and fight,[44] and when the allies entered Paris after Waterloo ;[45] on that occasion Wellington sharply put a stop to it, and the offending Royal Regiment played, instead, *Croppies lie down*. Apart from being played by military bands on every conceivable occasion, its "one tormenting strum, strum, strum"[46] was the delight of amateur pianists throughout Britain.

After Waterloo, and apparently despite Wellington's misgivings, Captain Blakeney of the 28th Regiment heard it in Paris and considered it "rather singular and wanting in delicacy that every band of music in the Austrian, Prussian and Russian armies, while they marched past the group of kings, played by us the tune called *The downfall of Paris*, but subsequently learned that among the nations mentioned, as also in France, it bore quite another name and meaning".[47] Blakeney's note of peeved surprise is not at first logical, and it seems that he is merely resentful of all Europe borrowing a tune that was "ours". The "want of delicacy" only begins to make sense if it is known – as Blakeney knew – that the tune serenading the most autocratic monarchs in Europe was, by its other name, the savage *Ça Ira* song of the first and bloodiest French Revolutionaries. The redcoats took the tune with them wherever they went. In Ireland it long survived as a jig, and American fife-and-drum corps, especially – it is said – those of New England, still play it.

25
The downfall of Paris

MUSIC Traditional
SOURCE A. Wyatt-Edgell –
A Collection of Soldiers' Songs

Ça Ira became a regimental march of the British Army, for the 14th Regiment won the right to play it in unique circumstances. During an assault on Famars in 1793 the 14th were getting the worst of the argument, and the embattled revolutionaries were encouraged by their drums pounding out the savage air. Colonel Wellbore Ellis turned to his musicians and ordered them to play so that the French might be beaten "to their own damned tune", which they duly were, and the 14th subsequently adopted it as their own. In 1833 Major-General Richard Goodall Elrington, who had been a lieutenant at Famars, committed the story to paper, and Sir Francis Doyle, Colonel Ellis' grandson, confirmed it as true, although Elrington has the band playing and Doyle the drums.[48] Supporting evidence also comes in 1849 from the recollections of Sir Francis Skelly Tidy, who joined the 14th in September 1807 when the story was still fresh in many soldiers' minds.[49]

Ça Ira was not the only tune acquired from the French although it is the only one that has survived. In 1813 when the opposing armies were encamped near Pampeluna the strains of French music drifted regularly into the British camp and when two bandsmen deserted from a French regiment they were promptly incorporated into the band of the 31st Regiment, to whom they taught one particular tune. "It was called Bonaparte's March, and a very fine piece of music it was. I remember the air of it to the present day", wrote Sir George L'Estrange proudly,[50] but without asking a musical friend to note the score in his autobiography. Today, Bonaparte's March, by that title cannot be identified.

In 1827 an anonymous writer who was interested in all the music he heard in the Peninsula — French, Portuguese and Spanish — claimed that many British soldiers knew a French song called Le sentinel, and gave his own stilted translation.

When o'er the camp the midnight moonlight beams,
And soldiers' eyes are sealed in happy slumber,
The wakeful sentinel his watch proclaims,
And silence sweetly swells the echoing number.
Oh, then to heaven he turns his eyes,
And murmurs with a glowing sigh,
'Angels bright, that dwell above,
Tell my country, tell my love,
For them, for them I watch, for them I'll die'.[51]

The idea of British soldiers picking up a tune whistled across no-man's land, or from prisoners, seems somewhat improbable until one hears the catchy and pleasant melody. It then becomes feasible that they knew it to hum or whistle, even without words. If this happened, The sentinel was well travelled, for it was composed in the first place by the Viennese J. N. Hummel.

E

26
The sentinel

MUSIC J. N. Hummel

REFRAIN

The possibility that *Sir Manley Power* was once a French air has been dismissed (p. iii) but another melody used by the army may have derived from an unfortunate incident with the Spanish or Portuguese. For many years the 12th Royal Lancers have played the *Vesper Hymn*, the *Spanish Chant*, and the old Russian national anthem. Various strange and conflicting legends surround the origin of the custom, most of them centering around a drummer who was either murdered or murderous, and either a sacked convent and ravaged nuns, or the theft of 104 bottles of wine from a monastery. Possibly as a penance the Lancers may have adopted the *Spanish Chant* and kept it after the period of obligation terminated. The earliest known corroboration of the story is in a letter written around 1910 by M. Larter, a former bandmaster of the 13th Hussars. "In 1862 when I was stationed in Aldershot I recollect the 12th Lancers playing hymns on Sunday evenings and was told that it was something that occurred in a convent during the Peninsular War".[52]

The redcoats' taste in songs was as varied as the origins of the men themselves. They put their own words to familiar tunes, sang traditional national songs and more recent compositions, and made up a number of regimental songs. *The British Grenadiers* being the popular march of the time invited improvisations ; one of these was *The British Bayoneteers*.[53]

Eyes right, my jolly field boys,
Who British bayonets bear,
To teach your foes to yield, boys,
When British steel they dare!
Now fill the glass, for the toast of toasts
Shall be drunk with the cheer of cheers,
Hurrah, hurrah, hurrah, hurrah!
For the British Bayoneteers.

Great guns have shot and shell, boys,
Dragoons have sabres bright.
Th'artillery's fire's like hell, boys,
And the horse like devils fight.
But neither light nor heavy horse,
Nor thundering cannoneers,
Can stem the tide of the foeman's pride,
Like the British Bayoneteers.

The English arm is strong, boys,
The Irish arm is tough.
The Scotsman's blow the French well know
Is struck by sterling stuff.
And when before the enemy
Their shining steel appears,
Goodbye, goodbye, how they run, how they
    run,
From the British Bayoneteers.

Another parody to the same tune is a whimsical blend of soldier humour and practical philosophy.

And all the gods terrestrial
Descended on their spears,
To view with adoration
The British Grenadiers.
While kept by guardian angels
From falling into harm,
They had their bayonets ready screwed
Upon the first alarm.[54]

The Scots had a preference for nostalgic ballads. After General Whitelocke's fiasco at Buenos Aires in 1807 (a forgotten sideshow of the war in which a general "notoriously known to have the greatest antipathy to the smell of gunpowder" surrendered at the moment of his own victory) one of the Highlanders considered staying on in the Argentine. But a few verses of the lament *Lochaber no more* sung by a fellow-Scot were all that was needed for him to abandon the idea.[55]

Farewell to Lochaber and farewell, my Jean,
Where heartsome with thee I have many
days been.
For Lochaber no more, Lochaber no more,
We'll maybe return to Lochaber no more.
These tears that I shed they are all for my
dear,
And no' for the dangers attending on war,
Though borne on rough seas to a far bloody
shore,
Maybe to return to Lochaber no more.

Though hurricanes rise, and rise every wind
They'll ne'er make a tempest like that in my
mind.
Though loudest of thunder on louder waves
roar,
There's nothing like leaving my love on the
shore.
To leave thee behind me, my heart is sair
pained,
By ease that's inglorious no fame can be
gained,
And beauty and love's the reward of the brave,
And I must deserve it before I can crave.

Then glory, my Jean, maun plead my excuse,
Since honour commands me how can I
refuse?
Without it I ne'er can have merit for thee,
And without thy favour I'd better not be.
I gae then, my lass, to win honour and fame,
And if I should luck to come gloriously hame,
A heart I will bring thee with love running
o'er,
And then I'll leave thee and Lochaber no
more.

After Wellington had defeated Massena at Fuentes d'Onoro in 1811,
a battle in which the 71st and 79th Highlanders distinguished themselves,
a group of these sad Scots were seen to squat upon the turf and gain a
measure of satisfaction from melancholy song.

Why did I leave my Jeannie
My daddie's cot and a',
To wander from my country,
Sweet Caledonia?[56]

Win or lose, the battling Scots wallowed in nostalgia. The night before
San Sebastian surrendered in 1813 an officer of the Black Watch
admitted to a terrible homesickness as he listened to his men singing songs
of their homeland.[57] Sometimes it seems as if the Scots relished misery
until it became insupportable, at which point they executed a smart
about-turn and became desperately jolly. There is the story of a Scottish
quartermaster and some cronies huddled together in a wet comfortless
bivouac, shattering the night with the chorus from Burns' song *Willie
brewed a peck o' maut*.

We are na fou, we're nae that fou,
But just a drappie in our e'e.
The cock may craw, the day may daw,
And ay we'll taste the barley bree.[58]

This was not the only Burns song the soldiers knew. Sergeant William Wheeler of the 51st Regiment pricked up his ears when he heard his messmate Brown intoning *The sodger's return*, "for he never sang this song but when he was elevated with the juice of the grape or he had met with good luck".[59] The words of this song were set to *The mill oh!* (which also carried a set of particularly earthy lyrics). It may have been this specific combination which led a Scots clergyman to say that "many of our airs or tunes are made by good angels, but the lines of our songs by devils", although *The sodger's return* is a fine honest ballad that could offend no one.

27
The sodger's return

WORDS Robert Burns
MUSIC The Mill Oh! – Traditional

When wild war's deadly blast was blawn,
And gentle peace returning,
Wi' mony a sweet babe fatherless,
And mony a widow mourning,—
I left the lines and tented field,
Where lang I'd been a lodger,
My humble knapsack a' my wealth,
A poor and honest sodger.

A leal light heart was in my breast,
My hand unstained wi' plunder;
And for fair Scotia hame again
I cheery on did wander.
I thought upon the banks o' Coil,
I thought upon my Nancy.
I thought upon the witching smile
That caught my youthful fancy.

At length I reached the bonnie glen,
Where early life I sported;
I passed the mill, and trysting thorn,
Where Nancy aft I courted:
Wha spied I but my ain dear maid,
Down by her mother's dwelling!
And turned me round to hide the flood
That in my een was swelling.

Wi' altered voice quoth I, sweet lass,
Sweet as yon hawthorn blossom,
O! happy, happy may he be,
That's dearest to thy bosom!
My purse is light, I've far to gang,
And fain wad be thy lodger;
I've served my king and country lang—
Take pity on a sodger!

Sae wistfully she gazed on me,
And lovelier was than ever:
Quo' she, a sodger ance I loved,
Forget him shall I never:
Our humble cot, and hamely fare,
Ye freely shall partake it;
That gallant badge, the dear cockade,
Ye're welcome for the sake o't.

She gazed—she reddened like a rose—
Syne pale like ony lily;
She sank within my arms, and cried,
Art thou my ain dear Willie?
By Him who made yon sun and sky,
By whom true love's regarded,
I am the man; and thus may still
True lovers be rewarded!

The wars are o'er, and I'm come home,
And find thee still true-hearted;
Tho' poor in gear, we're rich in love,
And mair we'se ne'er be parted.
Quo' she, my grandsire left me gowd,
A mailen plenished fairly;
And come, my faithful sodger lad,
Thou'rt welcome to it dearly!

For gold the merchant ploughs the main,
The farmer ploughs the manor;
But glory is the sodger's prize;
The sodger's wealth is honour:
The brave poor sodger ne'er despise,
Nor count him as a stranger;
Remember he's his country's stay
In day and hour o' danger.

Another Scots favourite that went well with a dram of whatever might be available was the story in six verses, to a now-forgotten tune, of an Irish lad who made good in Glasgow – *The banks of Clyde.*

1st verse

When I was young and in my prime,
Where fancy led me there to rove,
From town to town the nation round,
Through many a silent shady grove,
Till at length I came to Scotland by name,
Where beauty shines on every side.
There is no town there for to compare
To Glasgow fair by the banks of Clyde.

One salvationist in the ranks, complained that the Scots, who "instead of reading their bibles preferred taking a cheerful glass together", ended the evening with that song.[60]

The Irish loosed most of their musical energy on *St. Patrick's Day.* That was the tune the Irishmen of the 50th roared out with discordant variants as they grew by turns maudlin or bellicose during their liquorous stay at Ashford in Kent.[61] It was the same air that drew Lt. Woodberry of the 18th Hussars from his tent at 3 a.m. on March 17, 1813.[62] Even their enemies came to recognize *St. Patrick's Day*; after Napoleon's dismissal to Elba three men of the Rifle Brigade visited Montauban in the south of France, where they were royally entertained by French soldiers and then escorted towards their quarters to its rousing strains.[63]

But besides *St. Patrick's Day*, *Garryowen* and *Savourneen deelish*, the Irish had a beautiful air called *Love farewell*. It was particularly popular with the 88th Connaught Rangers,[64] and a regiment nicknamed the Black Belts sang it as they left Dublin in 1809 for the fever-ridden swamps of Walcheren.[65]

28
Love farewell

WORDS Traditional
MUSIC Traditional
SOURCE Sir C. Stanford –
Complete Petrie Collection

Come now brave boys, we're on for marching,
First for France and then for Holland,
While cannons roar and men are dying,
March, brave boys, there's no denying,
Love, farewell!

I think I hear the Colonel crying,
March, brave boys, there's no denying,
Colours flying, drums a-beating,
March, brave boys, there's no retreating,'
Love, farewell!

The mother cries, 'Boys, do not wrong me,
Do not take my daughter from me,
For if you do I will torment you,
And after death my ghost will haunt you'.
Love, farewell!

Now Molly dear, do not grieve for me,
I'm going to fight for Ireland's glory.
If we live we live victorious,
If we die our souls are glorious,
Love, farewell![66]

Yet this song, so unmistakably Irish in melody and words, almost certainly had its origin in an English nine-verse broadside ballad of the American War of Independence.

2nd verse
    The drums are beating to alarm them,
    We wish to stay still in your arms.
    But we must go and cross the ocean,
    The Americans keep us all in motion,
        A long farewell.

4th verse
    I think I hear my brother crying,
    'March, my lads, the colours flying.
    Our cause is just, we'll be victorious,
    If we're killed our death is glorious,
        A long farewell.

7th verse
    Dear mothers, weep not for us,
    We're going to fight for Britain's glory.
    Our country calls, our courage to display.
    The drums are beating, there's no delay.[67]

This ballad may have been written with an established Irish melody in mind, or the melody may have been composed for the words by some forgotten Irish fiddler or harpist, or words and tune may just have been thrown together because they happened to suit. Whatever the circumstances may be, *Love farewell* is certainly an Anglo-Irish hybrid.

Only one traditional English song was found in the redcoats' repertoire, but it is a melody of great beauty that belies the critics who pretended, throughout the 19th century, that the English soldier was incapable of singing any but the simplest tunes. In 1807 a needless campaign was undertaken in Egypt, then a province of the Turkish Empire. The British occupied Alexandria, but their attempts to venture further afield were effectively halted by an Albanian general named Mehemmet Ali. The night before a disastrous foray which ended in the Battle of El Hamed, an infantry commissary sang a "gay old English carol" in the cold of the desert, and twenty or thirty voices came in on the chorus.[68] The carol was called *The owl*.

29
The owl

WORDS Traditional
MUSIC Traditional

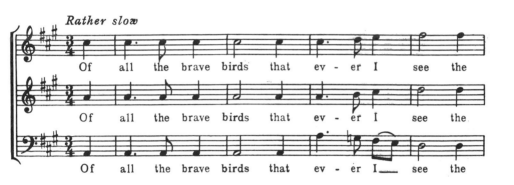

Of all the brave birds that ev - er I see the

Owl is the fair - est in her de - gree for

all the day long she sits in a tree and

when the night comes a-way flies she te whit te whoo

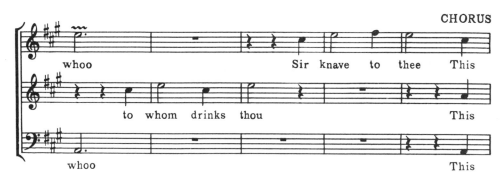

CHORUS

whoo Sir knave to thee This

to whom drinks thou This

whoo This

song is well sung I make you a vow and he is a

Soli ad lib.

knave that drink-eth now, Nose nose nose

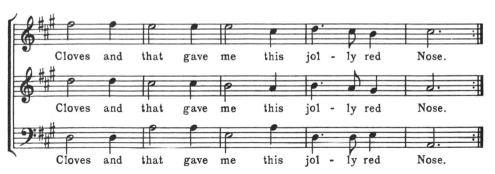

Of all the brave birds that ever I see,
The owl is the fairest in her degree.
For all the day long she sits in a tree
And when the night comes away flies she.
Tu whit, tu whoo, tu whit, tu whoo.
This song is well sung I make you a vow
And he is a knave that drinketh now,
Nose, nose, nose, nose,
And who gave thee that jolly red nose,
Cinnamon and ginger, nutmeg and cloves,
That's what gave me this jolly red nose.

A very rare gem is the "extemporaneous effusion" of a surgeon of the
12th Lancers – rare because these redcoats were strangely diffident when
it came to discussing their morals. It went to the tune, *Drops of brandy*.

Our grandfather's name was Sir Adam,
Who managed the king's nursery ground,
And was getting on well until Madam
Stealing pippins one morning was found.

The ladies they say have odd fancies,
But so have the gentlemen too.
I can guess pretty well what is Nancy's.
'Tis one that she never shall rue.[69]

Besides *Love farewell*, which was adopted by the 88th although not written for them, there were a number of regimental songs, of which some survive intact, and others in fragments or by name alone. The one that is most interesting because it was definitely written soon after the event it describes is called *Sahagun*, and is still sung by the 15th/19th Hussars. The Battle of Sahagun was fought on December 21, 1808, when General Sir John Moore made his audacious advance to strike Marshal Soult before the Frenchman could be reinforced by his colleague Junot. After a night ride in appalling weather Lord Paget decisively defeated the French under Dubelle, although it is debatable whether he was outnumbered 700 to 500 as some texts have it, 900 to 300 as the poet claimed, or whether (as Sir John Fortescue attested) it was the British who enjoyed a numerical superiority. But despite their victory at Sahagun the Hussars spent the first anniversary of the battle back in England, for Moore was forced to retreat. The adjutant's diary for December 21, 1809 laconically records the birth of the ballad. "The trumpets played *God save the King*. Gave three cheers and a party of the mess assembled in the officers' barracks yard and sang a song composed by themselves on the action at Sahagun".[70] Another regimental treasure that complements the diary is a faded document in the officers' mess bearing the original words of the song, which are less polished than those now sung. The words cannot all be deciphered, but it seems that the song as first sung was similar to this.

30
Sahagun

WORDS Traditional
MUSIC Traditional
SOURCE A. Wyatt-Edgell –
A Collection of Soldiers' Songs

As in quarters we lay, which you quickly shall hear.
Lord Paget came to us, and bid us prepare.
"Come saddle your horses, for we must ride soon
For the French are now laying in the town of Sahagun".

So we saddled our horses, and away we did go
Over rivers of ice, and o'er mountains of snow.
To the town of Sahagun, our course we did steer
For the 15th Hussars, my brave boys, never fear.

We marched all night until day it did break,
When eight of the French on a bridge we did take,
But two got away, and rode off to Sahagun,
To inform the French there that the Spanish had come.

The French then turned and from the town of Sahagun
Well mounted and armed, full 900 strong,
Whilst loudly they cried on Napoleon their king,
Three cheers from the 15th made the vineyard to ring.

They formed themselves up, and the play it began,
Thinking to dismay we brave Englishmen.
But with glittering broadswords upon them we flew
They went threes about, and away they did go.

We soon overtook them, as they rode at full speed
Cut through the brave helmets, they wore on their heads.
Have mercy, have mercy, we made them to cry
Have mercy, you English, or else we must die.

'Mid the snow in the vineyards many Frenchmen lay dead
300 were taken and the rest of them fled.
Their general likewise we took to the field
'Twas the 15th Hussars made the Frenchmen to yield.

The Spaniards came out from the town of Sahagun
With bread in their hands, and large jugs of wine,
With joy in their hearts, no tongue can express
Sing long live the English and down with the French.

Lord Paget came to us, and thus he did say,
"I thank you, 15th, for your valor this day,
Now dismount from your horses and feed everyone,
Then we'll be ready to fight them again."

On the 21st of December my boys, was the day,
When 300 of the 15th, made the French run away,
Although they consisted of 900 and more,
We'll drink and we'll sing now the battle is o'er.

Here's a health to Lord Paget, and long may he live,
Likewise Colonel Grant, and our officers brave.
With a full flowing bowl, we'll drink, and we'll sing,
Success to the 15th and God save the King.

Another regiment which commemorated its valour in song was the 87th, the Royal Irish Fusiliers. At Barrosa near Cadiz ("bright Barrosa", Byron called it, but to a veteran French officer it was "the most terrible bayonet fight I had ever seen") the 87th stabbing like demons and howling their war-cry – "Faugh a ballagh", ("clear the way") swung the balance of fortune to the British. Thomas Dibdin was one of several ballad writers who celebrated the victory which cost the French 2,000 casualties out of a force of 7,000, but the song that has survived is the one the Irish themselves wrote. Its precise origin is unknown, but the Royal Irish Fusiliers have a set of handwritten verses which appear to date from early Victorian times. The first version of the melody is in Sergeant Newman's book, where it is called *Barrosa plains*.

31
Barrosa

WORDS Traditional
MUSIC Traditional
SOURCE Sgt. F. Newman MS

'Twas on a Thursday morning that from Cadiz we set sail,
As many a gallant Frenchman had good reason to bewail;
Straight into Gibraltar Bay our gallant fleet did steer,
And on the Saturday we went ashore at Algesir.
    For we are the lads of honour, boys, belonging to the Crown,
    And death to those who dare to oppose the saucy "Prince's Own".

We marched along the coast until we reached Tarifa Bay,
Where waiting for the Spaniards in a convent long we lay;
But when the Spaniards joined us there we marched both night and day,
Determined when we met the foe to show them British play.
     For we are the lads, etc.

Our officers explained to us the hardships we should bear,
Well knowing British courage would triumph everywhere;
O'er plains and lofty mountains our army marched along,
And though our numbers were but few, our courage it was strong.
     For we are the lads, etc.

The Spaniards took the front, my boys, their country for to free,
And bid our troops bring up the rear, that glorious day to see;
But when Barrosa's plains appeared we never saw them more,
Their column drew behind the woods upon St. Petri's shore.
     For we are the lads, etc.

But Graham, our commander, didn't know of their design,
And swore that British infantry should never stay behind;
But as we marched to join the Dons, not dreading any snare,
The Frenchmen in an ambush lay, and closed upon our rear.
     For we are the lads, etc.

Some watchful eye the foe espied and to the general flew,
Which news an oath of anger from the gallant Graham drew;
"Oh cursed is my lot," he cried, "this is a wretched day,
When Britons must deplore their fate—by Spaniards led astray."
     For we are the lads, etc.

"Turn to the right-about, my boys—for Britons know no fear;
Extend your files, my Irish lads, and keep your out flanks clear;
Look back to Cape Trafalgar, boys, where Nelson bled before:
The blood that conquered on the sea shall triumph on the shore!"
     For we are the lads, etc.

We jumped into their lines, my boys; their ranks were overthrown,
And in confusion forced to fly, charged by the "Prince's Own";
Two generals left behind them their guns, and eagle, too,
Whilst the "Faugh-a-Ballaughs" cheered and charged, and boldly did pursue.
     For we are the lads, etc.

Here's health to Gough and Graham, and the soldiers on that field,
Who, though they fought them ten to one, soon taught their foes to yield;
Who put them in confusion and their eagle took away:
Long live our Irish lads to cheer on each Barrosa day.
     For we are the lads, etc.

Then this cup to all the living and in memory of the slain,
Who bravely fought for freedom's cause upon Barrosa's plain;
Pass it round beside the eagle which our soldiers bore away,
Long live our Irish lads to cheer on each Barrosa day.
     For we are the lads, etc.

From a literary point of view the best regimental song of the French Wars belonged to a regiment that never saw a shot fired in anger, although this was not their fault. The Royal Cornwall Militia – eventually the 3rd battalion, Duke of Cornwall's Light Infantry – first appear on the Army List in 1799, and although they volunteered twice for the Peninsula their offers were not approved. Instead, they seem to have been marched and quartered all over England, until at last in 1811 their offer for posting to Ireland was accepted and they were renamed, as an honour, the Royal Cornwall Light Infantry. On the occasion of their departure their commanding officer wrote some verses to the Cornish air, *One and all*. Among his men was James Lampier, with four years' service behind him and another 56 still to go. In 1872 Lampier, who rose to the rank of quartermaster and died in 1891 aged 95, bequeathed to posterity the verses that Lieutenant-Colonel James Brydges-Willyams had composed years before.[71]

32
One and all

WORDS   J. Brydges-Willyams
MUSIC   Traditional

Away, brave boys to Dublin jig,
The girls to kiss, the whiskey swig,
And each as merry as a grig—sing, one and all.
But he that will not with us jog,
Shall kiss no girls, and drink no grog,
For that he is a sorry dog—sing one and all.
    Then let the bells of Dublin ring,
    The Cornish boys are come to sing,
    With Irish lads, God save the King,
    Sing one and all.

To those who by their colours stand,
Great crowds shall shout throughout the land,
There goes true blue, and hark the band—plays one and all.
But they who are not of good heart,
And basely from their comrades part,
Shall have the *Rogues March* in a cart—hoot one and all.
    Then let the bells of Dublin ring, etc.

Whether we drink or play, or fight,
Or drunk or sober, if we're right,
We'll of our motto ne'er lose sight—of one and all.
This principle where e'er we go,
Will meet respect from friend or foe,
Then let the world our maxim know—'tis one and all.
    Then let the bells of Dublin ring, etc.

But see the transport crowd the strand,
We soon shall find on Irish land,
"Erin go bragh" go hand in hand—with one and all.
And as for French and foreign foes,
We'll twine the shamrock with the rose,
And pull old Boney by the nose—pull one and all..
    Then let the bells of Dublin ring, etc.

But when the din of war is o'er,
Our services required no more,
We'll hail again our native shore—with one and all.
And then the Cornish volunteer,
Shall meet kind welcome, hearty cheer,
Plenty of beef, and good strong beer—drink one and all.
    Then let the bells of Bodmin ring,
    The Cornish Irish lads shall sing,
    Drink to their sweethearts and their King,
    Drink one and all.

It is claimed that another song, sung by both the 60th and 95th Regiments at the end of the 19th century, originated in the Peninsula.[72] Its hero was sometimes General Dundas and sometimes Colonel Coote Manningham. The song has some claims to antiquity. In 1892 William Miller, former bandmaster of the 95th who had lived with the Regiment since 1820 when he was a child of five, said he knew *To fight for England's glory* (in this instance with Coote Manningham) when he was a boy.[73]

Private Phil Clay of the 95th recalled in 1890 that "several Waterloo men in our village.... used to sing *General Dundas*... about 1850–56".[74] The song may therefore well have been composed in wartime, although it is also possible it was composed later.

33
Riflemen's song

WORDS Traditional
MUSIC Traditional
SOURCE J. Farmer – Scarlet and Blue

Oh General Dundas, he was the man,
For he invented a capital plan,
He formed a corps of riflemen,
To fight for England's glory.

He dressed them all in jackets of green,
And placed them where they couldn't be seen,
And sent them in front, an invisible screen,
To fight for England's glory.

The number of regimental songs that existed (not songs about regiments but their own songs) may well have been legion. There was a song called *The Battle of Salamanca*[75] and a couplet survives which may have come from it. It was surely a popular air with the corps that it named.

The 61st and 79th great numbers they had slain.
They got their jackets dusted well on Salamanca plain.[76]

The 5th Regiment seem to have had their own song, written by Sergeant John Grey of the 2nd battalion, but his comrade-in-arms Stephen Morley thought a couplet on the title page of his own memoirs was enough to satisfy future generations.

Our streaming white feathers are plain to be seen,
And our facings are called the gosling green.[77]

Another regimental song, *The ragged brigade* of the 14th Light Dragoons, was too topical to outlive those whose condition evoked its composition and is long since lost.[78]

Although one cannot reason from the particular to the general and suggest that because a certain soldier had a taste for a particular sort of music his taste was widely shared, it is amusing to look at a pair of musical eccentrics thrown up by the records of the time. One officer who campaigned in the Low Countries and North-east France between May 1793 and March 1795, seemed more interested, if his diary is a true witness, in church organs than in the enemy. He never missed an opportunity to enter a church and inspect its organ, and if the occasion permitted he would play himself.[79] Then there was Lt. Woodberry of the 18th Hussars, a devotee of the flute who persuaded his regimental bandmaster McKennie to compose a *Woodberry waltz* which, according to the cavalier himself, attained considerable popularity. This young exquisite also translated into Portuguese for palpably devious purposes *My heart trembles with love, The flowers of the forest,* and *How happy I'd be with either dear charmer.*[80]

Song was also useful on the battlefield. At Barrosa, before the 87th made their epic attack, Colonel John Frederick Browne rode to the head of the composite battalion of the 9th, 28th, and 82nd Regiments that he commanded, having been ordered to make a close-order attack that was vital but seemingly suicidal. He removed his hat and in a voice of thunder announced to his "gentlemen" that he was the bearer of good news: "General Graham has done you the honour of being the first to attack those fellows. Now, you rascals, follow me". And pointing to the massed French he advanced chanting his favourite air, *Heart of oak.*[81]

> Now cheer up, my brave boys, to glory we steer,
> To add something more to this wonderful year.

That was precisely what the Colonel did, for aided by reinforcements that arrived in the very nick of time, his battalion drove 3,000 French before them.

There was also a famous solo at Waterloo when, around noon, it was said the British centre was a little shaken. (As the battle began about 11 a.m. and it was after 1.00 p.m. when Napoleon's eighty guns – including twenty-four 12-pounders – laid down one of the heaviest barrages of the great artillerist's career, the narrator might have been wrong in his timing). During a brief lull in the firing a voice was heard singing steadily in the ranks.

> Now's the day and now's the hour,
> See the front of battle lower,
> See approach Napoleon's power,
>   His chains and slavery!
> Lay the proud usurper low,
> Tyrants fall in every foe,
> Liberty in every blow,
>   Let us do or die!

The effect was electric. "I think it may be fairly doubted whether the speedy prospect of being succoured by the Prussians or the two verses of *Bruce's address* produced the most powerful effect on the hearts of our brave fellows".[82]

Robert Burns, who wrote the words that the singer adapted, would have gloried to hear his song sung at such a crisis for a persistent tradition among the country folk of Stirling maintained that the tune had been played by the army of Bruce as it marched to rout the English at Bannockburn. There is an interesting footnote to the history of *Bruce's address*. During the Indian Mutiny, forty-two years later, the Army believed that when the Scots Greys and the 92nd charged together at Waterloo, with the Highlanders hanging on to the cavalry stirrups, they were singing the same tune.[83] But this must be legend. It is physically difficult to run and sing, and there is no contemporary support for the story. Soon after the battle a number of ballads about Waterloo were published in Scotland, one reputedly by "a Royal Highlander" and another by "two soldiers of the Highland Brigade" but neither mentions the singing charge (which the patriotic Scots would surely have done had there been one), nor is the story included in a book published in 1859 entitled THE BATTLE OF WATERLOO FROM THE TRADITIONS OF THE SCOTS GREYS AND HIGHLANDERS.

In most anecdotal accounts of the French Wars the Highlanders figure rather larger than life. English writers were fascinated by their alien garb, their Gaelic, and their sometimes quaint use of English. They wrote about themselves for the same motives that prompted other veterans, and from the not unjust desire for glory that is found in every warrior society. Although Culloden had been fought half a century before, Highland society unlike any other in the British Isles, still thought in terms of martial prowess.

The Scots could and did sing readily, but their war music *par excellence* was of course the bagpipes. "There is no sound", a distinguished general is reputed to have told a Highland gathering in Edinburgh soon after Waterloo, "which the immortal Wellington hears with more delight or the marshals of France with more dismay, than the Highland pibroch".[84] Who this general was, or whether the Iron Duke ever heard any music with delight, is moot.

The role of the pipers in Highland regiments at this time was unconventional and peculiar, bearing comparison with no other institution in the Army. They were, in a way that no ordinary regimental band could be, a link with home and an integral part of a socio-economic pattern, albeit one that was already in a state of dissolution. Historically, the piper was closely leagued with his chief, well versed in the lore of his clan, and with a repertoire carefully chosen for its significance. Each piece had a proper time and place for performance, and many had associations and histories. The same piper played in triumph and disaster, at births and deaths, and he knew the correct, almost ritualistic, moment for any given tune. He was more than a mere minstrel; in battle it was his duty to animate his clansmen and to be with them where the blows fell thickest, so that he assumed something of the importance of a standard bearer. Although at the turn of the 18th century the days of the closely-knit patriarchal system in the Highlands were dwindling, the region was still comparatively isolated, particularism was strong and social customs died hard, so the regimental piper was not dissimilar from the piper who marched beside his chief. Moreover the Highland regiments were more homogeneous than most, and because men volunteered with their natural leaders, the affinity and affection between officers and men was greater than in the English corps. This song, kept alive by oral tradition and taken down by Major I. H. M. Scobie in the 1920's from an old man who had heard it seventy years previously, gives some idea of the Highland recruiting system.

> The brave Sir John Sinclair is a man of high renown,
> His dwelling is in Caithness, nigh to Thurso town.
> He came into this country to raise a noble train,
> And none would he accept but brave British men.
>> Wi' the Hieland lads of Scotland,
>> So merrily we'll go
>> With brave Sir John Sinclair
>> That valiant hero.

Our clothing is of red, my boys, all turned o'er with yellow,
A bonnet, plaid and black cockade, fit for a gallant fellow.
Five guineas of advance for to clip the wings of France
Wi' the brave Sir John Sinclair, that valiant hero.
    Wi' the Hieland lads of Scotland, etc.

When the time will come, my boys, we'll cross the raging sea
And face the daring foe in their ain country.
Wi' glittering gun and bayonet we'll do the best we can,
And make the French to tremble when they see a Caithness man.[85]

It is to be hoped that the brave Sir John's recruiters had better luck in Caithness than the recruiting squad of the 3rd Foot Guards that went, piper included, to Caithness Fair in 1796. After they had persuaded one man to enlist — by fair means or foul is not said — his friends raised a mob. "Being surrounded by the whole fair we were obliged to seek for safety in flight, but not until our piper, a stout young lad, was killed".[86] That, in the Highlands, was presumably an unusual and regrettable happening.

The regimental piper knew he held a special position. He was not officially carried on the regimental roster, but was supported by the officers because they recognised his value to morale and *esprit de corps*, and were prepared to pay for his services, and to pay handsomely. Captain Duncan Campbell, recruiting for Argyll's Highlanders in 1794, wrote : "If you can meet with one or two good pipers, handsome fellows and steady, you might go as far as 30 guineas for each",[87] which in the Highlands at that time — or anywhere else for that matter — was a massive bounty. With this sort of status accorded him the regimental piper rarely fell short of (and sometimes surpassed) the spirit of the pipers who had flourished in the near-legendary heyday of the clans. He was acutely conscious of his role and his position. "Shall a little rascal that beats upon a sheepskin take the right hand of me that am a musician?" asked one whose position was challenged by a drummer.[88]

If occasion arose the men had no qualms in pointing out to the piper where his duties lay. At the battle of Assaye where Wellesley beat the Mahrattas, the musicians were ordered to attend to the wounded and to carry them to the rear, and one of the pipers took himself to be included in this order, for which his comrades afterwards berated him. "For the piper, who should always be in the heat of battle, to go to the rear with the whistles was a thing quite unheard of." As a result of these reproaches the piper was desperately anxious to redeem himself and at Argaum his commanding officer was much afraid that the inspired ferocity of his music would provoke some rash action by the Highlanders.[89]

The paramount duty of the piper was indeed to play the men into battle and to keep playing so long as he was able. Even wounds could not silence a good piper. In the second charge of the 71st Regiment at Vimeiro, their piper George Clarke was brought low by a wound in the groin. Unable to run with his comrades he propped himself up on the ground, exclaiming, "The deil tak' ye, if ye hae disabled me frae following ye winna keep me frae blawin' for 'em," and blow he did until the battle was won. Long and loud his skirling must have been for several veterans of Vimeiro write of him. For his courage he was promoted to sergeant and pipe major and presented with a fine set of pipes by the Highland Society of Edinburgh.[90] A piper of the Gordons encouraged the troops at St. Pierre in the Pyrenees with *Johnny Cope* despite a broken leg.[91] When Badajoz was stormed on April 6, 1812, one of the first to mount the walls was John McLauchlan, piper of the 74th Regiment who played *The Campbells are coming*. McLauchlan died playing his pipes at Vittoria, but his exploits were the talk of common soldiers forty years afterwards.[92] Kenneth Mackay of the 79th earned immortality at Waterloo when he stepped outside the square and the protection of his comrades' bayonets and walked to and fro playing *Cogad na sith – Peace or war*.[93]

At Vittoria the 71st Regiment charged to the strains of *Johnny Cope*[94] driving the French before them and inspiring William Glen, the Scottish poet, to write to the tune of *Whustle o'er the lave o't*,

> If e'er they meet their worthy king
> Let them dance round him in a ring
> And some Scottish piper play the spring
> He blew them at Vittoria.

But the most famous occasion on which *Johnny Cope* was played was at Arroyo dos Molinos; the French lay in the village unaware of the closeness of the Scots until, at the crack of dawn, with a howling gale behind them, the Highlanders led by the Camerons stormed up the street, pipes playing. The French commander, aroused by their sound, tumbled out of bed and semi-nude emerged blinking into the pale light, to be rudely seized by a sergeant of the 92nd Regiment.[95] The whole episode, not least the wail of the pipes, must have seemed a horrid nightmare. After this incident various sets of topical words were improvised to the air, "more creditable to the patriotism and pluck than to the poetic powers of the 92nd."

> Go and tell Napoleon, go
> While Freedom's laws he tramples low
> That Highland boys will be his foe
> And meet them all in the morning.
> Hey! Monsieur Gerard are ye waukin' yet?[96]

There were times when the ardour inspired by the pipes was self-defeating. During the battle of Maya in 1813, the 92nd Regiment was moved into a position seemingly threatened by the French; their pipe-major, considering that an attack by the Scots would be timely and that they required some stimulation, struck up the *Gathering of the Camerons*. The result was as he had anticipated – the Highlanders could barely await the word of command. Lieutenant-General Stewart, whose tactical sense was more highly developed than that of the piper, warned the men against the danger of an unsupported attack and told the piper not to play again until he was ordered. This request the piper ignored and a second tune so inflamed the men that he was commanded to rest silent at the peril of his life. For a while he did so but then, moved beyond endurance by the appearance of Major-General Barnes' Brigade, he started *The haughs of Cromdale*. This famous battle song provided a stimulus that the Scots could not ignore, and led by a Captain Seton they charged the French, who "panic-struck at their audacity wheeled about and ran".[97] But it was not as easy an attack as these brief words imply, for the charge cost the regiment an appalling 330 casualties out of a strength of 750.[98]

Sometimes the request of a commanding officer for music dumb-founded his men. Lt. Campbell of the 72nd, sweltering with his troops in the trenches before Pondicherry on August 12, 1793, was surprised when the colonel who was his namesake called for music. But it was a day of unusual events, for "we were a good deal surprised to perceive that the moment the piper began the fire from the enemy slackened and soon after almost entirely ceased. The French all got upon the works and seemed more astonished at hearing the bagpipe than we with Colonel Campbell's request".[99] Before the wars were over Ronald Campbell would become accustomed to the strange effect the pipes had upon the Scots' opponents. When the Cape of Good Hope was captured from Napoleon's Dutch allies in 1806 the pipes added greatly to the consternation of the Dutch and their Hottentot levies. As they fled, looking back apprehensively, they saw one of the most improbable sights of any war. "The grenadier company requested that the pipers might strike up *Cabhar Feidh* to which they danced a reel". The Dutch and Hottentots were not the only stupefied troops on the scene, for the 59th Regiment, in close support of the Scots, watched their unorthodox performance with "utter astonishment".[100]

The pipes were a stimulus for the soldiers, but they were also recreation; the pipers played in camp to while away the hours and a correspondent of Sir Walter Scott describes how the night before Busaco he heard "in a low glen . . . the Highland bagpipe playing *The garb of old Gaul* and fell into the quarters of a Scottish regiment.[101] A more typical air to endear itself to the hearts of a Scottish corps cannot be imagined, for it was originally a Gaelic composition by an unknown soldier of the 42nd Regiment from Perthshire, supplemented by the regimental chaplain, and finally in the 1760's polished by Major Reid into the form in which it has ever since been played as a regimental march.[102] Sometimes the piper's task was a more sombre one. After the battle of Quatre Bras "the piper of the 92nd took post behind the garden hedge in front of the village and tuning his bagpipe attempted to collect the sad remains of his regiment".[103]

So many pipers were heroes that it comes almost as a relief to hear of one that was a rogue, in fact — a counterfeiter, for which crime he was condemned to be shot. At Vittoria however, his escort was loth to miss the fun and in the confusion Donald broke loose and wended his way towards the enemy lines, preferring to live with the French than die with the British. Some eighty yards from the French lines he began to play his pipes, to show that he meant no harm, but was shot dead as he gave his best tune. "We didna think muckle o' Donald," reported the laconic teller of the story, "but we thought less o' the French. 'Twas a poor thing to shoot a man with naething but a bagpipe."[104]

During the long struggle against France the redcoats found themselves associated with a range of allies, on whose music they frequently commented. As in previous wars they sometimes took part in combined operations with the Navy, when the Navy brought its big guns ashore for siege-work. Despite the rigours of life at sea, or perhaps because of them, Jack Ashore delighted to play the eccentric and show the Land Lobsters (as sailors irreverently called the soldiers), how things should be done – which meant, literally, with a song and a smile.

At the attack on Flushing in 1809 the sailors had selected as their target – for reasons best known to themselves – a church steeple. Whenever this was hit the tars cheered loudly, while their fiddler sawed away at *Rule, Britannia*.[105] In the battery before San Sebastian the sailors were on the receiving end of an artillery barrage – and just as jovially. Whenever a shell whistled overhead one was made to bend while the others leapfrogged over him and the inevitable fiddle played *Heart of oak*; when the French got the range each shell within the works was rewarded by a rendering of *Jack's alive*.[106]

But if the effect of sailors' music was humorous, the war music of the Germans, who fought with the redcoats on several fronts, was treated with an admiration that bordered on awe. Their bands – especially their buglehorn bands – were highly popular. On November 10, 1813, during the fighting around Biarritz, the conscripted regiments of Frankfurt and Nassau deserted from the French lines *en masse* and came over to the British with their bugles sounding a quickstep.[107] It was a "full band of trumpets and bugle horns sounding triumphal marches" that headed Blucher's progress through Paris,[108] and it was probably such a band that played *God save the King* amidst the carnage of Waterloo.[109]

But it was about German choral singing that the redcoat writers became truly ecstatic. "It was one of the romances of a soldier's life to hear them chanting their national war songs, some three or four voices leading and the whole squadron joining in the chorus".[110] One officer contrasted the English who were either silent or whistled and hummed "those tuneless airs in which the lower orders of our countrymen delight", with the Germans who "sang beautifully a wild chorus, a hymn . . . to the Virgin, different persons taking different parts and producing altogether the most exquisite harmony". This writer hoped to transmit the tune to paper but found himself "insufficiently master of the art of notation".[111] Another soldier adopted the same lyrical tone, when describing the Germans on their way to Walcheren in 1809. "It was not the least delightful of our pleasures to listen to the glees of the German riflemen who sailed in our division". Then he too turns on his less accomplished countrymen : "It has often been a matter of annoyance to me to think that the peasantry of Great Britain alone are the only people in Europe who cannot sing in harmony . . . Among my countrymen I have even heard an harmonious second condemned as 'not in tune' or 'putting the singer out'."[112] German hussars in Spain were heard "singing some delightful airs, their half squadrons at intervals joining in chorus".[113] With such praise thick in the air it needed a bold and shameless fellow to parody the hussars and suggest that they sang anything as trivial as –

> We have got schn—a—a—ps
> And the 73rd have got no—o—one.[114]

After Waterloo the British heard for the first time the singing of a German national army, not just German units in British service, and this naturally impressed them. "They were marching in columns of infantry and cavalry . . . and the men in front singing choruses of the most pleasing description. This is a custom among the German soldiery" – and here the routine rueful note creeps in – "which may perhaps be too national for us to adopt (although) there can be no doubt of its beneficial influence".[115] As they advanced through Gonnesse towards Paris an officer heard "hundreds singing songs of triumph as they move on".[116] This adulation of German war music is something that the English shared with their Anglo-Saxon cousins across the Atlantic. In the American Civil War the best Federal bands were those made up of Germans, and the best regimental singing was by Germans, whose favourite song seems to have been *Morgenroth*, written after the Napoleonic Wars. Because of the language difficulty, redcoat writers do not generally name or recognise the German songs that gave them so much pleasure. A German rifleman mentions that they used to sing *Auf, auf, ihr Bruder und seid stark*[117] and in the Peninsula they almost certainly sang the stirring, *Ein Schifflein sah ich fahren*, ("I saw a small ship sailing") sometimes called *Nimm das Madel bei der Hand* – ("Take the girl by her hand").

34
Ein Schifflein sah ich fahren

WORDS Traditional
MUSIC Traditional

Ein Schifflein sah ich fahren has a more chequered, and infinitely longer, history than *The sentinel* (p. 107). After its popularity with the German Legion in the Peninsula it received new words and became *La Parisienne*, the hit tune of the 1830 revolution that overthrew the Bourbon dynasty in France. The newly-raised Foreign Legion is said to have adopted it, and sung it when they landed at Oran in February, 1831. The French historian G. Kastner, who in 1855 established that it was sung by the

King's German Legion, thought *Ein Schifflein sah ich fahren* originated in 1757 when a French force in Harburg near Hamburg was forced to surrender. Although the Germans themselves do not generally accept this supposition their own theories establish a link with British military history that precedes the Peninsula, for they incline to the view that the tune was composed by German troops bound for North America during the American War of Independence. If true, this must have struck a responsive chord in some of the older British officers in Spain, recalling their youthful campaigns against the rebel Yankees. *Ein Schifflein sah ich fahren*, with its simple original words, has remained a constant favourite with German soldiers, and is still included in their song books.

The Spaniards too had distinguished choral singing and this description of Spanish guerrillas might have been composed by the director of a Hollywood epic. "Some were arrayed in green jackets with slouched hats and long feathers, others in blue, helmeted like our yeomanry or artillery drivers, while not a few wore cuirasses and brazen headpieces such as they had probably plundered from their slaughtered enemies . . . They were on the whole well mounted . . . Their whole appearance indeed, for they could not exceed 60 men, (resembled) a troop of bandits ; and the resemblence was not the less striking that they moved not to the sound of trumpets or other martial music, but of their own voices. They were singing a wild air as they passed, in which sometimes one chanted by himself, then two or three chimed in, and by and by the whole squadron joined in a very musical and spirited chorus".[118]

One of the favourite Spanish war songs was called *A la guerra, Españoles*. "Every guerrilla sang it . . . every peasant sang it . . . every child sang it".[119] The same heavy-handed officer who translated *The sentinel* tried his modest skill on this song, but without the music and the original words there is little chance of understanding its popularity.

> The curse of slavery's o'er us,
> And suffering freedom weeps.
> No hope—no hope's before us,
> While Spain's bright spirit sleeps.
> But if her slumbers lighten,
> Then freedom's glance will brighten,
> And lips shall cease to sigh and hearts to pain.

There is something more vigorous in the Spaniards' "*cancioneiros*" — vitriolic anti-French songs based on topical events whose choruses often imitated a Gallic cock clucking distressfully. These *cancioneiros* paid gracious compliments to Spain's allies. After Wellington's triumph at Salamanca the Spaniards sang —

> Adonde vayas, Marmont,
> Adonde vayas, Marmont,
> Tan temprano de la manaña
> Si te coge Velington,
> Ah, Marmont, Marmont, Marmont![120]

Not just English generals but also the ordinary redcoat made an impression on the Spaniards. The same sulphurous characteristic which impelled Joan of Arc's men to call the English "Godons", and which led Colonel Blackader to say that if devils had tongues they would talk like redcoats, was immortalized in a cancioneiro.

> Viva los Ingleses que dicen
> God damn you.
> Mueran los que dicen
> Sacré nom de Dieu.[121]

One baffling story concerns the soldier at Fuentes d'Onoro who heard "a song about Marlborough knowing how to make war and sung to the same tune as in England. The mothers lull their children to sleep with it, and when bodies of troops enter towns or the girls dance boleros this is the general tune". When he asked a girl where she learned it she answered, with a look of real or mock surprise, "Why, from my grandmother".[122] Despite his curiosity the soldier asked no one better informed than this girl, nor does he trouble to provide further information on this popular English song about Marlborough "knowing how to make war". Perhaps it was *Malbrouk s'en va t'en guerre* but the popularity of this melody in England at the beginning of the 19th century is unproven. The use of the song by either English or French in Marlborough's time has never been confirmed, otherwise it could be assumed it was taken to Spain by the redcoats of Peterborough or Galway, or by Berwick's French, and had survived there.

The Spanish zeal for singing led one writer to suggest that they "seem to have more taste for singing than fighting, while the poor Portuguese who sing little and write no bad verses fight like heroes".[123] Such a remark can scarcely go unchallenged, for it is at least two parts unfair. The Spanish regular troops, even when brigaded with British were all too often the despair of Wellington and his generals, but the guerrillas, who fought under their chosen and trusted leaders and in their own fashion were both brave and useful. The Portuguese, who were more consistently brigaded with the British, did fight like heroes, but they were far from being unmusical. They had their own marches, for when Wellington entered Elvas in May 1812 he did so to a medley of British and Portuguese tunes,[124] and they had their own bands to play these tunes, especially the one by Portogallo called *Vencer o morir* ("Conquer or die"). "I have heard it boldly played in the teeth of the enemy by the Portuguese bands," writes the musical enthusiast on whom this international section depends so heavily, "and I marked the countenances of the listeners with delight. It made all Portuguese hearts pant for the fight ... and as the voices joined the music, *Vencer o morir* was not sung without meaning".[125] The little green-jacketed Portuguese had less majestic songs which kept them happy on the hardest march, "the last mile even, singing along the road",[126] so the writer who found the "poor Portuguese" songless may, in his own unintentional way, have somehow depressed them into silence.

What Wellington thought about war music never emerges. His observation about the Highland pipes (see p. 136) is probably apocryphal, although in 1804, when he was still in India, he is supposed to have written: "the fiddlers of the dragoons and 78th and the bagpipes of the 74th play delightfully".[127] With his finely developed sense of diplomacy the Duke might forbid a tune for political reasons, as he did *The downfall of Paris* (see p. 105) and he once sat in conspicuously mute hostility to applause for the singer Catalani. "It was injudicious in every country but our own to give out a chorus of *Rule, Britannia*".[128] (He was not quite so extreme as Sir David Baird who as governor of the Cape of Good Hope once banished band and bandmaster to the guardhouse for celebrating the victory of Trafalgar beneath the very window where the peppery Baird sat with a Dutch general, Jansens. "It was an insult to a fallen enemy in the shape of his guest to show any symptoms of exultation").[129]

Just once, it appears, Wellington's mood was influenced – at least to a degree – by music. In the Waterloo campaign, despite the shortage of British infantry it was intended that the young and untried 3rd Battalion of the 14th Regiment should be withheld from the front. But their commanding officer, Colonel Tidy, had other views. He marched his 3rd Battalion to the Brussels hotel where Wellington and his staff were quartered, and had them beat *The Grenadiers March*. Lord Hill opened the window, and seeing "his old friends, the 14th" asked what they wanted. Tidy shouted up – courteously but determinedly – exactly what was required, and after a moment "Daddy" Hill returned to the window with the Duke. Wellington looked down at the fresh-faced young men so unconscionably anxious to get killed. "They are a very pretty little battalion," he murmured to Hill. "Tell them they may join the Grand Division if they wish." The window closed, and the battalion marched away cheering and happy, their fifes and drums again playing *The Grenadiers March*.[130]

If Wellington was not much concerned with music, choosing to leave relevant decisions about bands to his subordinates, his great rival Napoleon had fixed ideas. The Corsican's interest in military music is reflected not only in the splendid formal marches written while he was First Consul and then Emperor, but in orders that he issued, tastes he expressed, and even in jokes that he cracked with the veterans – his "Grognards" – about their songs. Before he departed on the Egyptian expedition he gave special attention to the formation of good bands, presumably to replace the enthusiastic but ragged music of the Revolutionary armies. In Cairo he ordered noon concerts daily by regimental bands stationed in public places near the hospitals, "playing various airs which will cheer the sick and recall to their minds the finest hours of past campaigns". In 1806 he ordered the performance at public concerts in Paris "of martial songs appropriate to the circumstances and easily retained". Sometimes Napoleon could demand the near-impossible. He invited the composers LeBrun and Rouget de Lisle "to compose a hymn to combat based on a familiar tune like that of the *Marseillaise* or the *Chant du Depart* which must contain sentiments for any and all circumstances of war". If the Muses and not Mars had decided who should win battles, Waterloo may well have gone the other way.

1. F. Markham, *Five Decades of Epistles of War* (1622), p.59.
2. T. S. St. Clair, *A Residence in the West Indies and America* (1834), I, p.2.
3. A. Alexander, *Life* (1830), I, p.71.
4. R. Butler, *Life and Travels* (1854), p.25.
5. J. Shipp, *Memoirs* (1829), I, p.12.
6. Sir G. B. L.'Estrange, *Recollections* (1874), p.20.
7. J. Harley, *The Veteran* (1838), p.64.
8. G. Cruikshank, *A Pop-gun fired off by George Cruikshank in Defence of the British Volunteers of 1803* (1866), p.11.
9. Sir Walter Scott, *The Antiquary* (1816), Note IV.
10. George Elliot, Earl of Minto, *Life and Letters* (1874), III, p.418.
11. J. Patterson, *Adventures* (1837), p.64.

F*

12. W. H. Maxwell, *Peninsular Sketches* (1845), II, p.205.
13. *The Diary of a British Soldier*, Sutro Library (undated), p.16.
14. J. Malcolm, *Reminiscences* (1828), p.251.
15. A. Neale, *Letters from Portugal and Spain* (1809), p.32.
16. J. E. Daniel, *Journal of an Officer in the Commissariat* (1820), p.454.
17. W. Stothert, *Campaigns of 1809, 1810, and 1811* (1812), p.219.
18. R. Blakeney, *A Boy in the Peninsula* (1899), p.211.
19. [Anon]., *Adventures of a Young Rifleman in the French and English Armies* (1826), p.308.
20. [Anon.], *Vicissitudes in the Life of a Scottish Soldier* (1827), p.213.
21. Sir J. S. Cowell Stepney, *Diary* (1854), p.35.
22. *JSAHR*, VI (1927), p.115.
23. *JSAHR*, II (1923), p.7.
24. C. Pearl, *Bawdy Burns* (1958), p.73.
25. *JSAHR*, II (1923), p.160.
26. *JSAHR*, II (1923), p.7.
27. *JSAHR*, XL (1962).
28. R. Cobbold, *Mary Anne Wellington* (1846), II, p.22.
29. *USM* (1832), Part I, p.199.
30. W. Grattan, *Adventures of the Connaught Rangers* (1847), I, p.270.
31. *The Soldier's Companion* (1824), I, p.96.
32. J. H. Stocqueler, *The British Soldier* (1857), p.122.
33. H. O'Donnell, *Historical Records of the 14th West Yorkshire Regiment* (1893), p.370
34. Sir H. Murray, *Memoir of Captain A. S. Murray* (1859), p.51.
35. W. Leeke, *Lord Seaton's Regiment at Waterloo* (1866), I, p.33.
36. Maxwell, II, p.257.
37. *JSAHR*, XXXII (1954), p.7.
38. Sir A. S. Frazer, *Letters* (1859), p.591.
39. Sir J. Kincaid, *Random Shots from a Rifleman* (1835), p.169.
40. H. R. Lewin, *Life of a Soldier* (1834), II, p.198.
41. W. Napier, *Life of Sir Charles Napier* (1857), I, p.172.
42. J. S. Cooper, *Rough Notes of Seven Campaigns* (1869), p.114.
43. Shipp, I, p.62.
44. Daniel, p.125.
45. Ward, p.109.
46. J. Patterson, *Camp and Quarters* (1840), I, p.120.
47. Blakeney, p.339.
48. O'Donnell, p.370.
49. Ward, p.108.
50. L'Estrange, p.117.
51. Officer⁻ of the Line [Pseud.], *Military Sketch Book* (1827), II, pp.3–8.
52. C. R. B. Barrett, *History of the XIII Hussars* (1911), II, p.306.
53. Officer of the Line, I, p.255.
54. Patterson, *Camp and Quarters*, I, p.324.
55. T. Pococke, *Journal of a Soldier of the 71st Regiment* (1819), p.45.
56. Pococke, p.142.
57. Malcolm, p.248.
58. W. Surtees, *Twenty-five Years in the Rifle Brigade* (1833), p.249.
59. W. Wheeler, *Letters* (1951), p.118.
60. Butler, p.161.
61. Patterson, *Camp and Quarters*, I, p.311.
62. G. Woodberry, *Journal* (1896), p.31.
63. E. Costello, *The Adventures of a Soldier* (1841), p.276.
64. Stocqueler, p.268.
65. *Bentley Ballads* (1869), p.237.
66. Stocqueler, p.268.
67. British Museum, 11621.c.2.
68. *USM* (1838), Part II, p.329.
69. J. G. Smith, *The English Army in France* (1831), I, p.230.
70. Regimental Archives.
71. J. H. T. Cornish-Bowden, *Notes on the History of the Duke of Cornwall's Light Infantry, No. 1* (1913), p.36.
72. J. Farmer, *Scarlet and Blue, or Songs for Soldiers and Sailors* (1896), p.207.
73. *Rifle Brigade Chronicle* (1894), p.156.
74. *Ibid*, p.125.
75. Daniel, p.125.
76. *Navy and Army Illustrated*, November 19, 1897.
77. S. Morley, *Memoirs of a Serjeant of the Fifth Regiment of Foot* (1842).
78. E. Mole, *A King's Hussar* (1893), p.100.
79. *The Diary of a British Soldier*.
80. Woodberry, pp.36, 123, 127.
81. Blakeney, p.187.
82. J. Hope, *The Military Memoirs of an Infantry Officer* (1833), p.426.
83. W. Forbes-Mitchell, *Reminiscences of the Great Mutiny 1857–1859* (1893), p.144.
84. A. D. Fraser, *Some Reminiscences and the Bagpipe* (1907), p.410.
85. *JSAHR*, VIII (1929), p.33.
86. G. Fraser, *Memoirs* (1808), p.230.
87. C. A. Malcolm, *The Piper in Peace and War* (1927), p.5.
88. Carr, p.181.
89. D. Stewart, *Sketches of the Highlanders of Scotland* (1822), II, p.239.
90. Lewin, I, p.227.

91. G. C. Bell, *Rough Notes of an Old Soldier* (1867), I, p.140.
92. T. Gowing, *A Soldier's Experience* (1883), p.166.
93. R. Jameson, *Historical Record of the 79th Regiment* (1863), p.55.
94. Pococke, p.180.
95. M. MacBride, *With Napoleon at Waterloo* (1911), p.188.
96. A. Clerk, *Memoir of Colonel John Cameron* (1858), p.51.
97. Hope, p.179.
98. Clerk, p.60.
99. Scobie, p.8.
100. *Ibid*, p.13.
101. Sir W. Scott, *Letters* (1932–1937), II, p.403.
102. Stewart, II, p.346.
103. Hope, p.235.
104. *Highland Light Infantry Chronicle* (October, 1893), p.148.
105. St. Clair, II, p.333.
106. Sir R. D. Henegan, *Seven Years Campaigning* (1846), II, p.35.
107. Cooper, p.107.
108. Daniel, p.455.
109. G. Jones, *The Battle of Waterloo* (1817), p.65.
110. Kincaid, p.162.
111. G. R. Gleig, *The Subaltern* (1825), p.277.
112. *An Officer of the Line*, I, p.187.
113. [Anon.], *Memoirs of the Late War* (1831), p.245.
114. Morris, p.235.
115. J. G. Smith, p.211.
116. Frazer, p.591.
117. *Adventures of a Young Rifleman*, p.24.
118. Gleig, p.220.
119. *An Officer of the Line*, p.107.
120. *Memoirs of the Late War*, p.241.
121. *USM* (1829), Part I, p.706.
122. *Memoirs of the Late War*, p.112.
123. An Officer (pseud.), *Personal Narrative of Adventures in the Peninsula during the War in 1812–1813* (1827), p.119.
124. Daniel, p.99.
125. *An Officer of the Line*, p.105.
126. F. S. Larpent, *Private Journal* (1853), I, p.216.
127. *Cabar Feidh*, VI (1932), p.200.
128. Lord W. P. Lennox, *Wellington in Private Life* (1853), p.19.
129. *USM* (1836), Part II, p.195.
130. Ward, pp.98–100.

Chapter 7

THE CRIMEAN WAR 1854–1856

"MAY I with right and conscience make this claim?" Shakespeare's Henry V asked the Archbishop of Canterbury, and being assured by the prelate that the French crown was his in the eyes of God and man, if not in the eyes of the obtuse French, he cheerfully went to war. And Henry's concern with moral sanction is typically English, for the English have always claimed that they, in contrast to less civilized peoples, were not naturally bellicose – either as individuals or as a nation. It was somehow *wrong* to go to war without just cause. And even if Britain did not always have that inevitable moral right to fight her wars that the Victorians self-righteously pretended, victory at least made common sense in terms of spheres of influence or useful territory. But the Crimean War was neither moral nor rational; it was as futile, senseless, and disorganized as a bar-room brawl.

Since the time of William Pitt the Younger it had been British policy to shore up the Turkish Empire in order to prevent the Russians from obtaining Constantinople and an exit from the Black Sea. In 1853 this question was re-opened. In essence, the Czar claimed the right to protect the Christian subjects of the Turkish Sultan, who were mostly concentrated in the Balkans and around Constantinople, which – as the British Ambassador there warned – would have given Russia the right to meddle almost at will in Turkey's internal affairs. While the diplomats bustled from one end of Europe to another, Russian troops occupied the Turkish-governed principalities of Moldavia and Wallachia on July 3 as "material guarantees" that the Czar's demands would be met. Angered at this violation of her territory Turkey declared war, confident in the last resort of material help from Britain and France. Diplomacy might still have prevented wide-scale escalation of the conflict but on November 30 the destruction by the Russians of a Turkish squadron at anchor in Sinope harbour created a great wave of anti-Russian feeling and on March 23–24, 1854 Britain and France declared war.

Troops had already been moving east to Malta and the first contingent of redcoats were in the vicinity of Constantinople by the end of April, but before they could come to grips with the Russians the principalities had been evacuated. The added fear of Austrian intervention and a cholera epidemic in the Czar's army had accomplished the objective that the British and French had set for themselves. It would have been sensible if not very glorious to bring the army back, but war fever still gripped the country. THE TIMES, which not long before had been denounced as "the Russian organ of Printing House Square," was now firmly for war, and the popular Lord Palmerston insisted that "the eye-tooth of the bear must be drawn", which was a poetic way of saying that Sebastopol, the base from which the Russians had sailed to victory at Sinope, must be razed. Queen Victoria's consort, Prince Albert, also expressed the inflated view that "on Sebastopol hangs the whole fate of European politics". But, in truth, there was little to be gained, and no lesson to be taught the Russians that they had not already digested; the Austrian demonstration and the manifest willingness of the British and French to fight would have deterred any future move by the Russians against the Turkish Empire. Why Britain chose to proceed with the quixotic venture of invading the Crimea is incomprehensible, but it has been suggested that after forty years without a major war, many British believed that a blood-letting would purify a nation grown effete, materialistic, and rent by internal discord. Tennyson, the Poet Laureate, managed to make the whole absurd and ugly proposition sound almost grand:

> And many a darkness into light shall leap,
> And shine in the sudden making of splendid
>   names,
> And noble thought be freer under the sun,
> And the heart of a people beat with one
>   desire.

To the diaries, letters, and memoirs of soldiers there can now be added as source material the despatches of war correspondents, for this was the first war dignified by the presence of this new type of journalist, who owed his effectiveness, if not his actual existence, to the newly-invented electric telegraph. Among these men William Russell of THE TIMES was foremost. There was also a new class of spectator at the war, what the Germans called a *"Kriegsbummler"* — civilians who roamed at will, dodging shot and abuse, appearing everywhere. If they were wealthy aristocrats they visited the theatre of war in their yachts and if they were not so wealthy, then by other means. Regardless of their class, the *Kriegsbummleren* were often prepared to recoup their expenses by selling the story of how the Bear's claws were being drawn.

The public could already see and hear how fit and ready The British Army was for war, singing and playing its way through the cheering crowds. The 7th Fusiliers left Manchester playing *Cheer, boys, cheer, The British Grenadiers, We're going far away*, and *The girl I left behind me*,[1] the Royal Artillery departed with *Rule, Britannia*,[2] and the 17th Lancers clattered through the cobbled streets of Portsmouth to the song that rang across America's prairies in the California Gold Rush of 1849, *Oh, Susannah!*[3] At Waterloo station dense crowds saw the Grenadier Guards off to, of course, *The British Grenadiers*,[4] and the 93rd Highlanders sailed out of Plymouth with the music of the 20th Regiment providing *Auld lang syne* and, prophetically, *Scots wha' hae wi' Wallace bled*, (*Bruce's address*).[5] One of the Naval Brigade which was to accompany the Army wrote a cheery song to the *Posthorn gallop*, which — allowing for poetic licence — gives a gay impression of Portsmouth at this time.

> And now to Portsmouth shoals of troops
> Are coming, coming, coming, coming.
> Fifes are squeaking and the drums
> Are drumming, drumming, drumming,
>   drumming.
> Bugles loud the buglers now
> Are blowing, blowing, blowing, blowing.
> And off in transports all the troops
> Are going, going, going, going.[5]

As the paddle steamer *Ripon* tossed uneasily in Lymington Roads, a Grenadier officer, George Cadogan, composed another bright song suggesting that sea-sickness was the worst thing that could befall a serving soldier.

> Southampton docks are reached at last,
> Our stout and gallant band
> Have trod the deck that wafts them from
> Their native British land..
> One more "hurrah"! The anchor's up,
> And now the ship so brave,
> As conscious of her gallant freight,
> Stems high the ocean wave.
> > But our Gren-a-dier
> > Feels a leetle queer,
> > For he really had no notion
> > Of the ocean's funny motion.
> > But "hurrah" cries he,
> > "Guardsmen are we,
> > And proud, I ween,
> > To serve the Queen
> > By land or sea".[6]

Private Edward Murphy of the Light Company of the 88th Connaught Rangers wrote and sang a song called *Come to the Danube*, of which only the first lines are given. Music probably gave it a vigour that the words alone cannot impart.

> Our allies to join, my boys,
> The English and French,
> Is going to combine, my boys.
> We'll fight to the last,
> And no mortals we'll spare my boys.
> What better fun could you ask,
> Than chasing the Bear, my boys?[7]

True to his words, Murphy fought to the last and was killed before Sebastopol.

The 88th still sang their old Peninsular song, *Love farewell*, with some new variants.

> Oh, Judy dear, ye're young and tender,
> When I'm away ye'll not surrender.
> But hold out like an ancient Roman,
> And I'll make you—an honest woman.
> > So love farewell.

> Oh, Judy, should I die in glory,
> In the papers ye'll read my awful story,
> But I'm so bothered with your charms,
> I'd rather die within your arms,
> > So love farewell.

For public occasions there was also a patriotic verse, apparently in case anyone felt disinclined to take the rollicking Rangers seriously.

> Eighty-eighth and Inniskillen,
> Boys that's able, boys that's willin'.
> Faugh-a-ballagh and County Down,
> Stand by the Harp, and stand by the Crown.
> > So love farewell.[8]

As the ships sailed away from England music kept the troops' morale high. A regimental band played daily aboard the *Trent*,[9] (even in the stormy Bay of Biscay), and on the *Oronoco* the band of the 7th Fusiliers kept "all on board quite merry".[10] Later, in the Black Sea, the four pipers of the 93rd Regiment aboard the *City of Carlisle* enabled the Highlanders to dance their reels.[11] But by the time the Army had arrived in and around Constantinople some of the euphoria had begun to seep away. The Turks scarcely seemed worth fighting for and there were ugly hints that British maladministration would be a more deadly enemy than the Russians. In addition the same cholera that had helped to drive the Russians from the principalities, was now decimating the redcoats and the *Dead March* was heard as frequently as *The British Grenadiers*. The troops at Gallipoli who had listened to the Rifles' band "playing the latest fashionable polkas or making the rocks acquainted with *Rule, Britannia* and *God save the Queen*"[12] became surfeited with the bands of the 79th and 93rd Highlanders playing the *Dead March*.[13] Gallipoli seemed an ideal place to escape from, and the Royal Regiment left willingly enough, singing *Hey, for the life of a soldier*. Although it sounds a bit insipid it was part of Thomas Simpson Cooke's "operatic anecdote" *Frederick the Great*, and a genuine soldiers' favourite.[14]

35
Hey for the life of a soldier

WORDS   T. S. Cooke
MUSIC   T. S. Cooke
SOURCE   A. Wyatt-Edgell –
      A Collection of Soldiers' Songs

When I was a youngster gossips would say
When I grew older I'd be a soldier.
Rattles and toys I threw them away
Except a drum and a sabre.
When I was older, as up I grew,
I went to see a grand review.
Colours flying set me dying,
To embark on a life so new.
    Roll, my merry drums, march away.
    Soldiers' glory lives in story.
    His laurels are green when his locks are grey,
    Then hurrah for the life of a soldier.

The thought of at long last actually fighting the Russians boosted the Army's spirits as it arrived in Bulgaria. The Light Division was welcomed to Varna by the bands of the 33rd Regiment playing *Cheer, boys, cheer* and the 77th playing *The British Grenadiers*. As the 8th Royal Irish Hussars rode past they were given a special welcome by their compatriots of the 88th, "a wild Irish screech" and a spirited *Garryowen*.[15] With these bands, and the nightly concert given by the 55th Regiment,[16] Varna must have been a friendly place until cholera caught up with the Army in Bulgaria. At Devno the *Dead March* had to be discontinued, "for to say the least of it, it was a most doleful noise".[17] There and at Aladyn other tunes were appreciated by the men, and when the bands were all silenced, "out of a humane regard for the feelings of the sick" wrote Russell, the disconsolate soldiers, with nothing else to take their minds off disease, "were wont to get up singing parties in their tents in lieu of ordinary entertainment".[18] Rather than engaging in a pointless pursuit of the Russians across the Pruth River the whole army was gradually withdrawn from Bulgaria and shipped to the Crimea. On September 12 some 28,000 men anchored off Eupatoria, which surrendered promptly next day, and the massed bands on the transports played first *God save the Queen* and then the French anthem, *Partant pour la Syrie*.[19] On September 18th, the southwards march began towards Sebastopol. "The colours were flying; the bands at first were playing; . . . but more warlike than trumpet and drum was the great quiet which followed the ceasing of the bands".[20] And as the army marched men were again dropping, from exhaustion, from dysentery – and from cholera.

When the British Army finally cornered the Russian Bear in his Sebastopol lair it became obvious that despite the musical noises made so far the bands of the British Army were as inadequate as every other service and supply in that blighted campaign. In his article BANDS IN THE CRIMEAN WAR[21] Dr. H. G. Farmer has chronicled how at the outbreak of war some of the regimental bandmasters, who were foreign civilians, not unnaturally tendered their resignations. They agreed with Charles Lever's fictional Irish dragoon.

> Now I like *Garryowen*
> When I hear it at home,
> But it's not half so sweet
> When you're going to be kilt.

Some bands were broken up before their regiments went on active service, some faded away under the vicissitudes of the campaign and bandsmen – as in earlier wars – often found themselves seconded to the Ambulance Corps. General Sir Evelyn Wood long remembered the words of Sir Colin Campbell before the storming of the Alma Heights : "Whoever is wounded must lie where he falls until a bandsman comes up to attend to him".[22]

The allied army waited – there was no siege, not even a blockade worth the name – before Sebastopol from September 1854 to September 1855. This period can be divided into two phases. Until about March 1855 an organizational shambles existed, but thereafter everything – including the bands and provision of music – improved. On October 9, 1854, Russell delivered himself eloquently on the miserable showing of the British bands. "The silence and gloom of our camp as compared with the activity and bustle of that of the French are very striking. No drum, no bugle call, no music of any kind is ever heard within our precincts, while our neighbours close by keep up incessant rolls, fanfaronnades and flourishes, relieved every evening by the fine performance of their military bands. The fact is, many of our instruments have been placed in store and the regimental bands are broken up and disorganized, the men being devoted to the performance of the duties for which the Ambulance Corps was formed . . . The want of music in camp is productive of greater consequences than appear likely at first blush from such a cause. Every military man knows how regiments, when fatigued on the march, cheer up at the strains of their band and dress up, keep step, and walk with animation and vigour when it is playing . . . It seems to me an error to deprive them of a cheering and wholesome influence at the very time when they need it most. The military band is not meant alone for the delectation of garrison towns or for the pleasure of the officers in quarters and the men are fairly entitled to its inspiration during the long and weary march in the enemy's country and in the monotony of a standing camp 'ere the beginning of a siege."[23]

The reason that Russell heard no music of any kind, not even for signalling purposes, was that there had been "some misunderstanding of orders" and only on November 22, when there were scarcely any musicians still surviving, did the British commander-in-chief Lord Raglan proclaim that music might be used whenever regimental commanding officers saw fit.[24]

Quite apart from organizational shortcomings before the war and wastage during it there occured two incidents that might have been laughable if they had not been part of more tragic circumstances. The band of the 55th Regiment which had given such satisfaction at Varna had lost its instruments. They had been kept together in a special tent, "for safety", and during the Battle of Inkerman the horse artillery, with diabolical precision, had managed to gallop into and over the tent.[25] During the great gale of November 14, the big drum of the 4th Regiment was among the many that bounded down the hill and into Balaclava harbour.[26] Since 21 ships were wrecked, and warm clothing, ammunition and food by the ton lost, the disappearance of the instruments went almost unnoticed at the time. It is easy to see why, when a detachment of the Guards arrived on November 20, their "drums and fifes kept the whole place alive . . . (with) the familiar squeaks of *Cheer, boys, cheer*, and *Willikins and his Dinah* aided by a rattling chorus",[27] for otherwise all was gloom and silent despondency. On March 3, 1855, THE ILLUSTRATED LONDON NEWS was still able to complain bitterly that "the French have shown their superiority to the English in the attention they have paid to the maintenance of their military bands as in everything else. While the English camp has been for months without any attempt to cheer the hearts of the men with inspiring martial airs our more mercurial neighbours have kept up regular practice of the bands, which has had an excellent effect on the soldiers". After the fall of Sebastopol in September 1855, British bands started to re-appear. The band of the 93rd which broke up because of numerous casualties was re-established, although not on its old grand scale.[28] In October the bands of the 14th and 39th were both playing regularly. "The 14th was an excellent band and on Thursday there was a full concert at 3 o'clock. Enlivening and inspiriting, although less refined, was the fife and drum music which was also played every night at 8 o'clock to call in soldiers who might be strolling about."[29] The Connaught Rangers were also able to put a band together to celebrate the first anniversary of the Battle of Inkerman, on November 5, 1855.[30]

Quite incredibly, during the very gloomiest days before Sebastopol a regimental march was written. Lieutenant-Colonel Stratton of the 77th Regiment, who might well have had other things on his mind, instructed his band sergeant, 35-year-old James O'Connor from Galway, to write a distinctive march for the regiment. As a compliment to the many Irish in the ranks (although this was nominally the East Middlesex Regiment) the march was to have an Irish flavour. The conditions were not conducive to great composing – inadequate furniture, paper, quietness and time – but Stratton would brook no argument and O'Connor buckled gamely to his task. Although he was no Carl Maria von Weber who managed to write two of the greatest German cavalry songs in one afternoon – *Lutzow's wild hunt* and *The sword song* – O'Connor produced a march that answered his colonel's requirements. As a tribute to the difficulties he had overcome, it was called *Paddy's resource*.

36
Paddy's resource

MUSIC P. O'Connor

The marked superiority of the bands of our allies stressed by the journalists was even confirmed by our soldier writers although this could not have pleased them. At Varna the French Army was said to have "the most beautiful bands . . . The Zouave is perfect, about 50 instruments, and so perfectly harmonized. The music is as soft as the most tender-eared person could wish for. They play every evening and throw ours into the shade".[31] The Zouave band did not disappear, like some of ours had done, when it was needed most. A soldier from the Light Division camp outside Sebastopol related how the Zouaves' "very fine band . . . play very often as they pass through our camp every day to relieve a strong picket they have . . . about 400 yards in front of our camp."[32] British soldiers thought it well worth their while to stroll across to the French camp and listen to bands such as that of the Chasseurs de Vincennes.[32] The French still used their music in battle and when they stormed the Mamelon bastion at Sebastopol their drums and bugles played the stirring refrain that had become popular during the Algerian Wars – *La casquette du Père Bugeaud*.[34] While it mortified British pride to admit the superiority of the bands of "the old enemy", it was almost worse to acknowledge that our other allies, the Piedmontese or Sardinians (who had argued themselves into the war to convince Europe they were a growing power), had fine bands too and the British had not previously reckoned them as a military nation of any sort. Lord George Paget wrote that "the Sardinian Army was the admiration of all; perfect in every detail", and this praise obviously extended to its bands. Officers galloped across the Balaclava plain to the Sardinian camp at Kamara, to hear "their excellent band . . . which played some nice operatic selections".[35] Only Mrs. Fanny Duberly who had accompanied her husband Captain Henry Duberly of the 8th Hussars to the Crimea, and is a delightful commentator on the war, had any reservations about the Sardinians, and it was feminine intuition rather than marked musical expertise that led her to a significant conclusion. Having heard them twice she decided that despite their technical efficiency they only put their hearts and souls into the business when playing to an Italian audience; for foreigners they contented themselves with a mechanical performance.[36]

The only (rather spiteful) satisfaction the British could derive was in reflecting that their own silence or near-silence was preferable to the hideous cacophony of the Turks. One Guardsman labelled the Turks as "the dirtiest, ugliest, most unsoldierly, cowardly brutes I have ever seen . . . Their instrumental music being exactly like penny trumpets, while the airs are nothing but tool - tool - tools".[37] Someone else thought their music "dismal in the extreme".[38] The Turks could do nothing right; whether they tried to copy Western-style bands or retained their own national music they were still widely derided and lampooned. "One regiment had a good brass band which almost alarmed the bystanders by striking up a quickstep (waltz) as they marched past and playing it in very excellent style, but the majority of the regiments was preceeded by musicians with drums, fifes, and semi-circular thin brass tubes with wide mouths, such as those which may have tumbled the walls of Jericho" wrote Russell, one of their least harsh critics.[39]

A Connaught Ranger noted "a band of harsh brass instruments . . . but as each musician appeared to play no particular tune – in whatever time he pleased – and to enjoy the same freedom in selection of key, the discord was painfully excruciating".[40] The assistant surgeon of a Scottish regiment thought their brass bands "an amusing burlesque of our English bands. Some of the tunes were, I presume, native melodies and barbarous enough. They got through, however, a selection from *I Puritani*", although the high notes were suspect.[41] Lord Paget found

Turkish music "uncouth . . . not altogether destitute of harmony, but peculiarly savage",[42] which was also the opinion on Anatolian irregular cavalry, "headed by a band of three drums which the musicians (?) played while holding the reins in their mouths."[43] Turkish war songs excited just as little enthusiasm. "One of their soldiers sang us a song and played with a quill on a pot-bellied guitar. I cannot say much for the music . . . The warrior's war song . . . was so simple that it was merely a howl succeeded by a gasp".[44] The one Turkish band held in any esteem was that of the commander-in-chief, Omar Pasha, which even Mrs. Duberly liked when it played excerpts from *Rigoletto* and marches composed by Madam Omar Pasha.[45] (Omar Pasha was a Croat, and Madam presumably a solitary Western wife, not one of a harem). What Mrs. Duberly might not have discovered was that the band, although dressed as Turkish soldiers, was Omar's own collection of German musicians, and although they were very good on opera – another listener liked their selection from *Il Trovatore*[46] – the only Oriental air they had mastered was the Turkish national anthem.[47]

Although British bands were in eclipse the voices of the redcoats were far from hushed. Their miserable circumstances inspired "original and extemporaneous verses apropos to . . . our government at home, to our generals at headquarters, to the Czar in his palace, and Johnny Russ at the front".[48] None have survived, although this couplet from "doggerel verses by a veteran" lambasting Britain's prime minister was possibly set to music.

> The French are well provided for,
> Their wants into are seen.
> The soldiers' friend is Bonaparte,
> And never Aberdeen.[49]

Not all the soldiers' songs were laments. One optimist, to the tune of *The British Grenadiers*, foresaw the imminent fall of Sebastopol.

> And soon a song of victory shall cheer the heart of all,
> And triumph float from every breeze, borne from Sebastopol.
> When Frenchman brave and black Zouaves—the men who know no fears,
> Have side by side like brothers fought with the British Grenadiers.
> The great Redan shall thunder find and we shall find the cheers.
> With a row-dow-dow and a row-dow-dow for the British Grenadiers.[50]

The British Grenadiers was also the tune of the best-known soldiers' song of the war, *The Battle of the Alma* by Corporal John Brown of the Grenadier Guards.

1st verse	Come all you gallant British hearts Who love the red and blue. Come drink a health to those brave lads, Who made the Russians rue. Fill up your glass and let it pass, Three cheers and one cheer more, For the fourteenth of September, Eighteenhundred fifty four.
2nd verse	We sailed from Kalamita Bay, And soon we made the coast, Determined we would do our best, In spite of brag and boast. We sprang to land upon the strand, And slept on Russian shore, On the fourteenth of September, Eighteenhundred fifty four.
10th verse	Here's a health to noble Raglan, To Campbell and to Brown, And all the gallant Frenchmen Who shared the day's renown. Whilst we displayed the black cockade, They the tricolour bore. The Russian crew wore grey and blue. In September, fifty four.
11th verse	Come let us drink a toast tonight Our glasses take in hand. And all around this festive board, In solemn silence stand. Before we part let each true heart, Drink once to those no more, Who fought their last fight on Alma's height, In September, fifty four.[51]

No regiment came out of the war with greater credit than the 93rd Highlanders, who at Balaclava, against the Russian cavalry, formed the original "thin red line". Over seventy years ago the Argyll and Sutherland Highlanders used to sing a song that they claimed was composed in the Crimea after Balaclava.

When they get the order off they go,
With lightsome hearts to meet the foe.
When they get the word, they scatter them like dirt,
The raw, braw laddies of the ninety-third.

Sir Colin Campbell kent good and weel
That his ain braw laddies were as true as steel.
Whenever he'd got any man's work to do,
He'd send for the lads wi' the bonnets o' blue.[52]

But the real hit tune of the Crimean War, which has already been mentioned several times was *Cheer, boys, cheer*, which enjoyed the same sort of popularity that *Tipperary* was to attain in World War One.

37
Cheer, boys, cheer!

WORDS   C. Mackay
MUSIC   H. Russell

fare - well En - gland much as we may love thee,

We'll dry the tears that we have shed be - fore.

Why should we weep who sail in search of for - tune? So

fare - well En - gland, fare - well for e - ver - more!

CHORUS
risoluto

Cheer! boys, cheer! for coun - try, mo - ther coun - try,

Cheer, boys, cheer! No more of idle sorrow.
Courage, true hearts, shall bear us on our way.
Hope points before, and shows the bright tomorrow,
Let us forget the darkness of today.

So farewell, England, much as we may love thee.
We'll dry the tears that we have shed before.
Why should we weep, who sail in search of fortune?
So farewell, England. Farewell, for evermore!

Cheer, boys, cheer! For country, mother country.
Cheer, boys, cheer! The willing strong right hand.
Cheer, boys, cheer! There's wealth for honest labour.
Cheer, boys, cheer! For the new and happy land.

Cheer, boys, cheer! The steady breeze is blowing,
To float us freely o'er the ocean's breast.
The world shall follow in the track we're going.
The star of empire glitters in the west.

Here we had toil and little to reward it,
But there shall plenty smile upon our pain.
And ours shall be the prairie and the forest,
And boundless meadows, ripe with golden grain.

Cheer, boys, cheer! For country, mother country,
Cheer, boys, cheer! For united heart and hand.
Cheer, boys, cheer! There's wealth for honest labour.
Cheer, boys, cheer! For the new and happy land.

The words were written by Charles MacKay and the music by Henry Russell, (who also wrote *A life on the ocean wave*, the regimental march of the Royal Marines). "It was played by every naval and military band, sung in every ship and regiment, and whistled by every whistler".[53] A contemporary sketch shows an old Crimea veteran, a muffled ragbag of a soldier, watching the immaculate Johnny Newcomes disembarking at Balaclava and the picture is called, ironically one supposes, *Cheer, boys, cheer*.[54] The song became almost a second national anthem and on one occasion a drunken merchant seaman tried without success to fight a French officer who declined to join him in singing the rousing chorus.[55] It was still sung in the Indian Mutiny and during the American Civil War, but its heyday was undoubtedly 1854–1855. At one time 39 presses were working non-stop to meet the demand but Russell himself made little enough from the hit. He received £3 for the copyright, and when the success of the song was assured his publishers sent a further princely £10 plus a piece of plate inscribed, "Cheer, boys, cheer".[56]

For their numbers the sailors of the Naval Brigade who manned several of the batteries confronting Sebastopol probably made more noise than anyone else. Before the batteries were of any use the huge naval guns had to be dragged up from Balaclava, but this daunting work merely inspired songs. "From a distance you hear some hearty rough English chorus, borne on the breeze over the hillside," said William Russell. "As you approach, the strain of an unmistakable Gosport fiddle, mingled with the squeaks of a marine fife rise up".[57] A lieutenant of the 20th Regiment thought "it was cheering to hear our jolly tars hauling the heavy guns to camp, singing every tune under the sun. You could hear them a mile off."[58] General Sir Evelyn Wood, who — oddly — was a midshipman at the time, explained how it was done. "We put fifty men on three drag ropes, placed a fiddler or fifer on the gun, and if neither was available a tenor was mounted to give the solo of a chorus song".[59] Jack Tars were accounted "curious animals in camp", and the redcoats seemed slightly perplexed to find them eternally "cheering and singing songs, and all delighted to begin the fight once more".[60]

One phenomenon of the Crimean War was the comparative eclipse of the piper, whose valour and knack for the improbable makes him such a frequent centre-piece in the history of British war music. Not that the pipes were entirely still. *Johnny Cope* was heard as the regular reveille before Sebastopol,[61] and as the winter of 1854 blossomed into the spring of 1855 Russell was glad to report that "the men have commenced tuning up their pipes and chanting their old familiar choruses once more".[62] When an amphibious raid was launched against Kertch the men of the 93rd aboard the *Stromboli* were permitted to dance reels of an evening.[63] So too, when the officers of the Highland Brigade entertained the Sardinian officers they had the pipers in "and innumerable beautiful reels were danced",[64] and when they gave a farewell dinner for Sir Colin Campbell the pipers played – *The Campbells are coming, See, the conquering hero comes*, and *Auld lang syne*.[65] But all this is tame when compared with the wild and inspired exploits of pipers in other wars.

Although the Crimea had revealed that the British Army was creaking, deficient in nearly everything except courage, it led to few significant reforms. It was only in 1868, when Edward Cardwell became Secretary for War, that the process began by which Britain developed a modern army.

But for the Army bands the Crimea inaugurated a revolution. The disappearance of so many civilian bandmasters (and bandsmen) at the beginning of the war, the peculiar role of the bandsmen in the Crimea (neither musician, rifleman, nor stretcher-bearer but a bit of each), and the famous (or infamous) silence of the camp had all been noted. There was also the debacle at Scutari in 1854 when, in celebration of the Queen's birthday, the massed regimental bands played the national anthem before the entire staffs of the British, French and Turkish armies, "not with that perfect unanimity which could be desired".[66] Put less charitably, there was total lack of uniformity in instrumentation, arrangement, and even key. Among the audience on that embarrassing occasion stood George William Frederick Charles, Duke of Cambridge, amateur musician, professional soldier, commanding officer of the

Guards Brigade, and cousin to the Queen. In 1856 he was appointed Commander-in-Chief of the British Army, and although he did not prove amenable to many needed reforms, in one matter he acted with lightning speed. In 1857 under his directive a Military Music Class was established at Kneller Hall, Twickenham, which became in due course the Royal Military School of Music. From that day forward regimental music was in the hands of soldiers, not civilians, and the bands of the Army could never again fall apart when they were needed most. Although commanding officers were still allowed a good deal of latitude in musical matters the days of autonomous, and sometimes eccentric, individualism were over ; as time went by the increasing influence of Kneller Hall ensured not only a high degree of professional competence in the bands of regiments, but also a reasonable conformity in everything pertaining to regimental music.

1. T. Gowing, *A Soldier's Experience* (1883), p.4.
2. T. Faughnan, *Stirring Incidents in the Life of a Soldier* (1885), p.203.
3. D. H. Parry, *The Death-or-Glory Boys* (1899), p.201.
4. Sir G. Harrison, *Seventy-one Years of a Guardsman's Life* (1916), p.79.
5. F. M. Norman, *At School and Sea* (1899), p.337.
6. Harrison, p.81.
7. H. F. N. Jourdain, *Ranging Memories* (1934), p.54.
8. E. H. Maxwell, *With the Connaught Rangers* (1883), p.55.
9. Sir D. Lysons, *The Crimean War from First to Last* (1895), p.2.
10. W. Jowett, *Diary* (1856), p.11.
11. J. A. Ewart, *The Story of a Soldier's Life* (1881), p.222.
12. Sir W. H. Russell, *The War* (1856), I, p.27.
13. Ewart, p.213.
14. G. C. Bell, *Rough Notes by an Old Soldier* (1867) II, p.151.
15. F. I. Duberly, *Journal of the Russian War* (1855), p.42.
16. J. R. Hume, *Reminiscences of the Crimean Campaign with the 55th Regiment* (1894), p.23.
17. A. Mitchell, *Recollections of One of the Light Brigade* (1885), p.29.
18. Russell, I, p.205.
19. W. Baring Pemberton, *Battles of the Crimean War* (1968), p.26.
20. A. W. Kinglake, *The Invasion of the Crimea* (1863), II, p.207.
21. *JSAHR*, XLI (1963), p.19.
22. Sir H. E. Wood, *The Crimea in 1854 and 1894* (1895), p.377.
23. Russell, I, p.204.
24. C. C. Taylor, *Journal of Adventures with the British Army . . .* (1856), I, p.148.
25. Hume, p.76.
26. *The British Bandsman*, (Sept 1889) No. 34 p.280.
27. Russell, I, p.277.
28. Ewart, p.400.
29. G. Buchanan, *Camp Life as seen by a Civilian* (1871), p.238.
30. N. Steevens, *The Crimean Campaign with the Connaught Rangers* (1878), p.297.
31. A. Brooksbank, *Letters from the Crimea* (1873), p.20.
32' Sir R. D. Kelly, *Letters to his Wife during the Crimean War* (1902), p.150.
33. G. S. Peard, *Narrative of a Campaign in the Crimea* (1855), p.116.
34. Wood, p.280.
35. Steevens, p.252.
36. Duberly, pp.201, 206.
37. *USM* (1855), Part I, p.372.
38. Ewart, p.207.
39. Russell, I, p.412.
40. Steevens, p.23.
41. F. Robinson, *Diary of the Crimean War* (1856), p.48.
42. Lord George Paget, *The Light Cavalry Brigade in the Crimea* (1881), p.61.

43. Steevens, p.21.
44. T. Kelly, *From the Fleet in the Fifties* (1902), p.63.
45. Duberly, p.190.
46. T. Buzzard, *With the Turkish Army in the Crimea and Asia Minor* (1915), p.122.
47. *Ibid*, p.122.
48. W. H. Logan, *Pedlar's Pack of Ballads and Songs* (1869), p.110.
49. Kelly, p.74.
50. Logan, p.110.
51. W. Forbes-Mitchell, *Reminiscences of the Great Mutiny, 1857–1859* (1893), p.141.
52. R.S.M. F. C. Devereux, (Argyll and Sutherland Highlanders). Interview, 1954.
53. Norman, p.336.

54. Wood, p.236.
55. E. Bruce Hamley, *The Story of the Campaign of Sebastopol* (1885), p.146.
56. H. Russell, *Cheer, Boys, Cheer* (1895), p.199.
57. W. H. Russell, I, p.213.
58. Peard, p.111.
59. Wood, p.79.
60. D. A. Reid, *Memories of the Crimean War* (1911), p.61.
61. Ewart, p.334.
62. W. H. Russell, I, p.377.
63. Ewart, p.347.
64. *Ibid*, p.420.
65. *Ibid*, p.439.
66. Russell, I, p.74.

Chapter 8

THE INDIAN MUTINY 1857–1858

ON May 10, 1857, the Indian regiments at Meerut, 40 miles north-east of Delhi mutinied, slaughtered every European they could lay hands on, and the following day in Delhi, proclaimed the senile old king, Mogul Emperor. Their action triggered off a series of uprisings throughout Central India, mainly in May and June, but continuing sporadically, as late as October.

The ostensible cause of the Meerut mutiny was a new type of cartridge, supposedly greased with a mixture of pig and cow fat, which offended the religious sensibilities of both Moslems and Hindus. But throughout India many classes had become dissatisfied with British rule and the new cartridge was merely the final excuse. The sepoys, for instance, feared that a plan was afoot to ship them overseas for service, which would lead to a loss of all-important caste. Sepoys from Oudh (some 40,000 men) were further discontented for their province had been annexed by the East India Company in 1856. Princes feared that under the new Doctrine of Lapse their states would be seized by the Company if they died without issue, for the adoption of heirs had been arbitrarily forbidden. Some client rajas had seen their pensions pared. Further, many Indians – both Moslem and Hindu – felt that their faiths were taken too lightly by the British. Christian missionaries were given many prerogatives, railways did not distinguish caste so that a Brahmin and a lowly sweeper might be seated together side by side, and the enforced abolition of infanticide and suttee (the burning of widows) seemed unpardonable encroachments on their religious beliefs. Finally, landowners resented the Company's sudden interest in land tenure and frequent seizures if title could not be proved satisfactorily.

The Indians had long been disillusioned about their white overlords. They knew that the British had won many wars, but also that the British had always relied on sepoy help. They had seen the Afghans, and more recently the Sikhs, tax British fighting capability to breaking point, and accounts of the Crimean War had filtered through, with British ineptitude probably magnified in the telling. Further, with their own eyes the Indians noted that the 300,000 native troops, trained and armed, outnumbered the white armies by over 7 to 1. The time was ripe for the overthrow of the British Raj, and holy men took pains to remind the superstitious that it was exactly 100 years since Clive had begun the era of British domination by winning the Battle of Plassey.

The Indian rebels – "Pandies" to the British – included retainers of the princes, and "badmashes" from the slums and bazaars, but the nucleus of their forces were often the sepoys, still fighting in regimental units created by the British. It is ironic to find them persistently playing British marches "as if in defiance".[1] At Lucknow where over 10,000 sepoys besieged 1,000 British troops, plus some civilians and loyal Indians, their regimental bands were much in evidence. They gave a regular morning performance, plus an occasional evening encore that included *The standard-bearer's march*, *The girl I left behind me*, and *See, the conquering hero comes*, concluding in dubious taste with *God save the Queen*.[2] The bands also played the besiegers into action and it must have been a bizarre and fearsome nightmare to see sepoys, ragged badmashes, and the picturesque retainers of the thalukadars (barons), sweeping in "like so many demons in human form" to the strains of some well loved English air.[3]

One of the keys to the overall strategy of the Mutiny was the recently-conquered Punjab. Here 10,000 British troops, 36,000 sepoys, and 13,000 local irregulars were stationed; if the Punjab stayed quiet some of the British could be released for duty elsewhere, and indeed it was possible that the Sikhs and other Punjabis might be persuaded to fight for the British against the Indians of the Central Provinces for whom they had no traditional affection. Conversely, if the Punjab flared into insurrection the 10,000 British would be fully occupied there and this involvement in the north-west would encourage further outbreaks in Central India. Fortunately the Punjab stayed loyal, generally speaking, and a Movable Column was drawn from garrisons there and sent to help the British watching Delhi. As for the princes of the Punjab, they provided all manner of fierce irregulars who relished the opportunity to return to pastures they had happily pillaged and looted before.

Most of the sepoy regiments in the Punjab were immediately disarmed but some which seemed trustworthy marched with the Movable Column until suspicion grew as they approached their mutinous brethren, and it was thought best to disarm them. On June 23, the 33rd and then the 35th Native Infantry were drawn into a virtual trap by the 52nd Light Infantry Regiment with Royal Artillery guns in the background positioned to blow the sepoys to shreds if they declined to lay down their arms. As the 35th marched unwittingly on their music was heard playing a familiar air that the 52nd also used.[4] It was a sublimely sentimental, inconsequential ballad filled with evocations of babbling English brooks, dear old English schoolmasters, and sighing girls. Nothing could have been less appropriate from the hell-bent sepoys than *Don't you remember sweet Alice, Ben Bolt?*

38
Don't you remember sweet Alice?
(Ben Bolt)

WORDS   N. Kneass
MUSIC   N. Kneass

Sentimentally

Oh! don't you re-mem-ber sweet A-lice, Ben Bolt, Sweet A-lice with hair so—

brown! She wept with de-light, when you gave her a smile, And

trem-bled with fear at your frown In the old church yard, in the

val-ley, Ben Bolt, In a cor-ner ob-scure and a lone, They have

fit-ted a slab of— gran-ite so gray, And sweet A-lice lies un-der the

stone. they have fit-ted a slab of— gran-ite so gray, And sweet

A-lice lies un-der the stone.

colla voce.

Oh, don't you remember sweet Alice, Ben Bolt?
Sweet Alice with hair so brown.
She wept with delight when you gave her a smile,
And trembled with fear at your frown.
In the old church yard in the valley, Ben Bolt,
In a corner obscure and alone,
They have fitted a slab of granite so grey,
And sweet Alice lies under the stone.
They have fitted a slab of granite so grey
And sweet Alice lies under the stone.

Oh, don't you remember the wood, Ben Bolt?
Near the green sunny slope on the hill.
Where oft we have sung 'neath its wide spreading shade,
And kept time to the click of the mill.
The mill has gone to decay, Ben Bolt,
Silence and gloom reigns around,
See the old rustic porch with its roses so sweet,
Lies scattered and fallen to the ground.
See the old rustic porch with its roses so sweet,
Lies scattered and fallen to the ground.

Oh, don't you remember the school, Ben Bolt?
And the master so kind and true.
And the sweet little nook by the clear running brook,
Where we gathered the flowers as they grew.
O'er the master's grave grows the grass, Ben Bolt,
And the clear running brook is now dry.
And of all our friends who were schoolmates then,
There remain, Ben, but you and I.
And of all our friends who were schoolmates then,
There remain, Ben, but you and I.

On August 14, the 52nd and the rest of the Movable Column joined the British troops who had been observing Delhi from the ridge overlooking the city since June 8, but who had lacked the numerical strength and siege guns necessary for an assault. As they swung into camp the band of the 8th Regiment greeted them.[5] It must have been a welcome duty for the musicians, for all too often recently their music had been played (sometimes with the band of the 61st)[6] to enliven a camp scourged by cholera. One of the tunes they would have played was *Cheer, boys, cheer*, the Crimean favourite which is mentioned in several accounts of the Mutiny. It was played by the 61st when they first marched on to Delhi Ridge,[7] and it was sung at a party in Lucknow when the defenders learned from a spy that help was on the way.[8] There was no widely popular tune in the Mutiny comparable to *Cheer, boys, cheer* in the Crimea. Apart from songs and marches mentioned so far there are only passing references in contemporary works to *Far upon the sea*, and *I'm Ninety-five*, the march of the Rifle Brigade.[9]

Instrumental music was greatly appreciated on the seemingly endless marches across the sub-continent. In his old age General Sir Richard Harrison remembered the departure of the expedition to reconquer Rohilkhand. "The country was more open than usual and the whole of the Highland Brigade was deployed in line, and in that formation with bands in front of the battalions, moved steadily over the broad plain."[10] Pipes too were invaluable in keeping troops on the move. On a 42-mile march to the Banass River in August by three Highland companies their three pipers "played alternately and almost without a break during the 13 hours of the march".[11] Bands also played when the troops moved through inhabited areas, to sustain the loyal and cow the disaffected, actual or potential.[12]

Apart from the sepoys' regimental bands (of both the insurgents and those who stayed loyal) a variety of native music was heard during the Mutiny. The Sikhs who arrived with the Movable Column and were played in by the 8th Regiment had a band[13] as did the Sikhs and hillmen who arrived from Kashmir on September 7, in spectacular fashion. Captain Griffiths of the 61st was sitting with the regimental bandmaster, a German called Saüer, when "we were saluted with the sound of distant music, the most discordant I have ever heard. The bandmaster jumped up from his seat exclaiming, 'Mein Gott ! Vat is dat ? No regiment in camp can play such vile music,' and closing his ears rushed out". On came the Sikhs, playing or distorting an unspecified English air, and although their music was atrocious Captain Griffiths was more than pleased to see these 2,200 men "of good physique", and their 4 guns.[14] The Indian regiments all had 'bhats' (rather like the traditional Highland bards) "whose business it was to encourage the men in action . . . to celebrate their achievements and to sing their praises".[15] Another ex-officio but indispensable attachment to each regiment marched in the vanguard with a small drum ; when the camping ground for the night had been reached he would plant a little flag and beat out a welcome to the arriving soldiers, thereby earning gratitude for his glad tidings of rest, and a shower of small coins.[16]

Music was also provided by the sailors, the same happy breed who made merry before Sebastopol. One of the officers who had distinguished himself there was Captain William Peel, third son of the former prime minister. Peel had fought with the Guards at Inkerman and had led an assault party at the Redan, and in August he arrived at Calcutta aboard H.M.S. *Shannon*. Disembarking with 450 sailors and ten 8-inch guns (soon re-inforced by a further 120 bluejackets) he organized the Naval Brigade. When the 93rd marched into Bunterah they were happy to find "Peel's Naval Brigade lining the road to welcome us and their band of fiddlers ready to play us into camp".[17] The tars considered any time music time, and once they appropriated "a French piano which was kept going all day by anyone who was not actually on duty".[18]

The defence of Lucknow (p. 173) was one of the most dramatic events in Britain's military history, and it is probably the fight about which the greatest quantity of musical anecdote has been found, surpassing both Quebec and Waterloo. The siege began on June 30, and on September 22, a relief force, under the joint but uneasy command of Brigadier General Havelock and Major General Outram was within striking distance. Next day they penetrated the Alumbagh, "the gardens of the world", a walled pleasure park of the former kings of Oudh four miles south of Lucknow. It appears that a ceremonial entry into Lucknow had been intended "with bands playing and colours flying" but the rebels did not melt away after their first defeat, and so, "colours had to be brought in with difficulty, the bandsmen had to be converted into soldiers and their instruments had to be left behind at Alumbagh".[19]

This did not seem to have bothered the Scots, who still had their pipers and when the relief force broke through on September 25, there was a great deal of emotion and merriment. "The piper of the 78th sprang up on a chair and he and Mrs. A. fraternized," wrote one lady.[20] (Fraternization standing on a chair sounds uncommonly difficult, but anything may have been possible on that day). After the ice had been thus broken the piper asked Mrs. A. where she came from and learning it to be Edinburgh, "he shouted out — 'So do I, from the Castle Hill' — and then gave us another tune on his bagpipes." Although the garrison had simply been reinforced, not rescued, and the rebels were still thick around Lucknow the mood of gaiety continued to find expression in music, "some of us dancing the hornpipe to the sounds of the High-landers' pibroch".[21] The relief force had lost so many men, partly as a result of shortcomings in the joint command, that withdrawal with the

G*

many Lucknow civilians would have been impractical, and the original defenders and the new arrivals settled down to await further help.

When the city was finally relieved by Sir Colin Campbell on November 17, it was again done to music. Among the first of the 93rd Highlanders (Campbell's Crimean pets, it will be recalled), into the Secundrabagh, a fortified stone compound, was pipe major John Macleod, blowing *The haughs of Cromdale* with great nonchalance, "as if he had been walking around the officers' mess at a regimental festival". When Campbell complimented him Macleod took it in his stride. "I thought the boys would fecht better wi' the national music to cheer them on".[22] Another strongpoint to be taken was the Shah Najaf, a domed mosque surrounded by a walled garden. Once the 93rd were inside (with the help of Captain Peel's guns and rockets which thoroughly demoralized the defenders) their pipes struck up *The Campbells are coming* to let Sir Colin know they were inside and to inform the besieged of their whereabouts.[23] Thinking this might not be sufficient they hoisted their regimental colours and a feather bonnet, and a tiny twelve-year-old drummer named Ross was sent aloft with a bugle and orders to sound the regimental calls and *The cock o' the north*. Then, if the story can be believed, despite injunctions to come down, he began to sing:

> There's not a man beneath the moon,
> Nor lives in any land he,
> That hasn't heard the pleasant tune
> Of *Yankee Doodle Dandy*.
> In cooling drinks and clipper ships
> The Yankee has the way shown,
> On land and sea 'tis he that whips,
> Old Bull and all creation.

Little Ross was back to the redcoats' old trick of singing Yankee songs in derision. He later explained that he was born when the regiment was in Canada and his mother was visiting her sister in the United States and he could not come down from his perch on the roof until he had sung *Yankee Doodle*, "to make my American cousins envious when they hear of the deeds of the 93rd".[24]

Lucknow was also the supposed scene of one of the most controversial stories about bagpipes – the story of Jessie Brown. The tale was popularized in THE TIMES of December 14, 1857, which in turn is quoting the JERSEY TIMES of December 10, which in turn is supposedly quoting a letter that appeared in LE PAYS of Paris, datelined Calcutta, October 8.

The writer was M. de Banneroi, a French physician in the service of Mussur Raja, who related an anecdote he had been told by an officer's wife rescued from Lucknow. Her husband served with some unspecified Highland corps.

During the siege this lady had witnessed the decline of a certain Jessie Brown, "the wife of a corporal in my husband's regiment", who had "languished in a state of restless excitement" as her mind became deranged through terror and privation. On September 25, when others heard nothing but guns, screams and oaths, Jessie started up from her reverie. "Dinna ye hear it? Dinna ye hear it? It's the slogan o' the High-landers!" She then "darted to the batteries, and I heard her cry incessant-ly to the men. 'Courage, courage! Hark to the slogan, to the Macgregor, the grandest of them a' ". Her cries went unheeded, for "dull Lowland ears heard but the rattle of musketry". Jessie made a fresh appeal to the troops, who might well have been exasperated with this hysterical woman. "Will ye no' believe it noo? The slogan has ceased indeed, but the Campbells are coming!" And despite their initial lack of faith in the Highland Sybil the troops were soon convinced. "Now there was no longer any doubt of the fact . . . It was indeed the blast of the Scottish bagpipes, now shrill and harsh as threatening vengeance on the foe, then in softer tone seeming to promise succour to their friends in need". The relief force arrived, and Jessie — happy and suddenly freed from both lethargy and excitement — "was presented to the general on his entrance into the fort and at the officers' banquet her health was drunk by all present while the pipers marched round the table playing once more the familiar air of *Auld lang syne*". The JERSEY TIMES does not make clear whether M. de Bannerois' original correspondence was in English, or whether by some clever system of phonetics he had managed to translate Scots dialect directly into French.

In February of the following year R.S.F. wrote to NOTES AND QUERIES, which was then approaching its magnificent heyday, and asked with great earnestness precisely what Jessie had meant by "Hark to the slogan — to the Macgregor"? Was it the war cry "O' ard choille" or pipe music or something else again?[25] R.S.F. pursued the question on his own and in May reported back to NOTES AND QUERIES that he had obtained the views of the Calcutta correspondent of THE NONCONFORMIST, who had talked with one of the Lucknow garrison. THE NONCONFORMIST's correspondent asserted first, that it would have been impossible for information of the sort quoted in the letter of October 8, to have been known in Calcutta at that date. Next, there had been no Jessie Brown in Lucknow. Thirdly, the 78th Regiment neither played their pipes nor howled their slogan when they came in, "as they had something else to do". (At first sight this was a poor argument, for the Scots were likely to play their pipes in the hottest circumstances). Finally, there was no marching round the dinner table to pipe music that evening.[26] Apart from the stand taken by THE NONCONFORMIST against Jessie's existence it is remarkable that none of the people who published their experiences of the siege soon after it had been raised referred to her.

But the story had a popular appeal and there was no killing it. Dion Boucicault wrote a three-act drama, JESSIE BROWN, OR THE RELIEF OF LUCKNOW which ran at Wallach's Theatre in New York for 80 nights and had its English première at the Theatre Royal in Plymouth in November, 1858.[27] Alexander Maclagan wrote "Dinna ye hear it?" – "it" now being positively identified with *The Campbells are coming*[28], R.T.S. Lowell brought Jessie into his poem *The Relief of Lucknow*[29] and Vandenhoff wrote how she, "bore orders to the wall, the wounded nursed".[30] From a distraught, rather unpopular, neurotic she had developed into another Lady with the Lamp. Jessie was even immortalized by Frederick Goodall who painted the scene for all to wonder at.[31]

But other people had serious doubts about Jessie's existence. "Alexander M'Kellar who was pipe major of the 78th Highlanders on the occasion of the memorable relief in a letter to the ARMY AND NAVY GAZETTE fairly disposes of all doubts which may have existed as to the accuracy or otherwise of the romance. The veteran piper denies that his pipes played on the day of the relief, and even if they had done so the women and children of the Ross-shire Buffs were left behind at Poona when the Regiment marched up-country. Jessie Brown is reported to have been the wife of a soldier of the 78th. What, therefore, was she doing at Lucknow ... ?"[32] If Alexander M'Kellar was the piper who had so acrobatically fraternized with Mrs. A. he seems to have grown noticeably less high spirited and certainly more forgetful with the passage of time (p. 179). The only other evidence that suggests Jessie Brown actually existed is from Sergeant Forbes-Mitchell who claimed to have heard the story in Lucknow some time during November 1857, and who also claimed acquaintance with a certain Mrs. Gaffney who shared Jessie's shell-proof, but not pipe-proof cellar.[33]

The last word lies with F. J. Crowest, writing in the NATIONAL REVIEW on May 3, 1889.

"This Highland lassie never lived in the flesh but was an imaginative creation of a lady who had cultivated her ruling faculty by much writing for the newspapers and magazines." That let M. de Banneroi off the hook, for a start. "The Highland lassie of Lucknow, in fact, made the tour of the world of print and though there is absolutely not one word of truth in her she probably will not receive her official and final contradiction until Judgement Day".

With the exception of the story about Ross, little has been said so far about singing, but there was apparently plenty of that during the Mutiny. The Lucknow defenders, as was noted, sang *Cheer, boys, cheer* to keep their spirits up. When Delhi fell a band of Scots was found clustered around a fire in the middle of a street intoning *Annie Laurie*,[34] and on at least one occasion song featured prominently in battle. During the attack on Cawnpore by the 53rd, the 93rd, and the Naval Brigade, Sgt. Daniel White of the 93rd tilted into Corporal Brown's Crimean song, *The Battle of the Alma*, as the rebels' fire became hotter and soon the whole line, and skirmishers out in front joined in. Later on White explained his inspiration ; the cheers of the bluejackets as they came under a hail of grapeshot reminded him that when the Scots Greys and the 92nd Highlanders charged at Waterloo they had sung *Scots wha' hae wi' Wallace bled*. (In fact this is most unlikely, see p. 135). It seemed to White that this was also an occasion when troops might be stimulated by a rousing song, and so he had begun *The Battle of the Alma*.[35]

Singing was also popular on the long marches. "As soon as the sun was up and the pipes finished" (tobacco pipes that is) "the men usually began to sing, by companies generally, one man taking the solo and the rest the chorus."[36] In 1895 an elderly gentleman by the name of R. G. Wilberforce who had been a subaltern of the 52nd Light Infantry during the Mutiny published his memoirs, AN UNRECORDED CHAPTER OF THE INDIAN MUTINY. His book yields a fair idea of singing and marching for, as he says, the regiment marched from Sialkot to Delhi, 900 miles, between May and August. They would regularly start after midnight, to avoid the heat of the day, and "the band used to go on playing and when the bandsmen were tired our bugle band would take it up and play. When they had finished, some individual somewhere in the centre of the regiment would start a song, and so the hours whiled away". One song was the traditional *We'll drink old England dry*.

> For our broadswords shall glitter and our grapeshot shall fly,
> Before the French shall come and drink old England dry.

Two others sound more like genuine rankers' verses, the first with its reference to the "Light Bobee", being obviously a regimental song.

> As we were marching down the street,
> We heard the people say,
> There goes a gallant regiment,
> A-marching on its way.
> Away go those brave heroes,
> The like we'll never see more.
> And with them goes the Light Bobee,
> The lad that I adore.

The other anticipated an ideal girl who would keep the soldier in the state to which he felt he should be accustomed.

> Neither pot nor pipe shall grieve me,
> Nor yet disturb my mind,
> When I come rolling home
> To the girl I left behind.
> Happy is the girl that will keep me,
> When I come rolling home.

Mr. Wilberforce also recalled that "one of the favourite songs was of a most revolutionary character; it had about 30 verses and a long chorus. I forget the song, but I recollect that 'confound our officers' held a place in the chorus and used to be shouted lustily. At first the men would not sing this song – they thought it would hurt our feelings – but it had so good a tune that nearly every night one of our captains would call for it".[37]

When the book was published it immediately became clear that this "unrecorded chapter" might have been better left unrecorded, for the other elderly gentlemen who had fought with the 52nd in the Mutiny turned on Wilberforce with one accord, and a display of savagery that, in their youth, they had reserved for the Pandies. The OXFORDSHIRE LIGHT INFANTRY CHRONICLE of 1895 spends sixteen pages administering the death of a thousand cuts to Wilberforce's book. It tabulates statement after statement and disproves or derides them one by one, as well as quoting a morsel of character assassination from the UNITED SERVICE MAGAZINE. The editor managed to enlist the support of Michael Johnson, a former bugler of the regiment, who on his own showing was "the individual who wrote the music and accompaniments to all the road songs, as we used to call them." When it came to *Confound our officers*, Johnson quivered with indignation. "How a gentleman who was once a British officer can so far forget himself as to write such rubbish it is indeed hard for me to understand. No such song was ever heard in the regiment, much more sung on the march". Rarely can a personal account of war, written solely to entertain and inform, have aroused such hostility.

None of the road songs composed by Michael Johnson have survived, although one Mutiny ballad of the 52nd was fortunately resurrected in 1907, when the regimental veterans of the Mutiny were guests of honour at a Sergeants' Smoking Concert. It must have been with great pleasure that they heard again, after many years, former Private William McKenna sing a song writen by a soldier of 'C' company soon after the recapture of Delhi.[38]

The British had been driven from Delhi in May and although they began operations from the Ridge the following month they were not strong enough to attempt an attack until September 14. Of the five storming columns formed on that day the third included 200 men of the 52nd (led by Colonel George Campbell), 750 Indians, and a handful of British and Indian sappers whose duty it was to blow in the Kashmir Gate for the assault troops. Despite heavy fire the Gate was blown – four of the dynamiters received the V.C. – and although the bugler of the 52nd who was with them to blow the charge, and who also received the award, could not be heard above the noise of the explosion, the 52nd and their supports surged forward before the dust had fairly settled. Fighting their way through the debris of the Gate the third column penetrated further into Delhi than any other, and although a partial withdrawal became necessary through lack of flank support Colonel Campbell had every reason to feel proud of his men. The storming of the Kashmir Gate was the sort of event that merited commemoration in song.

> Come, fill up a bumper,
> Our toil at length is done,
> Since the Pandies are defeated,
> And Delhi has been won.
> Great men they were in their own eyes,
> At least, then so they thought.
> So we took the shine out of them
> On the 12th at Trimmu Ghat.
>> When a-hunting we did go, my boys,
>> A-hunting we did go.
>> To chase the Pandies, night and day,
>> And levelled Delhi low.

> A-thirsting to avenge, my boys,
> The bloodshed that was done.
> On poor defenceless women,
> 'Ere Delhi had been won.
> We made the Pandies for to know,
> And caused them for to feel,
> That British wrongs should be avenged,
> By sterling British steel.
>> When a-hunting we did go, my boys, etc.

> On the 14th of September,
> I remember well the date,
> We showed the Pandies a new hit,
> When we stormed the Kashmir Gate.
> Their grapeshot, shell and musketry,
> They found but little good.
> When British soldiers were outside,
> A-thirsting for their blood.
>> When a-hunting we did go, my boys, etc.

Another ballad was written about the victory of Fatehpur won by Sir Henry Havelock, but only a fragment has survived.

> With our shot and shell,
> We made them smell hell,
> That day at Fatehpur.[39]

One particularly lugubrious ballad may date from the Mutiny, although this is by no means certain. The difficulty arises because the song was discussed in 1898 by the NAVY AND ARMY ILLUSTRATED, a journal with an unsurpassed editorial talent for rendering its correspondents faceless and anonymous. One such anonymous correspondent asked on August 27 about the origin of a ballad said to have been sung in the Mutiny, and another – equally disguised – replied on October 1 that it had been composed in India by a Captain Darling who later died of cholera. Whether the questioner was well qualified to suggest it had been sung in 1857 or the replier to attribute it to Captain Darling never emerges, but *Here's to the last to die* is a fine example of the Victorian penchant for morbidity.

39
Here's to the last to die

WORDS   Captain Darling
MUSIC   Traditional
SOURCE   Scottish Students Song Book c. 1892

We meet 'neath the sounding rafters,
And the walls around are bare;
As they echo to our laughter
'Twould not seem that the dead were there.
So stand to your glasses steady,
'Tis all we have left to prize,
Quaff a cup to the dead already,
And one to the next who dies.

Who dreads to the dead returning,
Who shrinks from that sable shore
Where the high and haughty yearning
Of the souls will be no more?
So stand to your glasses steady, etc.

Cut off from the land that bore us,
Betrayed by the land we find,
When the brightest have gone before us,
And the dullest remain behind.
So stand to your glasses steady, etc.

There's a mist on the glass congealing,
'Tis the hurricane's fiery breath,
And 'tis thus that the warmth of feeling
Turns ice in the grasp of death.
So stand to your glasses steady, etc.

There is many a head that is aching,
There is many a cheek that is sunk,
There is many a heart that is breaking,
Must burn with the wine we have drunk.
So stand to your glasses steady, etc.

There is not time for repentance,
'Tis folly to yield to despair,
When a shudder may finish a sentence,
Or death put an end to a prayer.
So stand to your glasses steady, etc.

Time was when we frowned on others,
We thought we were wiser then;
But now let us all be brothers,
For we never may meet again.
So stand to your glasses steady, etc.

But a truce to this mournful story
For death is a distant friend;
So here's to a life of glory,
And a laurel to crown each end.
So stand to your glasses steady, etc.

1. V. D. Majendie, *Up among the Pandies* (1857), p.222.
2. L. E. R. Rees, *A Personal Narrative of the Siege of Lucknow* (1858), p.343.
3. H. Metcalfe, *Chronicle* (1953), p.38.
4. *Oxfordshire Light Infantry Chronicle* (1907), p.61.
5. H. H. Greathed, *Letters Written During the Seige of Delhi* (1858), p.191.
6. *Ibid*, p.189.
7. C. J. Griffiths, *A Narrative of the Siege of Delhi* (1910), p.136.
8. Rees, p.168.
9. Majendie, p.112.
10. Sir R. Harrison, *Recollections of a Life in the British Army During the Latter Half of the 19th Century* (1908), p.43.
11. Scobie, p.26.
12. R. W. Danvers, *Letters from India and China* (1898), p.82.
13. Greathed, p.191.
14. Griffiths, p.136.
15. Seaton, p.47.
16. *Ibid*, p.49.
17. W. Munro, *Records of Service and Campaigning* (1887), II, p.239.
18. S. H. Jones-Parry, *An Old Soldier's Memories* (1897), p.200.
19. Rees, p.257.
20. R. C. Germon, *Lucknow Diary* (1870), p.97.
21. Rees, p.226.
22. Forbes-Mitchell, p.210.
23. W. Gordon-Alexander, *Recollections of a Highland Subaltern* (1898), p.123.
24. Forbes-Mitchell, pp.102–104.
25. *NQ*, Second Series, V, p.147.
26. *NQ*, Second Series, V, p.425.
27. *NQ*, Eleventh Series, IV, p.439.
28. *NQ*, Seventh Series, III, p.482.
29. *Ibid*, p.482.
30. *NQ*, Eleventh Series, IV, p.325.
31. *Ibid*, p.325.
32. British Museum, Add. MSS 37151, F.68.
33. Forbes-Mitchell, pp.114–119.
34. R. M. Coopland, *Escape from Gwalior* (1859), p.277.
35. Forbes-Mitchell, pp.141–144.
36. [Anon.] *Reminiscences of School and Army Life, 1839–1859* (1875), p.61.
37. For all quotes from Wilberforce, see R. G. Wilberforce, *An Unrecorded Chapter of The Indian Mutiny* (1895), pp.83–84.
38. *Oxfordshire Light Infantry Chronicle* (1907), p.67.
39. A. Owen, *Recollections of a Veteran of the Days of the Great Indian Mutiny of 1857* (1916), p.37.

Chapter 9

EGYPT AND THE SUDAN
1882–1898

LTHOUGH no 19th century British statesman spoke of Egypt with the lyrical praises that Napoleon used in his conversations about that land, Britain maintained a wary eye on happenings there. Egypt, romantic concepts apart, was for Britain the half-way house to India.

Lord Palmerston was worried by the growing power of Mehemmet Ali, the Albanian adventurer who had beaten the redcoats at El Hamed in 1807. Palmerston feared that the "ignorant barbarian" was becoming too independent of his nominal overlord, the Anglophile sultan of Turkey, and was inclining towards either Russia or France at Britain's expense. In 1840 during a confused international crisis 1,500 Royal Marines landed in Syria, which was part of Mehemmet's "Empire", but there was no direct confrontation with the wily Albanian who, in fact, genuinely admired and wanted friendly relations with Britain.

With the opening of the Suez Canal in 1869 Egypt became still more important to Britain and in 1874 Disraeli, who had once derided the project as "a most futile attempt" was delighted to buy a block of Canal shares worth £4 million from the spendthrift khedive of Egypt, Ismail. But even then it was not Britain's policy to become directly involved in Egypt's internal affairs. The original dream of the old East India Company was being relived – economic advantage, even mild exploitation, but no worries of empire. Fortune, however, decreed differently.

In 1882 British troops were again sent to Egypt, the same Egypt which — wracked by dysentry, blinded by ophthalmia, and live free men only by courtesy of Mehemmet Ali — they had left so gladly in 1807. The cause of their return was a nationalist rising led by an Egyptian officer named Arabi Pasha in which a number of Europeans were slaughtered. Both Britain and France saw fit to support the rightful ruler, the khedive Tewfik, against his insurgent subject, especially as they feared that Arabi might try to block the Canal. On August 2 British troops landed at Suez, and on September 13 Arabi's army was routed at Tel el Kebir, 50 miles from Cairo, by Lieutenant-General Sir Garnet Wolseley.

Regimental histories of the Scottish regiments involved in this short campaign mention rather commonplace tunes played by the pipes, but one unique and now-forgotten song should be remembered. It was both cause and effect of a bruising feud between the Buffs and the East Surreys. According to a soldier who took part in several of the affrays,[1] the simplest way to brighten up a dull canteen or pub was to chant, to the air of *Pop goes the weasel*, this simple doggerel:

> The men of Kent were battered and bent,
> But tottered as far as Malta.
> The 'Gippies fired, the Buffs retired,
> You couldn't see an arse for water.

The rendition would promptly be followed by rapid unbuckling and what Kipling called "belts, belts, belts, an' that's one for you." The Buffs had every reason to come out fighting when they heard these words, for they were totally untrue. The origin of the song was that by the time the Buffs reached Malta from England, Arabi's revolt had been crushed, and so they turned about, but not in the undignified manner, or for the reason, claimed by the East Surreys.

One piece of advice given to Tewfik the impoverished khedive, was that he should abandon the Sudan, the immense country conquered by Mehemmet Ali, which now cost more to administer than it was worth and where a Messiah, the Mahdi, had since 1881 made things increasingly awkward for the Egyptian administration. The Sudanese backed him for various reasons. Some admired the austerity of his Islamic faith compared with the more effete Mohammedanism of the Egyptians; others resented the way that the khedival government, through its English governor-general Charles Gordon, had embargoed slave raiding and trading. As for the nomads, they equated a change of government, at best, with a chance for plunder and, at worst, with a chance to avoid paying taxes until things quieted down.

Although the British made it clear to Tewfik that his slender exchequer could not afford the luxury of the Sudan, and that British troops would not be used in expeditions on his behalf, individual Britons were, willy-nilly, being drawn into the Sudan problem. One was an ex-Indian Army officer, Hicks Pasha, who with an army of 10,000 wretched Egyptian conscripts was cut to pieces in a two-day battle south of El Obeid in 1883. Another was F. M. Upton who, compelled to surrender his khedival forces in the Bahr al Ghazal, died in captivity.

On an official level the British government at last agreed to send General Gordon back to the Sudan to work out a way of extricating the Egyptians there – troops, dependents, and others – and it was in this atmosphere of rapid disintegration that Gordon arrived at Khartoum on February 18, 1884. Whether he could have organised an evacuation if he wished, or whether he even wanted to abandon the Sudan to the Mahdi and his followers is immaterial, because before he reached Khartoum circumstances had dragged Britain a little deeper into the Sudan morass. One of the Mahdi's ablest lieutenants, Osman Digna, hovering around Suakin on the Red Sea, induced the port's defender, General Valentine Baker, to come out after him. At El Teb, Baker's 3,500 Egyptians panicked, and Baker retired to base with a disproportionate loss among the English officers who had tried unavailingly to rally their troops.

While Gordon, without British troops, was committed to one operation on the Nile, Sir Gerald Graham was sent to Suakin with troops, but seemingly shackled by a strict order to use them only defensively. He found an excellent excuse for circumventing this command – the ostensible need to relieve an Egyptian garrison – and met the dervishes in two hard fought actions, at El Teb (February 29) and Tamai (March 19). The British Army was once again in an official war, with an enemy who was to be immortalized by Kipling's poem – the Fuzzy Wuzzy. As the troops sailed for Suakin they sang current hits like *So near and yet so far* and *Where is now that merry party?*[2] apparently oblivious to the tragic relevance of those words to Gordon, trapped in Khartoum with a demoralized and starving Egyptian garrison. There is a very real impression that these redcoats (and they were still carting their scarlet tunics with them) had the idea that the expedition was little more than a topping lark. There were many "jolly singing evenings" at Suakin in 1884, where it was remarked how well the Highland officers sang,[3] and one soldier reminisced that he had never been in a happier garrison than Suakin in '85.[4]

Meanwhile the British government had decided that although Gordon had exceeded his brief by dallying in Khartoum, he could not be left to his fate and an expedition led by Garnet Wolseley (created a peer after his exploits against Arabi) was sent to his relief. Wolseley's troops, with the band of the Royal West Kents "discoursing sweet music,"[5] pressed up the Nile on steamers – and by camel. Men of the Guards regiments, plus some Marines, were formed into the Guards Camel Regiment, which sported red serge jumpers, yellow cord breeches, dark blue putties, white pith helmets, and brown leather bandoliers and cross-belts. Once the men had mastered their smelly and unlovable mounts they became quite cheerful and a description of their night ride to the wells of El Howeiyat is not without charm. "As soon as it became known that we had entered the New Year the whole column struck up *Auld lang syne* . . . After *Auld lang syne* songs of all sorts were started and by the time everyone had shouted themselves hoarse with choruses we had arrived at the wells."[6] One of the most comical army songs of the century, its tune unfortunately lost, was composed by Sergeant Eagle of the Marines who rode with what Ian Hamilton enviously called "that band of patricians".

When years ago I 'listed, lads,
To serve our gracious queen,
The sergeant made me understand
I was a Royal Marine.
He said sometimes they served in ships,
And sometimes served on shore,
But never said I should wear spurs,
And be in the Camel Corps.

Chorus:

I've rode in a ship, I've rode in a boat,
I've rode on a railway train.
I've rode in a coach, and I've rode a moke,
And I hope to ride one again.
But I'm riding now an animal,
A Marine never rode before.
Rigged up in spurs and pantaloons,
As one of the Camel Corps.[7]

Many of the cheerful riders on the trail to El Howeiyat were singing their last song. On December 30 Wolseley, both to make up lost time and to avoid following a great bend of the Nile, pushed the Camel Corps and the 19th Hussars across 176 miles of desert, and on January 14, just short of the river and the longed-for wells of Abu Klea their path was barred by 10,000 dervishes. One corner of the square in which the dismounted troops advanced crumpled under pressure and before the situation was repaired 170 men were dead and wounded, among them Colonel Fred Burnaby, commanding officer of the Royal Horse Guards, the Blues. Burnaby had won fame as a cross-Channel balloonist, a TIMES war correspondent in Spain, a traveller who had penetrated to Khiva in Central Asia, and a great bohemian. More recently he had taken part, without permission, in the Suakin campaign, and before Wolseley's expedition had been approved had offered to lead 2,000 camel-riding volunteers to rescue Gordon. The commander-in-chief, the Duke of Cambridge (of Kneller Hall renown), detested him and refused Wolseley's request to have him in the relief force. Not at all discomfited, "Galloping Fred" simply applied for leave, nominally to visit the Cape of Good Hope, and caught up with Wolseley's columns. This giant of a man with his bravery, initiative and loathing of conformity was a natural soldiers' darling, and one of his men composed a eulogy on his death which seems to have survived in the Army for some years.[8]

40
Colonel Burnaby

WORDS   W. Stubbs
MUSIC   Traditional
SOURCE   J. Farmer – Scarlet and Blue

Come, listen to my story, lads,
There's news from over sea:
The Camel Corps have held their own,
And gained a victory!
　　Weep not, my boys, for those who fell:
　　They did not flinch nor fear;
　　They stood their ground like Englishmen,
　　And died at Abu Klea.

No more our Colonel's form we'll see;
His foes have struck him down.
His life on earth, alas! is o'er,
But not his great renown.
No more his merry voice we'll hear,
Nor word of stern command;
He died as he had often wished—
His sabre in his hand.

Now, Horse Guards Blue, both old and young,
Each man from front to rear,
Remember Colonel Burnaby
At sandy Abu Klea!
And when Old England calls the Blues
To battle, soon or late,
We shan't forget how soldierly
The Colonel met his fate.

　Weep not, etc.

　　　　　Weep not, etc.

But Burnaby's death and many others were in vain for on January 26
Khartoum was penetrated and Gordon slain, and the relief force headed
north again.

For the next 14 years a slow relentless war was waged against the
Mahdi and his successor the Khalifa. The songs of the period were *John
Brown's body*,[9] *Boys of the Old Brigade*, and *Soldiers of the Queen*.[10] There
was also an unctuous ballad, *Roll on to Khartoum*, which despite its shortcomings was sung.

Come, forward march and do your duty,
Though poor your grub, no rum, bad 'bacca.
Step out for fighting and no booty
To trace a free red line through Africa.
No barney, boys, give over mousing,
True Britons are ye from hill and fen.
Now rally, boys, and drop all grousing,
And pull together like soldier men.

Chorus:
Then roll on, boys, roll on to Khartoum,
March ye and fight by night or by day.
Hasten the hour of the dervishes' doom.
Gordon avenge in old England's way.[11]

A far more interesting song, said to have been written by a soldier,
and heard not only in Egypt and the Sudan but wherever the troops got
together, was *The Whitechapel Polka:*

Now ladies all, beware.
Or you'll get caught in a snare.
They tell me that the devil's running loose.
With a big knife in his hand
He trots throughout the land
And with all the ladies means to play the deuce.

He's a knockout, I declare,
He's here and everywhere.
To catch him we know they've had a try.
He comes out of a night,
To put us in a fright,
And manages somehow to get away.[12]

The subject of this edifying ditty was, of course, Jack the Ripper, whose forays against the street-walkers of Whitechapel in the autumn of 1888 gave him great notoriety and a tally of five bedraggled harlots. (If the composer was a soldier, the rhyme of "try" with "away" suggests that he may well have been a neighbour of Jack's, in East London).

The commission for the reconquest of the Sudan had by this time devolved upon Major-General Sir Herbert Kitchener, and one of his logistical imperatives was that a railway line must be built steadily southward so that the Sudan would not remain an isolated land penetrable only through the vagaries of the Nile and the desert. This task was accomplished by Egyptian peasants and convict gangs working under British supervision, and the construction inspired a good song by an officer of the Royal Engineers.

We're convicts at work in the Noozle.
We carry great loads on our backs.
And often our warders bamboozle,
And sleep 'neath mountains of sacks.

Ri-tooral-il-looral, etc.

We convicts start work at day dawning.
Boilers we mount about noon.
Sleepers we load in the morning.
And rails by the light of the moon.

Ri-tooral, etc.

Our warders are blacks who cry Masha!
And strike us if we don't obey.
Or else he's a Hamla Ombashi
Who allows us to fuddle all day.[13]

For the uninitiated, the ominous sounding "Noozle" was the commissariat depot, "Masha" an exhortation, "Hamla Ombashi" a transport service corporal, and "fuddling" the gentle art of dodging the column.

One ballad of which more would be happily known was written about the black soldiers of the Anglo-Egyptian army. At the same time as a handful of dedicated British officers and NCO's were drilling the supposedly spineless Egyptian fellah into an honest soldier who beat the dervishes at Sarras, Toski, Suakin and Tokar, other battalions of black Sudanese were being raised, and brigaded under Lieutenant-Colonel Hector MacDonald, one of the few rankers in the old army to reach such an exalted rank. An officer named Townshend who had distinguished himself in the Chitral campaign on the North West Frontier of India arrived to serve with one of these battalions, about which he wrote a song, seemingly accompanying himself on the banjo. Its gist was, that "with MacDonald to lead" the black brigade would do its share, and the recurrent line — surely relevant to the campaign and not to the battalion —

was "We wonder how long it will last?"[14]

If these Sudanese knew that they were the subject of a song it would have pleased them beyond measure, for no troops ever, anywhere, can have loved music as they did. "The first thing these black troops do when they get into camp is to strike up some of their unearthly tunes", wrote a war correspondent, "and in the absence of more normal appliances they have been known to fashion old tin biscuit boxes into a species of wind instrument".[15] The music of the black battalions excited more comment than any other music in the Sudan. The old khedival Army had established a fine tradition for noise, and regiments of conscripted Egyptian peasants, the dreaded Turkish Bashi Bazouks, and the Sudanese, all had bands, ranging from primitive collections of horns and tom-toms to those equipped with the latest cornets-à-piston, playing Arab airs arranged by Italian bandmasters.[16] This musical tradition was carried over into the new army created by Kitchener for it was astutely realized that rhythm was life itself to the black soldier. "Barbaric Ethiopian, darky American, or English music hall it is all the same".[17] They liked *Oh, them golden slippers*,[18] and specialized in the songs of Gus Elen. After the victory at Atbara (1898) they strode along to his apposite air *Catch 'em alive-oh!*

> Catch 'em alive-oh, catch 'em alive-oh!
> If once they gets off the gum,
> They'll pop off to kingdom come.
> Catch 'em alive-oh, catch 'em alive-oh!
> For I am the flyest man around the town![19]

If the band of a Sudanese regiment was temporarily silent on the march the company buglers had only to blow a few notes and the whole column would break into a chant on some topical theme. "Thus marching to alternate music of the bugles and their own voices they swung along as if they were strangers to weariness".[20] In 1898 the hard work of the British, Egyptians and Sudanese was rewarded. They routed the dervishes at Omdurman outside Khartoum and marched triumphantly into the Khalifa's mud capital, with regimental drums and fifes, Highland pipes, and Sudanese bands playing regimental marches.[21] As the 13th Sudanese Regiment appeared the defeated Khalifa's personal band of drums and horns provided the honours of war, striking up a melody which, if discordant to British ears, delighted the brave 13th,[22] for they had become men of two worlds and versatility was their pride. So much so, that when a memorial service was held for Gordon on September 4 the contribution of these black pagans was a fine performance of *Toll for the brave* and *Abide with me*.[23]

1. Lance-Corporal E. Norman (The Buffs). Interview, 1954.
2. E. A. de Cosson, *Days and Nights of Service* (1886), p.13.
3. B. Burleigh, *Desert Warfare* (1884), p.120.
4. Sir N. Stewart, *My Service Days* (1908), p.146.
5. A Macdonald, *Too Late for Gordon and Khartoum* (1887), p.84.
6. A. E. W. Gleichen, *With the Camel Corps up the Nile* (1888), p.80.
7. Macdonald, p.83.
8. J. Farmer, *Scarlet and Blue, or Songs for Soldiers and Sailors* (1896), p.183.
9. Interviews at Royal Hospital, Chelsea, 1954.
10. O. S. Watkins, *With Kitchener's Army* (1899), p.241.
11. B. Burleigh, *Khartoum Campaign* (1899), p.50.
12. Gunner J. Austin (Royal Field Artillery). Interview, 1954.
13. B. Burleigh, p.50.
14. A. H. Atteridge, *Towards Khartoum* (1897), p.154.
15. Sir E. N. Bennett, *The Downfall of the Dervishes* (1898), p.119.
16. J. Colborne, *With Hicks Pasha in the Soudan* (1884), p.120.
17. G. W. Steevens, *With Kitchener to Khartum* (1898), p.190.
18. Burleigh, *Khartoum Campaign*, p.43.
19. G. W. Steevens, p.161.
20. Watkins, p.51.
21. Bennett, p.195.
22. Burleigh, *Khartoum Campaign*, p.215.
23. Watkins, p.228.

Chapter 10

THE LITTLE WARS OF THE NINETEENTH CENTURY

THE Napoleonic Wars, the Crimea, the Mutiny, Egypt and the Sudan, were the principal, but not the only wars of the 19th century. Although it is blandly said that the Crimean War ended forty years of peace, "peace" merely meant that Britain was not fighting another major power. So far as the redcoats were concerned there had been a campaign somewhere every year since Queen Victoria came to the throne in 1837, as well as a number of campaigns between Waterloo and her accession. According to VICTORIAN MILITARY CAMPAIGNS (edited by Brian Bond, 1967), there were only two years in which British soldiers were not fighting (1869 and 1883) during the Queen's sixty-four year reign.

The lesser wars of the century are grouped together as "Little Wars", although for a redcoat storming a Maori pah, facing a Sikh charge, or battling through a Kaffir ambush, these wars were big enough. Such enemies were no less dangerous than Napoleon's exalted Garde, and a Kaffir assegai or a Gurkha kukri could be every bit as fatal as a Russian cannon ball.

The main theatre of action for the Little Wars was India, where the British had been involved more or less continuously since the mid-18th century, but the earliest known ballad from the Little Wars commemorates General Lake's victory over the Mahrattas at Laswari in 1803. The battle was fought on November 1 – not the 6th as the ballad states – and there were only 15,000 Indians, not 50,000. Their guns may well have been "ponderous" and they were certainly numerous – seventy-two in all. The ballad ran to some twenty-five verses of which the first five and the final one survive, while the tune is unknown.

It was on the sixth day of November
We met the gallant foe,
The day they well remember,
And long will live to woe.

Fifty thousand warlike men
In battle's awful 'rray,
That victory thought to win
On that very day.

They three solid lines did form,
With guns of ponderous size,
The battle was fierce and warm—
The bravest shut their eyes.

We had but one small band
But those were often tried,
We faced them hand to hand,
And of victory would not be denied.

Our gallant Lake on Brown Hope did ride,
Who flew along the battle's plain,
It was that horse's pride
To see the foes of England slain.

Then push the flowing can about,
Let notes of victory ring,
These are Britons' shouts,
'Our country and our king!'[1]

The Mahratta War was concluded with a peace conference at which British military bands entertained the Rajah of Berar and the Divan of Sind with the national anthem, *The British Grenadiers*, and *The Grenadiers March*.[2]

A rather better set of verses than those on General Lake was written by George Calladine of the 19th Regiment while he was on sentry duty in Ceylon in 1818. His comrades were taken with this song, sung to the tune of *The Battle of Waterloo* (which may be either the *Plains of Waterloo* in Sergeant Newman's MS book or *The Battle of Waterloo* as in A. Wyatt Edgell's COLLECTION OF SOLDIERS SONGS p. 7) and Calladine recorded in his diary that they almost drowned him with arrack and porter.[3]

41

Ceylon ballad

MUSIC Sheepskin and Beeswax – Traditional
SOURCE A. Wyatt-Edgell –
A Collection of Soldiers Songs

Come all ye lads of courage bold and listen to my song,
I'll sing to you a ditty which will not keep you long.
Concerning of our late campaign shall here related be
When Britons fought like heroes in the Kandian country.

Our forces then proceeded to where this fray begun,
And many a day we've marched from rise to set of sun,
O'er Dombra's lofty mountains and Wellasses' watery plain;
But Britons' sons, like heroes bold, all dangers still disdain.

Our enemy we did pursue for many a weary day.
Along with those black rebels we'd many a bloody fray,
O'er hills and lofty mountains where troops ne'er marched before
And many a rebel Kandian lay in his bloody gore.

The rebel chiefs whene'er we met before us soon did fly,
And Keppitipola taken was sentenced to die.
According to his sentence beheaded soon was he
Which closed this rebellion in the Kandian country.

> Come all ye lads of courage bold and let a toast go round,
> Here's a health to Governor Brownrigg who put rebellion down,
> And unto every officer who fought in freedom's cause,
> For the honour of old England, her liberty and laws.
>
> Come all ye lads that's faced with green, here's a bumper unto you
> Who have done your duty manfully and to your cause stood true.
> Now this rebellion's over we'll sing so merrily,
> Our Nineteenth lads have bid adieu to the Kandian country.

John Shipp, the soldier who preserved Lake's song for us, fought against the Gurkhas of Nepal and when his regiment entered the surrendered fort of Muckwanpore he was surprised to find a drummer and fifer saluting them with *The Grenadiers March*. "The drum and fife were of British manufacture", he added darkly, and one suspects he would have welcomed an investigation of how they came to be in Gurkha hands.[4]

Lake was not the only general to be remembered in song. Sir Charles Napier who annexed Sind ("a very advantageous, useful, humane piece of rascality," he admitted) was bearded to the waist, luxuriantly moustached, and sported a great fringe down the back of his neck. With a beak-like nose, huge spectacles, and a peculiar helmet of his own design he was a natural subject for rhymers, and his soldiers sang about him to the tune of *Billy Barlow*.[5]

Popular songs in India during the first half of the century were *Love farewell*[6] of Peninsula fame, *John Barleycorn*,[7] *Out of the way for old Dan Tucker*, *The rakes of Mallow*, and

> A soldier courted a farmer's daughter
> That lived convenient to the Isle of Man.[8]

Of all the enemies that the British met in India none were more worthy than the Sikhs, whose physical strength and bravery were enhanced by a discipline and professionalism not often found in Asia. In two wars and half a dozen hard-fought battles they proved their mettle in a style which receives scant justice from the one soldiers' song about them that is preserved.

> There was Loll Singh and Foll Singh and Roll Singh,
> And every great Singh of them all,
> But before the day was half over,
> By my faith, they sang mightily small.[9]

An incident involving a military band reflects a more accurate evaluation of the Sikhs. At the Battle of Sobraon (1846) the band of the 10th Regiment was sent to fight in the ranks, and after the bloody contest their colonel said he would never repeat his action.[10] There is a suggestion that one regiment actually used its band in action against the Sikhs. Some time around 1850 Colonel Smyth of the 16th Lancers found himself at loggerheads with a vicar who disliked the regiment marching to church to the strains of martial music. Smyth told him that during the Sikh War "the band had many times played his regiment in and out of battle, and so long as he remained its commander it should play him and his men to and from church".[11] But Colonel Smyth led only one charge of the 16th against the Sikhs – when he was a Major at Aliwal – and there are no records of a band playing there, so he may have been exaggerating.

The Sikhs relied on Europeans to train their armies and they even imitated the British bands. As a consequence the drums which beat the charge against us often bore startlingly irrelevant legends which the Sikhs, may have considered to be magic symbols – legends such as "Waterloo" and "Pinsular" [sic].[12]

The natural proclivity of many Indian tribes and classes for a warrior society lead to a life that hovered between war and banditry. One practitioner of this dubious career was Doonga Singh, who claimed he had been driven to violence through the red tape which denied him his rightful dues. Although advanced in years he raided the government treasury at Nuseerabad, cut down a sergeant's guard of the 19th Punjab Regiment, and escaped with £30,000 loaded on camel-back. His daring on this occasion threw the British into confusion, as the song grudgingly admits.

> Then raise your voices, let us sing
> Confusion to this robber king,
> Who made all Rajputana ring
> By looting the buckshee khana.
> Some officers ran as hard as they could,
> Intending to do no end of good,
> But devil a one was there who could
> Order out the cavalry, sirs![13]

Doonga Singh's success was short lived. He was betrayed by a woman – a common fate throughout history for fast-living bandits – tried, and hanged.

Regiments which had fought together in the French Wars often renewed acquaintanceship in India, and special friendships would then be cemented. When the 16th Lancers and the 40th Regiment returned from the Gwalior campaign in 1843, the 40th NCO's gave a ball at Meerut for which they wrote a special song to the tune of *Auld lang syne*.

> Welcome here our gallant friends,
> Thrice welcome to this hall,
> Where beauty and where valour meets,
> To grace the Fortieth ball.
> Then gaily circle round the bowl,
> Sure mark for fortune's boons;
> In love or war, for ever first,
> Our gallant Light Dragoons.

> The old Sixteenth, the bold Sixteenth,
> The Fortieth love the name,
> For records bright of many a fight
> Identify our fame.

> We've met on Talavera's plain,
> At Salamanca too,
> Vittoria and Peninsula,
> And then at Waterloo.
> We've seen Kabul and Kandahar,
> And many a triumph more
> In Sind and through Afghanistan,
> And bled at Maharajpore.

> In many a proud and happy day
> The two old corps have shared,
> For many more as proud and gay
> I trust they may be spared.
> And if in England we should meet,
> As gaily rolls old Time,
> We'll hand in hand as brothers greet,
> For Auld Lang Syne.

> Then let us pray, where move we may,
> That those loved friends we miss
> Have found that day—that endless day—
> In brighter lands than this.
> And 'ere from valued friends we part,
> We'll fill with roseate wine,
> Embalming friendship in the heart,
> And drain to Auld Lang Syne.

> The old Sixteenth, the bold Sixteenth,
> The Fortieth famed in story;
> Where'er we move our mottoes prove
> Fidelity and glory.[14]

During the 19th century, regiments often did long tours of duty in India, and the novelty of life in cantonments soon wore off for them and their families. Boredom was a perpetual problem, which regimental bands did something to solve. Band night in India was a welcome social occasion and a spectacle, with a double or treble row of carriages laagered around the musicians, and with the garrison's brave paying respects to the garrison's fair.

Nevertheless, it seems to have been common practice to criticize the musicians. Long service in India supposedly lead to a band's decline,[15] since it would then include Indians and half-caste children of the regiment among its members. "The natives are naturally enough slow in adapting their ears to European strains," said one officer generously, before adding his contribution to the capricious lore of Victorian physiological myths. "They seem not to possess that strength of lungs necessary for filling our wind instruments".[16] But half-caste musicians had to face occupational hazards besides criticizm. A group of half-castes playing *Rory O'More* at Secunderabad were assaulted by "a drunken Irish soldier, irritated at blacks playing one of the most popular tunes of his beloved country".[17]

During their long stay in India the British could not remain oblivious to native music although they tended to speak of it disparagingly. British bandmasters were rarely interested in native melodies, although early in the century the bandmaster of the 33rd Regiment took a Hyderabad nautch girl's song and arranged it as *Chundah's song*, by which name it became quite popular.[18] When J. Mackenzie Rogan was with the Queen's Regiment at Calcutta in 1885 he composed marches on Indian themes which were played when the regimental band performed at Indian weddings.[19] The best-known tune which the British acquired in India was *Zachmi dil, The wounded heart*, a Pathan song of homosexual love said to begin,

> There's a boy across the river,
> With a bottom like a peach,
> But alas—I cannot swim.

This entered the repertoire of the North Staffordshire[20] and Liverpool Regiments, and the latter used it for many years as an unofficial march.

42
Zachmi dil

MUSIC Traditional

Just as the loyal Indians had entertained their British comrades with
military music during the Mutiny so they did again on the North West
Frontier where they served against the hill tribes and the Afghans.
During the Second Afghan War of 1879–1880, the 4th Gurkha Regiment took its band to Jellalabad and the Sikhs had their tom-toms and
native bagpipes.[21] During the Tirah Campaign of 1897, when there
was little regimental music, the irregular Khyber Rifles provided melody

with their extraordinary surnas, which looked rather like clarinets and had a range somewhere between that instrument and the bagpipes. These accompanied the drums, and on most nights the Pathan musicians gave two performances – one after the British had turned in. They preferred their own tunes, with *Zachmi dil* rating high, but they occasionally varied the programme with Scots and Irish airs (or versions thereof?) and loyally they always ended with *God save the Queen*.[22]

Twice during the 19th century fear of Russian penetration into Afghanistan led to British intervention in that country, while even in time of official peace the frontier smouldered. The first British adventure in Afghanistan began in 1839. The army fought its way through mountains and deserts – with *St. Patrick's Day* reviving exhausted troops once again[23] – and the British puppet, Shah Suja, was duly crowned at Kabul while regimental bands played *God save the Queen*[24]. But Suja could not be propped up by British arms and in 1842 a British force, hopelessly encumbered by camp followers and its own women and children, was cut to ribbons retreating from Kabul. Only one man survived to reach the British garrison holding out at Jellalabad. This was an unparalleled disaster for British arms, and when relief troops were ordered to Afghanistan they played *The British Grenadiers* instead of *The girl I left behind me* – an ominous indication of their mood.[25]

By the time a relief force under General Pollock arrived at Jellalabad the tide had turned; the defenders had sallied out and won a decisive victory, which entitled the 13th Regiment to greet the newcomers with a slightly derisive refrain, *Ye're o'er long o' coming*[26].

43
Ye're o'er long o' coming

MUSIC Traditional
SOURCE Queen's Own Highlanders Standard
Settings of Pipe Music

(Pipe music)

This gesture entered army lore and when the Sikhs were beaten at Multan in 1848 the 32nd Regiment wanted to play the old tune for belated arrivals from the Bombay Presidency army, but tact prevailed and the plan was dropped.[27]

The British did not return to Afghanistan until 1879–1881 when the Russian bogey again spurred them to action. They took their regimental bands with them and one long column winding its way through the inhospitable Khyber uplands saw fit to play *Home, sweet home*[28] Of all the regiments stationed at Jellalabad only the 10th Royal Hussars — temporarily — had no band. It was rumoured that Afridi raiders had massacred the caravan bearing the 10th's precious instruments and that the frightful noises echoing down the pass at night were made by tribesmen struggling to master trombones and other brass instruments.

Fortunately for the pride of the Hussars this was all ugly rumour, and the missing instruments eventually arrived.[29]

On December 31st, 1897 the 72nd and 92nd Highlanders in Kabul ushered in the New Year with their pipes,[30] and if Englishmen shuddered and grimaced, the local inhabitants relished the performance to the last man. As early as 1789 Captain Innes Munro noted that the Indians had no taste for anything but pipe music,[31] and another soldier said that "they looked upon bagpipes as the nearest approach white men have made to harmony divine".[32] The Sikhs and Afghans had pipes of their own, and in the First Afghan War a hill outside Jellalabad was named Piper's Hill by the redcoats in honour of a tribal musician who, in best Scots manner, "stood his ground so bravely and tried to rally his countrymen when they fled".[33] The Highland pipes made such an impression on the Amir of Afghanistan that in 1888 he ordered 200 sets.[34]

Sing-songs – known as "free-and-easies" – were often held on the frontier and in Afghanistan, and the sentimentality which became musically fashionable as the century progressed left its mark on soldier – singers as well as civilians.

Describing "the hit of the Kohat season" in 1878, a writer notes how "the saddest of songs unearthed from goodness knows where were chosen".[35] When *The vacant chair* was sung at Jellalabad, "there were only a few who could join quietly in it, and those with a certain tremor in their voices".[36] Fortunately, when the Irish were on hand they would liven up the proceedings with revolutionary songs like *Cruiskeen lawn* and *The shan van vocht*,[37] and a fine rowdy chorus.

> Then you ought to've seen us there,
> The truth I do declare,
> All so frisky, drunk on whisky,
> Drive away despair.
> There was fightin' to be sure,
> Indeed it was a squall,
> The night was spent in devilment,
> At Paddy Carey's ball.[38]

Besides sad songs at Kohat there was a number of parodies, but the reporter of this particular free-and-easy, who rambles on interminably about a fresh-faced corporal drawing tears with "the simple old English ditty" (*The vacant chair*), makes only a fleeting aside to "a very clever topical song" by Sergeant Moon of the 10th Hussars about Sher Ali, the disputed frontiers, and the Russians.[39] The reader must rest content with two other frontier ballads, one a parody on Gilbert and Sullivan.

> So ring the banjo all day long,
> And away with your old delusions,
> The eleventy-third, upon my word,
> Are the boys to fight the Rooshians.[40]

The other song is what was then called a "grouser".

> Wanted a soldier-boy, very warlike,
> Straight and smart and bold.
> To be drilled all day while he is young
> And kicked out when he's old.
> Warranted tough, though he doesn't eat
> enough,
> And very skilled in shaving,
> Twopence a day is all the pay
> That he'll get when he thinks of leaving.[41]

A song whose text indicates that it was written during the Second Afghan War, which began with an attempt to foist British advisers on Sher Ali, survived into the South African War of 1899–1902,[42] and was called *The Elephant Battery*.

44
The elephant battery

WORDS Traditional
MUSIC Traditional
SOURCE J. Farmer – Scarlet and Blue

I love to see the sepoy, and to hear his martial tread;
And the sound of cavalry galloping goes through and through my head;
But sweeter than the sweetest music band has ever played,
Is the ringing tramp of the buffalo as he's going to parade.

Aya, aya, aya, aya, twist their tails and go!
Hathi, hathi, hathi, hathi, oont, and buffalo!
Aya, chel, chel, chel, chel, chel, chel, aya bhai chelo!
Oh, that's the way we shout all day as we drive the buffalo!

H*

I love to see the hathis with their trunks all in a row;
I love to see the haughty and high-stepping buffalo;
It's sweet to see the sergeants on their dashing kangaroos,
As they gallop past the general and the ladies at reviews.

   Aya, aya, etc.

See that rough-riding bombardier with the pole-axe for a whip,
Such a seat upon an elephant—good heavens, what a grip!
And see the farrier-sergeant's camel's stopped as if he knew
A shoe'd come off the battery sergeant major's kangaroo.

   Aya, aya, etc.

Now watch that careful trumpeter come spurring through the dust;
He's got firm hold of his camel's hump, or else come off he must;
And see the bheesti's katcha, how he tugs with might and main
At the rope which keeps his mussuck on, as he's pani on the brain.

   Aya, aya, etc.

When the byles went out to fight against Amir Sher Ali Khan,
What a fearful time they had of it in the pass they call Bolan!
The major swore he'd do his best, and press the buffalo,
But the byles heard what the major said, and were damned if they would go.

   Aya, aya, etc.

Although music was not played in battle, pipers went wherever the Scots soldier did, and one famous incident resurrects memories of the colourful Peninsula days. During the Tirah Campaign of 1897 the Gordon Highlanders were ordered to storm the Dargai Heights. The Afridi tribesmen were well entrenched, and good marksmen who paced out the distances on potential battlefields to take the guesswork out of range-finding. Not surprisingly the pipers who led the charge were singled out for attention and Piper George Findlater went down, shot through both legs. Like George Clarke of the 71st at Vimeiro, he was undaunted, propped himself against a boulder, and continued to play *The cock o' the north*.[43] His gallantry earned him a well-merited V.C.

According to Chelsea Pensioners, the last decade of the 19th century saw the use, if not the actual origin, of a number of soldiers' songs that have survived into our own day – *I've got sixpence*, *The quartermaster's stores*, *Bless 'em all*, and *Roll me over*. Nevertheless a certain haziness surrounded discussion on these songs, and it was never possible to fix a time or place which anyone could *positively* associate with them. The same group of veterans however all recalled a mildly crude song about the famous music hall star.

Lottie Collins got no drawers,
Will you kindly lend her yours?
For she's got to go away,
To sing ta-ra-ra boom-de-ay![44]

Obscene songs were mostly in the Anglo-Indian argot that Kipling occasionally used in his ballads, and the most famous was a minatory epic which described in minute detail the fate of the unwary soldier who ventured too deep into the Indian labyrinths. Its title could be translated, *Watch out when you're in the bazaar.* Ex-soldiers pleaded amnesia when this song was discussed, and the venereal perils confronting Tommy Atkins on his travels can only be guessed.[45]

India's eastern neighbours, the Burmese, were not as fierce as the tribes of the north-west or the Afghans, but three Little Wars were fought against them. The first, in 1824–1825, proved that the climate was more dangerous than the Burmese. When the troops at Kemmendine were dispirited by fever, Colonel Tidy did what he could for their morale on March 17, by having the band of the 13th Regiment put aboard a large barge to drift past the camp playing – inevitably – *St. Patrick's Day.*[46] Other marches heard during this campaign were *The British Grenadiers, Blue bonnets over the border,* and *Over the hills and far away.*[47]

One officer with a good ear for music noted, with apparent irritation, that the Burmese listened to "one of our best regimental bands without expressing either by words or gestures the least satisfaction at what they heard".[48] As the Burmese naturally considered their own harmonies infinitely superior to western music, their lack of comment was diplomatic, for they were certainly indifferent neither to music nor redcoats. Long before Kipling wrote about Supi-yaw-lat "by the old Moulmein Pagoda" the enthusiasm of the British soldiers for dainty Burmese girls was reciprocated, and many redcoats knew a song composed to honour, and lament, them. The redcoats called it *Tekien, tekien me me no songolah* – a butchering of Burmese. The translation of what they were trying to say is *My benefactor, why are you leaving?*

45

Burmese tune

MUSIC Traditional
SOURCE T. A. Trant – Two Years in Ava

There is little reference to music in the Second Burmese War of 1852. It can only be said that when the 18th Royal Irish Regiment arrived at Martaban *St. Patrick's Day* was played, and *The British Bayoneteers* was still being sung.[49]

The Third Burmese War, in 1886, was less of a campaign than a coup. Fortunately, the indefatigable J. Mackenzie Rogan was at hand to do some musical research and one of his discoveries was the ten-man band of the exiled king Thibaw fallen on lean times and playing in the bazaars.[50] Rogan had already decided that Oriental music had its own charm and persuaded the band to play their national melodies which he wrote down and then re-arranged with happy results. The band of the Queen's Regiment added the Burmese national anthem *Kayat than – The sound of the trumpet* to their repertoire, and their rendering on one occasion proved particularly impressive. Among the Burmese who fought on after Thibaw's exile was Boh Hymat Maung who gave a lot of trouble before he surrendered. With his men he showed great pleasure at the surrender when the band played familiar airs and, obviously encouraged and impressed, "came inside the band circle and went slowly round, listening to each player in turn. At the drum and cymbals he came to a halt, picking him out as the best player of all — doubtless because he made the most noise". Of Rogan the Boh had a poor opinion, "pointing out the uselessness of a large man with a tiny stick . . . A bigger stick would be necessary if I needed to chastise any of the players".[51]

Among the troops used to hunt down Boh Hymat Maung and guerrillas like him were Mounted Infantry, and one of these — Private D. May, ordinarily a member of the Rifle Brigade — described his unaccustomed status in song, rather as Marine Sergeant Eagle, the unwilling cameleer, had done in the Sudan.

> I crave your notice for a time, pray listen to my song,
> It is about the gallant corps to which we now belong.
> We had to serve in Burma for months, it might be years,
> They dished us out with breeches, coats, bandooks and bandoliers.
>
> > Then come along, my hearties, together we will ride,
> > Together we will conquer, together we will die.
> > We ride o'er hills, we ride o'er vales,
> > We have no foolish fear.
> > For free from care are those who bear
> > Bandooks and bandoliers.
>
> All mounted upon Burmese tats to the jungles off we go,
> Some sturdy steeds are found too fast and others far too slow,
> The friendly villagers depart and quickly run with fear,
> When they see us ride, and by our side, bandooks and bandoliers.
>
> > Then come along, etc.
>
> The fierce dacoit is a creature strange, his life is doubtless gay,
> He does no work and spends his time in boozing and in play.
> When The Mounted scour his jungle haunts he flees away in fear,
> When the bullet flies and the look-out spies bandooks and bandoliers.
>
> > Then come along, etc.
>
> Now I must bid you all goodnight, I can no longer stay,
> For fear a runner might come in to summon us away
> By shouting "damiah sheethe!" It may be far or near,
> Away we ride and bear with pride bandooks and bandoliers.
>
> > Then come along, etc.[52]

"Damiah sheethe!" is Burmese for "dacoits are here!" and "bandook" soldiers' slang for a rifle.

If India (with its flanking countries, Afghanistan and Burma) was the major theatre for the Little Wars, South Africa easily ranked second. There were no fewer than nine wars against the assorted tribes labelled "Kaffirs", two Matabele campaigns, the Zulu War, and a Little War with the Boers before the full-scale South African War of 1899–1902.

The Kaffirs were no one's idea of an attractive enemy — they were cruel, cunning, and devoid of chivalry; fighting them was a hard and dangerous business. They were elusive too, and the notion of hunting them down "by beat of drum and sound of bugle" or with "shrill bagpipes sounding strangely indeed among those plains and echoing valleys" was derided.[53] Nevertheless, the Highlanders insisted on their music. The band of the 74th, in 1852, played the regiment's combatants out of Ft. Hare to *Hielan' laddie, Auld lang syne,* and *Over the border.*[54]

In 1847 the 91st Highlanders marched out of Fort Beaufort with pipes and drums playing *The Campbells are coming,*[55] and with the 75th they gave a hearty welcome to new arrivals at Grahamstown. Their music on that day consisted of three gay airs which delighted the Hottentot wagon drivers and sent the native girls whirling in appreciative pirouettes — *Rory O'More, The sprig of shillelagh,* and *Nix, my dolly pals.*[56]

Rory O'More, written by Samuel Lover, was the hit tune of 1837. Lover claimed that "on the occasion of Her Majesty Queen Victoria's coronation every band along the line of procession to Westminster Abbey played *Rory O' More* during some part of the day and finally it was the air the band of the Life Guards played as they escorted Her Majesty into the park on their return to Buckingham Palace."

46
Rory O'More

MUSIC S. Lover

The sprig of shillelagh was less refined in origin and associations. The words went to the tune of *How happy the soldier*, and the recurrent phrase in 19th century memoirs "to spend half a crown out of sixpence a day" proves the long lasting popularity of the original. Oddly enough, only one soldier's memoirs actually refers to the song being sung, but this proves only the arbitrary way the redcoats chose to ignore or mention their favourites. The music also appears in Sergeant Newman's collection.

47
The sprig of shillelagh

MUSIC Traditional

Nix, my dolly pals had no military relevance but provides an interesting aside on social history. The words appeared in W. Harrison Ainsworth's ROOKWOOD (1834), the Gothic and wholly unrealistic novel which gave Dick Turpin a fame that eluded him in real life. Set to music, *Nix, my dolly pals* was a great success; young ladies who would have fainted at an encounter with the genuine Newgate gallows-bait trilled its underworld slang to piano accompaniments in polite drawing rooms.

Music was the only defence a marching column had against boredom, and varying the repertoire was essential if the music itself was not to become tiresome. Regiments were grateful if they had in their ranks someone like Nicholas McCarthy of the 11th, who was not just a drummer but a capable ballad writer and improviser. During the 10-day march from Grahamstown to Capetown he sang some 40 songs. "The band would play a march on leaving camp, then the drums and fifes would play, and the same order would be repeated. After four marches which would take us along the road for about two miles we would rest for about half a mile, when there would be a call for Nicholas to sing us one of his latest ditties. This would be followed by somebody singing one of the newest popular songs from home such as *Champagne Charlie* or *Tommy Dodd*".[57] Other popular songs at this time were *Not for Joe*, *Pretty Polly Perkins of Paddington Green*, *I wish I were a bird*, and *She doted on Leybourne*.[58]

One tune became a regimental march because it was so effective in keeping the men buoyant on the road. Bandmaster William Miller had introduced the comic song *I'm ninety-five* into the Rifle Brigade, the 95th Regiment, when they were at Malta in 1842, but without anyone particularly noticing. "But when we got to the Cape in 1846 there were long marches and sore feet and I now made use of *Ninety-five* to help the men into camp. The first day the battalion marched into it there was not a limping man amongst the lot, so I continued it during the First Cape War (1846–1848). I did the same in the Second Cape War (1851–1853). During our stay at Fort Beaufort (1852) it became the regimental quick march. The march before it was the *Huntsman's Chorus* from the opera of *Der Freischütz*".[59]

I'm ninety-five, I'm ninety-five,
And to keep single I'll contrive.
I'll not get married—no, not I—
To have five brats to squall and cry.
A furtune teller told me so
But I'll resist her tale of woe.

I'm ninety-five, I'm ninety-five,
And to keep single I'll contrive.
I'll not be bound, to be for life,
Some man's mere toy or wedded wife,
To bake and brew, to screw and save,
And be my husband's humble slave.

I'm ninety-five, I'm ninety-five,
And to keep single I'll contrive.
And I will let the fellows see,
That none can make a fool of me,
To darn their socks and mend their clothes,
To suit their whims and take their blows.[60]

McCarthy of the 11th was one of several regimental bards in South Africa. The 88th Connaught Rangers had Private Kenny who rose from the ranks to become captain and quartermaster, and whose compositions ranged from the fairly simple to the near-lyrical.

> Now all you Irish boys,
> Who are fond of fun and noise,
> We will face the Kaffirs and all other dangers.
> I am sure we will never shame
> The old immortal name
> Of the glorious 88th, the Connaught
> Rangers.[61]

When the Rangers were prevented by orders from going in pursuit of the chief Kreli he wrote:

> But little contented,
> Here we remain,
> Nothing to fight for,
> No glory to gain.
> That being the case, boys,
> I'm sure you'll reply,
> It is not our intention
> To capture Kre—li.[62]

Kenny's best effort was inspired by the successful stand of forty-five Rangers under Major H. G. Moore against 700 Kaffirs at Draaibosch on December 30, 1877.

> Stand, sons of Erin! Stand, men, I say!
> Rangers prepare to fight, carry the day.
> Though they count numbers, we but a few,
> Just show them, my lads, what the Rangers can do
> Test but our courage, praise up our land,
> And the Rangers before any number will stand.
> Let a brave man but lead us, that's all we require,
> And this charge of our bayonets shall make them retire.
>
> Stand, Rangers, stand! The Kaffirs are nigh,
> Though forty we number yet bravely we'll die.
> There's hundreds before us, yet we'll never yield.
> No, we fight for our honour or die on the field.
> Raise up your Irish hearts! Now men, prepare!
> Fix your bayonets, my lads, in the sun let them glare.
> Charge, Rangers charge! Give one hearty cheer.
> Hurrah, boys, we've done it! The road is clear.
>
> Stand, Rangers, stand, and see what you've done!
> Seven hundred Kaffirs before you have run.
> Raise up your hearts and thank Him on high,
> That you, like so many, that day did not die.
> You've kept up the name of our brave Irish corps,
> And words can't express our thanks to brave Moore,
> For if forty could make so many men run,
> If we'd all been together, what should we have done?[63]

Another noted ballad composer and singer, rather earlier in the 1840s, was Private Buck Adams of the 7th Dragoon Guards. He was much in demand at concerts and officers' parties, but his work is lost except for two titles — *Swart coppiges* — (*Black hills*), and *Paddy among the Kaffirs*.[64]

Whatever other criticisms might be delivered against the Kaffirs they were certainly not impervious to the charms of music. In 1847 the chief Macomo listened intently to the band of the 7th Regiment playing polkas and a selection from *Lucrezia Borgia*.[65] A particularly villainous character, Umhala, would weep like a baby when he heard military bands and might even withdraw, exhausted by emotion.[66] When Hintza and Bokoo surrendered after the war of 1834–1835 they were intrigued by the bagpipes, although it is doubtful if they believed the story that these instruments were constructed in such a way that they could not sound the retreat.[67] During the fighting in 1880 against the Basuto chief, Lerothodi, the band of the Duke of Edinburgh's Own Volunteer Rifles began to play and the troops held their fire. "Whether the Basutos thought we were coming to attack them or as the old adage goes 'music hath charms' they ceased firing at us".[68]

The Africans had no difficulty in assimilating European music. In 1881 a friendly Fingo chief called Veldtman, resplendent in the full-dress uniform of a naval officer, paid a formal visit to Ibeka near Butterworth. He was preceded by his drum and fife band consisting of "about thirty boys and young men dressed in a uniform of white with red braid, and forage caps on the side of their heads. The big drummer flourished his drumstick in the orthodox manner, evidently acquired after long study of the drummer of an infantry regiment".[69] Malay troops at the Cape in 1846 also imitated British bands. They made their own drums and rude flutes, clarinets, and horns, "shaped hurriedly from bamboo but emitting not unpleasant music in most perfect time". The tune they played and sang was *Garryowen*.[70]

The finest warriors in South Africa were the Zulus, at last provoked into war in 1879. Nothing is known about the songs of this campaign, although the 94th Regiment marching from Durban to Zululand "stepped along cheerily whistling or singing popular airs" helped by the concertina of a certain Halligan.[71] The war began with a notable Zulu victory at Isandhlwana. Lord Chelmsford was tricked into leaving his camp under-garrisoned and when he returned it was to find that over 800 white troops and about the same number of tribal auxiliaries had been butchered in a Zulu attack. Most of the British casualties were from the 24th Regiment (South Wales Borderers), and the disaster inspired G. C. Anewick to write *The noble 24th* or *Vanquished, not disgraced*. Although the four verses were soon forgotten, the chorus, which was jaunty and easily retained, has been sung by the regiment ever since.[72]

48
The noble 24th

WORDS G. C. Anewick
MUSIC V. Davies

CHORUS

A story came one morning
From a far and distant land
That savages had massacred
A small but gallant band.

1st
verse

'Gainst twenty thousand foreign foes,
'Mid thunder, shot and shell,
Five hundred valiant English fought,
And nobly fighting fell.
Five hundred valiant English fought,
And nobly fighting fell.

Chorus

All honour to the Twenty-fourth
Of glorious renown.
England, avenge your countrymen,
And strike the foemen down.

Anewick's praises were less than accurate. There was precious little "thunder" or "shell" at Isandhlwana — it was primarily a battle of rifles and cold steel — and none of it came from the Zulus, while the "valiant English" were mostly Welsh. But the vengeance he demanded was exacted, at least in part, the very day of Isandhlwana, and by soldiers of the 24th. When the triumphant Zulus swept on to Rorkes Drift, held by 103 fit men and 35 hospital cases, they were repulsed with massive losses in the famous action which won eleven V.C.'s for the tiny garrison.

Six months after Isandhlwana the Zulus were defeated at Ulundi and their kingdom broken up into eight tribal areas each under a chief. But before the Zulus were finally pacified a crisis arose, which music helped first to create and then to dispel. General Sir Evelyn Wood had called a meeting of some of the chiefs and intending to impress them and their warriors he ordered the band to play *God save the Queen* and the troops to cheer. Either the sombre national anthem or the rousing 'hurrah' upset the Zulus, and it was only their chiefs' calm demeanour that held them in uneasy check and the atmosphere became so tense and forbidding that discussion was clearly impossible. To clear the air the bandmaster was ordered to play a lively tune, and being an Irishman he obliged with *St. Patrick's Day*. "First a few of the Zulus rose, then a few more, and then the whole lot, as if the Pied Piper of Hamelin was after them and they could not help themselves. In less than five minutes the whole of the dusky host were swaying to and dancing to the music . . . all in the best of humours".[73]

It was poetic justice that the Zulu War, provoked by the British, should lead them to the one Little War which they lost, which was also the only conflict of its type against a white nation. The Boers of the Transvaal had been more than happy to be annexed by the British when the threat of Zulu invasion hung over them, but when the Zulu menace disappeared they demanded the restoration of their independence. When this demand was ignored they resorted to arms and the first shots of the war were fired on December 20, 1880. Lieutenant-Colonel Anstruther and 250 men of the 94th Regiment were on the march when they were stopped by a Boer commando of 150 riders. There was a brief parley, Anstruther refused to turn back, and within twenty minutes he and over seventy men were dead or dying. His last act was to order a surrender, saying that "he had better leave a few men to tell the story" – a handsome tribute to the fighting ability of the outnumbered Boers. It was ironic that the 94th had been playing, at the instant they caught sight of the commando, *Kiss me, mother, kiss your darling*.[74]

49
Kiss me, mother, kiss your darling

WORDS L. C. Lord
MUSIC G. F. Root

Kiss me, mother, kiss your darling,
Lean my head upon your breast.
Fold your loving arms around me,
I am weary let me rest.

Scenes of life are swiftly fading,
Brighter seems the other shore
I am standing by the river,
Angels wait to waft me o'er.

   Kiss me, mother, etc.

Kiss me, mother, kiss your darling,
Breath a blessing on my brow,
For I'll soon be with the angels,
Fainter grows my breath e'en now.

   Kiss me, mother, etc.

Tell the loved ones not to murmur,
Say I died our flag to save,
And that I shall slumber sweetly
In the soldiers' honoured grave.

   Kiss me, mother, etc.

Oh, how dark this world is growing,
Hark, I hear the angel band.
How I long to join their number,
In that fair and happy land.

   Kiss me, mother, etc.

Hear you not that heavenly music,
Floating near so soft and low?
I must leave you. Farewell, mother,
Kiss me once before I go.

   Kiss me, mother, etc.

Anstruther's defeat at Bronkhurstspruit left the British with just four small garrisons in the Transvaal, all hemmed in by Boers. The defenders of Pretoria were supported by the pipes of the Royal Scots Fusiliers, although one dignitary would possibly have foregone their help. This dignitary was the Bishop of Pretoria who on "New Year's Eve carried through a midnight service successfully despite the fact that the band and pipers of the Scots Fusiliers in the square immediately adjoining were ushering in 1881 with all the ardour of brazen notes and skirling pipes, effecting serious collisions of *Auld lang syne* with *Nunc dimittis*".[75] Besides their band and their pipes, the Fusiliers boasted an orchestra under the direction of a Mr. Daniels ; the orchestra entertained regularly, although a loyal soul might well have asked what it was doing playing "with great effect" a "sweetly plaintive air . . . suggested as the national anthem of the South African Republic".[76]

The war was short. In August the Pretoria Convention restored the Transvaal's independence, although the ambiguities of this document were certainly a contributory factor to the South African War of 1899–1902.

Not all the Little Wars inspired anecdotal histories or even the presence of newspaper correspondents but two of these minor campaigns were covered by the American journalist H. M. Stanley. Stanley travelled with the British force that invaded Abyssinia to rescue the prisoners held by mad King Theodore, and noted that when the troops set out for Magdala on April 13, 1868, they were preceded by "a small army of musicians". The 33rd Regiment marched to *Yankee Doodle*, which doubtless pleased Stanley, the 4th King's Own to *Garryowen*, and the 45th to *Cheer, boys, cheer*.[77] This is the last mention in British military history of the spirited Crimean favourite and one wonders why – after its wide popularity in the Crimea, the Mutiny, and Abyssinia, and without competition from a new favourite – it should have fallen from grace. When Magdala fell *Rule Britannia* and the national anthem were played, and the arrival of Sir Robert Napier, the successful general, was met with *See, the conquering hero comes*.[78]

In 1874, undeterred by the coolness of the commanding officer Sir Garnet Wolseley who thought reporters "drones" and "a curse to modern armies", Stanley was back with the British Army on the jungle road to Kumasi, the capital of the Ashantis. He has nothing to say about bands or singing soldiers, although he did hear the pipes of the Black Watch playing at the Battle of Amoaful,[79] and recognized two Civil War songs sung by the Naval Brigade – *When Johnny comes marching home* and *John Brown's knapsack is number ninety two*.[80] Like many other commentators before and after, Stanley also found "joyous chorus and . . . roaring songs which made the evenings lively and pleasant at the camp of the Naval Brigade".[81]

Two regimental songs were written by serving soldiers during the period of the Little Wars, although they are not derivative of any particular campaign. *The jolly Die-hards* of the 57th (West Middlesex) Regiment was written by the regiment's bandmaster, C. Moore,[82] soon after the Maori Wars of 1861–1866, and traces the 57th's history up to that time. The words were transcribed in 1874 by J. Grove-White,[83] who had just joined the regiment and rose to become its commanding officer. The tune disappeared, quite literally, during World War Two when the greater part of the 1st Battalion were being shuttled to Japan as prisoners of war after the fall of Hong Kong. Their transport ship, the *Lisbon Maru*, was torpedoed by an Allied submarine and the regimental music was among the documents that were lost. Efforts to re-discover any one who remembers the tune have proved unsuccessful. It is just remotely possible that it was the same melody used for *The bold King's Hussar*, a 19th century ballad lauding the 15th Hussars, but not included in this book because its provenance could not be definitively established. *The jolly Die-Hards* and *The bold King's Hussar* certainly echo each other — with a summons to battle in the opening couplet, an invitation to a toast in the last verse and a common metre.

> When our bugle for battle so merrily sounds,
> In the ranks of the Die-Hards each heart then rebounds,
> As fearless of danger, right onward we go,
> When up go our colours and down go the foe,
> Be they Russians or Prussians or Spanish or French,
> At scaling a rampart or guarding a trench,
> Neither bayonet nor bullet our progress retards,
> For its just all the same to the gallant Die-Hards.
>> For Highlanders, Riflemen, Lancers or Guards,
>> Are not like the boys called the jolly Die-Hards.
>
> Our regiment has conquered, but never in vain,
> Bear witness those hills and the mountains through Spain,
> Bear witness the shades of those hundreds who fell
> At red Albuera, and our victory can tell
> How Soult and his Frenchmen were beaten and sank,
> As we fell on them fiercely, rank after rank,
> Invincible seemed those brave children of Mars,
> When Lord Beresford styled us the "Gallant Die-Hards".
>> For Highlanders, etc.
>
> I wish you had seen them at famed Inkerman,
> Or heard their wild shouts at the gory Redan,
> 'Midst lightning and thunder their spirits ne'er quailed,
> 'Midst bloodshed and carnage their hearts never failed;
> Why weep for the loss of brave Goldie our chief,
> Why weep for brave Shadforth, away with that grief,
> They died like true heroes as history records
> While leading to glory the gallant Die-Hards.
>> For Highlanders, etc.
>
> When black-hearted savage with treacherous guile,
> Slew our comrades in arms, did they reckon the while
> That our steel was as sharp and our arms were as strong,
> As the days when we hurled the wild Cossack along?
> The Die-Hards advance—how fiercely they cheer
> The Pahs—they are taken, without dread or fear,
> And the Maoris are vanquished and got their reward,
> And our chief, like his men, was a gallant Die-Hard.
>> For Highlanders, etc.

What harm if we suffer from hardship at times,
What harm if we're bronzed by those hot Eastern climes,
Such trifles as these our spirits can't damp
For we're jovial in barracks and more so in camp,
Watch the girls, how they smile when we march through a town,
When they hear we're the Die-Hards of far-famed renown,
So fill up your glasses and show your regard
By drinking the health of each jolly Die-Hard.
        For Highlanders, etc.

The other song composed by a soldier serving in the time of the Little Wars presents no scholarly difficulties. It was written by Charles Martin, a lieutenant in the 88th Connaught Rangers from 1888 to 1893, and the descendant of one of those Rangers who stood before Badajoz in 1812 while the band played *Savourneen deelish*. It was sung to the air *Killaloe*.[84]

50
The Connaught Rangers

WORDS C. Martin
MUSIC R. Martin

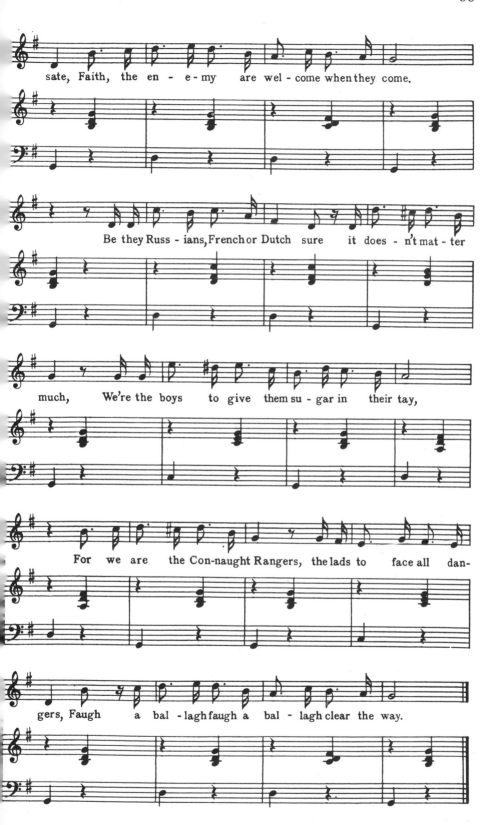

sate, Faith, the en - e - my are wel - come when they come.

Be they Russ - ians, French or Dutch sure it does - n't mat - ter

much, We're the boys to give them su - gar in their tay,

For we are the Con - naught Rangers, the lads to face all dan-

gers, Faugh a bal - lagh faugh a bal - lagh clear the way.

CHORUS

You may talk a-bout your Guards, boys your Lan-cers and Hus - sars, boys, Your Fus - i - liers and Roy - al Ar - til - le- rie *with-out the guns!* The girls we drive them cra - zy The foe we bate them ai - sy The Ran-gers from Old Con-naught *yarrrgh!* the land a - cross the sea!

rall. *a tempo*

In our Army we're the best, from the north, south, east and west,
The best of boys are following the drum;
We're mighty hard to bate, I may say without consate,
Faith, the enemy are welcome when they come.
Be they Russians, French or Dutch, sure, it doesn't matter much,
We're the boys to give them sugar in their tay,
For we are the Connaught Rangers, the lads to face all dangers,
Faugh-a-ballagh, faugh-a-ballagh, clear the way.
      You may talk about your Guards, boys, your Lancers and Hussars, boys,
      Your Fusiliers and Royal Artillerie—without the guns!
The girls we drive them crazy, the foe we bate them aisy,
The Rangers from Old Connaught—yarrrgh—the land across the sea!

Now allow me here to state, it is counted quite a trate
In Ould Ireland just to fight for friendship's sake.
To crack your neighbour's head, or maybe your own instead,
Faith, 'tis just the fun and glory of a wake!
So you see all Irish boys are accustomed to such noise,
It's as natural as drinking whisky nate,
For there's none among them all, from Kingston to Donegal,
Like the gallant Connaught Ranger on his bate.
      You make talk about, etc.

'Twas Bonaparte who said, as the Frenchmen on he led,
'Marshal Soult, are them the Rangers, do you know?'
'Faix', said Soult, 'There's no mistake, to our heels we'd better take,
I think it's time for you and I to go!'
When the colleens hear their step, it makes their hearts to leap,
'Arragh, jewels, will ye whist to *Patrick's Day?*'
For they are the Connaught Rangers, the boys that fear no dangers,
And they're the lads that always take the sway.
      You may talk, etc.

Now you haven't far to search for the lads that best can march,
The lads that never fear the longest day;
Faith, you easily will know, their dashing step will show,
'Tis the Connaught boys that always lead the way.
If me words, perhaps, ye doubt, go and join them on the route,
I'm thinking you'll not find it quite a treat;
You'll see them in the van, you may catch them if you can,
Faith, you'll have to travel fast, or you'll be late.

1. Shipp, III, p.103.
2. J. Welsh, *Military Reminiscences* (1830), I. p.199–200.
3. G. Calladine, *Diary* (ed. 1922), p.73.
4. J. M. MacMullen, *Camp and Barrackroom* (1846), p.211.
5. Shipp, II, p.137.
6. *NQ*, Third Series (1863), III, p.459.
7. N. W. Bancroft, *The Bengal Artillery of the Olden Time* (1885), p.101.
8. *USM* (1852), Part III, p.211.
9. A. J. Macpherson, *Rambling Reminiscences of the Punjab Campaign* (1889), p.3.
10. T. Malcolm, *Barracks and Battlefields in India* (1891), p.28.
11. F. Trenchard, *The Young Dragoon* (1870), p.124.
12. J. A. Bostock, *Letters from India and the Crimea* (1896), p.116.
13. J. Ruggles, *Recollections of a Lucknow Veteran* (1906), p.23.
14. R. H. Raymond Smythies, *Historical Records of the 40th (2nd Somersetshire) Regiment* (1894), p.232.
15. Bostock, p.73.
16. F. B. Doveton, *Reminiscences of the Burmese War in 1824–1826* (1852), p.222.
17. J. Creagh, *Sparks from Camp Fires* (1901), p.252.

I

18. J. Blakiston, *Twelve Years Military Adventure* (1829), I, p.257.
19. J. M. Rogan, *Fifty Years of Army Music* (1926), p.97.
20. Interviews at Royal Hospital, Chelsea, 1954.
21. A. Male, *Scenes through the Battlesmoke* (1891), p.127.
22. R. G. Thomsett, *With the Peshawar Column* (1899), p.156.
23. W. Taylor, *Scenes and Adventures in Afghanistan* (1842), p.48.
24. *Ibid*, p.96.
25. J. Greenwood, *Narrative of the Late Victorious Campaign in Affghanistan* (1844), p.126.
26. Seaton, I, p.327.
27. J. Ryder, *Four Years Service in India* (1853), p.114.
28. R. G. Thomsett, *Kohat, Kuram and Khost. Experiences and Adventures in the Late Afghan War* (1884), p.77.
29. Male, p.127.
30. B. P. Crane, *The Ninth Lancers in Afghanistan* (1884), p.50.
31. I. Munro, *Narrative of Military Operations* (1789), p.33.
32. A. S. H. Mountain, *Memoirs and Letters* (1857), p.98.
33. Seaton, I, p.255.
34. *The British Bandsman* (March 15, 1888), No. 34, p.101.
35. Thomsett, p.55.
36. Male, p.126.
37. *Ibid*, p.124.
38. Thomsett, p.196.
39. Male, p.125.
40. Thomsett, p.58.
41. *Ibid*, p.64.
42. Major G. Tylden, 1st Battalion, Imperial Yeomanry. Interview, 1969.
43. H. D. Hutchinson, *The Campaign in Tirah, 1897–1898* (1898), p.74.
44. Interviews at Royal Hospital, Chelsea, 1954.
45. *Ibid*.
46. Ward, p.173.
47. Doveton, p.223.
48. T. A. Trant, *Two Years in Ava* (1827), p.221.
49. W. F. B. Laurie, *The Second Burmese War* (1853), p.55.
50. Rogan, p.102.
51. *Ibid*, p.103.
52. *Rifle Brigade Chronicle* (1894), p. 157.
53. *USM* (1844), Part III, pp.183, 505.
54. W. R. King, *Campaigning in Kaffirland* (1853), p.44.
55. H. Ward, *Five Years in Kaffirland* (1848), II, p.264.
56. *Ibid*, I, p.83.
57. Rogan, p.22.
58. *Ibid*, p.29.
59. *Rifle Brigade Chronicle* (1894), p.104.
60. *Rifle Brigade Chronicle* (1934), p.311.
61. Jourdain, p.34.
62. *Ibid*, p.34.
63. *Ibid*, p.21.
64. A. Gordon-Brown, *The Narrative of Private Buck Adams* (1941), pp.90, 235.
65. Ward, II, p.87.
66. *Ibid*, p.87.
67. Scobie, p.19.
68. H. V. Woon, *Twenty Five Years Soldiering in South Africa* (1909), p.184.
69. *Ibid*, p.239.
70. Ward, II, p.121.
71. W. E. Montague, *Campaigning in South Africa* (1880), p.74.
72. Letter from Lt. Colonel I. Jarman, MBE, South Wales Borderers, 1969.
73. Mole, p.286.
74. C. Duval, *Personal Reminiscences of the Transvaal War* (1882), II, p.42.
75. *Ibid*, p.59.
76. Lady B. Bellairs, *The Transvaal War* (1885), p.181.
77. H. M. Stanley, *Coomassie and Magdala* (1874), pp.439–440.
78. *Ibid*, pp.450–453.
79. *Ibid*, p.197.
80. *Ibid*, p.128.
81. *Ibid*, p.137.
82. *The Diehards* (June, 1959), p.293.
83. *The Diehards' Doings* (1903), III, No. p.3.
84. Jourdain, p.50.

Chapter 11

THE SOUTH AFRICAN WAR
1899–1902

IT may appear strange that there has been so little sociological comment in SONGS AND MUSIC OF THE REDCOATS — so few attempts to relate what soldiers sang in response to economic circumstance, social environment, or political mood. The explanation is simply that few songs with sociological value were found from earlier wars, and no valid assertions about the relationship between army music and its contemporary culture could be made. The Civil War, with the Roundheads' hymn-singing a manifestation of the godliness of Cromwellian England, is one exception ; the South African War is a second. Enough is known about both the society and the war music to make three points.

While one is forced to suppose that the music of Vauxhall and Ranelagh pleasure gardens influenced the musical tastes of the redcoats who fought in the American War of Independence, one is certain that the flourishing late Victorian music hall influenced the singing of soldiers in South Africa. The most popular of the music hall songs reached audiences which were not as large as those of today's mass media but which were still big, and since it was not customary to launch a new hit each week songs were less ephemeral. A good tune had the chance to establish itself in public esteem, and to become an element in popular culture.

Secondly, the Victorian "evening at home" was a recognized form of entertainment among all classes. Organized musical evenings were nothing new even in the days when Samuel Pepys relished them, but by the 1890s it was desirable, rather than merely permissible, to take one's harp to the party, and it was a poor guest who was unable to sing a party-piece or recite. It was considered that anyone who could not, lacked the social graces, just as 1200 years before Caedmon had been despised by his fellow Saxons because he could offer no contribution. In South Africa home customs endured, and soldiers were not bashful about taking banjos or accordions to sing-songs and concerts.

Finally, it is easy to see how the mood of the nation influenced what the soldier sang. A noisy patriotism blended with an atypical but temporarily strong royalism was ascendant, as if the Boers were threatening the aged Widow at Windsor personally. Patriotism was not new, nor writers to express it, but in Rudyard Kipling Britain found someone who captured the very essence of national sentiment and translated it into poems which were often set to music. If he did not inspire the citizenry to the same degree as the war songs of Tyrtaeus inspired the Spartans, or Rouget de Lisle and Theodor Körner moved their French and German compatriots, he nevertheless influenced what the soldiers sang. He was not alone in reflecting the patriotic-royalist mood, and songs like *Soldiers of the Queen* were genuinely popular among the soldiers.

The music of the war was varied because the Army in South Africa was not only large but also cosmopolitan. Of 450,000 men about half were British regulars but the remainder were, in every respect, a mixed lot. At first the War Office had been reluctant to accept volunteers, but after the Black Week in December 1899 when three British generals were beaten in three separate engagements with proportionately heavy losses, a change of heart followed. All types of volunteer corps came into existence, rather like the numerous fencible units that mushroomed during the invasion scare of the Napoleonic Wars.

The volunteers came from every social class, and Kipling's quartet — sons of cook, duke, belted earl, and Lambeth publican — was wholly credible. One of the City Imperial Volunteers described the concerts that were held aboard the *Ariosto* en route to South Africa as "illustrative of the representative character of the regiment as regards the many classes and stations of life from which the rank and file are drawn . . . Music-hall songs with 'lodger' and 'mother-in-law' complete are sandwiched between madrigals and Tennysonian recitations . . . sentimental ditties with valse refrain such as are beloved of regular Tommies . . . Good old cavalier marching tunes are contrasted with the lilt of modern war songs, whose triumphant and bellicose words are somewhat marred by the eccentricities of their rhymes".[1]

These City Imperial Volunteers were recruited from the London volunteer regiments, and consisted of a 1,000-strong battalion of infantry, 300 mounted infantry, and a six-gun battery of the Honourable Artillery Company. Many regular regiments raised short-service volunteer battalions, and it was a unit of this sort from the Royal Welch Fusiliers which at Southampton "relieved the monotony with singing – as Welsh-men always do when they get the chance".[2]

Although the value of mounted troops had been underestimated it soon became clear that they were better able to catch and cope with the Boers than footsloggers and a committee was appointed by Army Order to raise 8,000 volunteer horse called the Imperial Yeomanry. And apart from these, wealthy patriots were given the privilege of forming their own units – such as Earl Dunraven's battalion, Lord Lovat's Scouts, and Lord Lathom's Roughriders. In addition to British volunteers, regiments of Australians, New Zealanders and Canadians, and white residents in essentially non-white colonies, plus 30,000 South Africans fought with the Imperial army.

These half-million-odd men were no "scum of the earth enlisted for drink" as Wellington described his own troops, but highly respected citizen-soldiers and there was a corresponding increase in concern for the private soldier's welfare. Generals might kill him in homicidal frontal assaults on well-entrenched Boers, but before they killed him they looked after him, and even considered his recreation. For the first time official concerts were organized on a wide scale.

The war music of the British Army in South Africa can be learned from the writings of soldiers, non-combatant participants, and journalists. But of still greater value are the memories of survivors. Just ten years ago it would have been possible to interview enough of them to demonstrate irrefutably that South Africa inspired as many soldier songs as World War One, but the past decade has drastically reduced their number and often numbed the memories of those who remain. There were only a handful of Pensioners at the Royal Hospital, Chelsea, who could recall the South African songs, and attempts to reach other veterans through newspaper advertisements in Britain and Ireland were not particularly fruitful. But these few contacts were nevertheless sufficient to substantiate the literary evidence that this war was rich in music, and especially in parodies.

The soldiers' own lyrics to familiar tunes range from the sophisticated to the infantile and cover a spectrum of attitudes, although cynicism predominates. Among the best are the verses written by one of Roberts' own staff and sung by the author at a concert in the Pretoria Soldiers' Home in front of the commander-in-chief and his three daughters. The song was described as "sensational" and went to the tune, *Long as the world goes round*.[3]

> Of all the Boers we have come across yet,
> None can compare with this Christian de Wet,
> For him we are quite unable to get—
> Though Hildyard and Broadwood
> And our Sudanese Lord *should*—
> Long as the world goes round.

This verse refers to the remarkable Boer leader who led the British — including Kitchener the "Sudanese Lord" — a dance more bloody than merry. The song continued with an oblique reference to Lt. Hans Cordua of the Transvaal State Artillery who planned to set fire to Pretoria and amid the confusion kidnap Roberts and his staff.

> Though the Boer some say is a practised
>   thief,
> Yet it certainly beggars all belief
> That he slimly should try to steal our chief—
> But no Hollander mobs
> Shall kidnap our Bobs—
> Long as the world goes round.

The charges against Cordua were many and black for after breaking his parole he donned British uniform in an attempt to slip through the British lines to General Louis Botha. He was duly caught, tried, and hanged in Pretoria Jail, regarded by the Britons as the type of Boer of whom the song said:

> He'll bury his Mauser,
> And break all his vows, sir.
> Long as the world goes round.

Among the less sophisticated parodies were simple doggerels like this plaint to a purging doctor.

> Oh doctor, oh doctor,
> You're a doctor so fine.
> But for every ill that we have,
> You give us a Number Nine.[4]

Equally simple was the chant of a Connaught Ranger.

> There was a Colonel B.
> Who had some tired men.
> So he marched them up to the top of the hill,
> And marched them down again.[5]

The Canadians also had a "singular marching song".

> We will follow Roberts,
> Follow, follow, follow.
> Anywhere, everywhere,
> We will follow him.[6]

Rather better than this was an observation on the Boers composed and sung by Major H. Corbyn, of the Royal Artillery.

> A wicked old uncle was guardian left,
> To a wicked republic of morals bereft.
> He called for his burgers and bribed them with gold
> To turn the poor British out into the cold.
> With a pom-pom, whizz-crash-bang,
> Tooral-ay-ay.[7]

This was another observation on the Boers.

> When the war is over I shall love you, Johnny Boer,
> But riding in the saddle makes my rear parts sore.
> Without Long Toms, pom-poms, Mausers,
> You can bet your Sunday trousers,
> That is when I'll love you, Johnny Boer.[8]

Sweet Rosy O'Grady was the tune for another song which looked forward to the end of hostilities.

> Lord Roberts and Kitchener, French, Buller and White,
> All out in the Transvaal, all ready to fight.
> Now when we catch Kruger, how happy we'll be,
> We'll all have a swing on his whiskers,
> And a damned jolly good spree.[9]

Cynicism is a recurrent theme in many of the parodies. The soldiers might sing the professionally-composed *Why did I leave my little back room in Bloomsbury?* but when it came to expressing disillusionment with the war they could write more poignantly than any professional. The Rifle Brigade reworked their traditional regimental song, briefly but eloquently.

> I'm ninety-five, I'm ninety-five,
> I'd just as soon be dead as alive.[10]

Ranking with a famous parody from the American Civil War* was a widely known gem sung by, and possibly written by, Major H. Corbyn.

*(Just before the battle mother,
  I was drinking mountain dew,
  When I heard the rebels coming,
  To the rear I quickly flew.)

Riding in the ammunition van,
Amidst the shot and shell I've been.
While my comrades fought,
(As comrades ought)
I was nowhere to be seen.
I was covered over with the flag,
Listening to the din and strife
When the fight was o'er, out once more,
And that's how I saved my life.[11]

It was this verse that moved a volunteer to write : "It illustrates the difference between the French and the English that the former would not for a moment tolerate a song reflecting on the honour and glory of a soldier".[12] The writer might have broadened the statement and said that no nation anywhere, except the British and their Anglo-Saxon relations, would joke about cowardice.

Another song, *The wagon loafer*, was sung by the 55th Imperial Yeomanry (Northumberland Hussars) and was even more specific in condemning the high proportion of battle-shy volunteers who were seized by a sudden desire to become batmen or otherwise non-combatant.

A little song, it's all my own, I'm going to sing to you,
About our wagon loafers who've got easy jobs to do;
Jobs like driving Cape carts, when we've kaffirs not a few,
Bur wait till we get home.
    Glory, glory halleluia, oh wait till we get home!

Now what these chaps left England for, the dickens only knows,
Every night beneath a wagon they sleep in sweet repose,
But who is it when we reach the line that gets the pick of the clothes?
Oh wait till we get home.
    Glory, glory etc.

Now if these chaps would chuck their jobs, and come back to the ranks,
Come and share the fighting with the boys upon the flanks,
Earning with brave comrades, their country's grateful thanks,
To sweeten Home Sweet Home.
    Glory, glory etc.

Now at home in old Newcastle, wagon loafers in a bar,
Will sponge a drink and spin a yarn about the great Boer War,
How they made the Dutchmen run – by thousands. Ha, ha, ha!
Oh wait till we get home
    Glory, glory etc.[12a]

Hymn tunes were convenient for parodies and *Holy, holy, holy* became the horseman's

Grooming, grooming, grooming,
All the bloody day I'm grooming,
From reveille to lights out
I'm grooming all the day.[13]

Refusing to be deprived of the use of this bit of philosophy the infantry changed "grooming" to "grousing", and the Oxfordshire Yeomanry sang :

> Grousing, grousing, grousing,
> Always bloody well grousing,
> Grousing till the ship we see
> When we shall grouse no more.[14]

The Oxfordshire men must have come from devout homes, for they also knew a second hymn tune.

> All good things are sent to us
> From friends across the sea,
> They're at the base, they're at the base,
> And there they'll always be![15]

Onward, Christian soldiers was also adapted, and with a cockney accent.

> Sons of the Empire marching on to war,
> With our brave Colonials going on before.
> C.I.V. will conquer and break old Kroojer's jaw.[16]

Nothing was sacred to hard bitten troops who even turned the fighting, gallant Seventh Fusiliers of a well-known song into "those gallant boozaliers".[17]

Rank was an obvious target of satire, and this malediction has the sound of being far older than the South African War.

> It's captains and colonels and lieutenants too,
> Sergeants, colour sergeants, and corporals likewise.
> With their hands in our pockets they rob us poor men.
> May the Lord damn and blast them,
> Says the soldier 'amen'.[18]

Money problems were viewed with a clear eye.

> We are two soldiers mild and meek,
> We only get seven bob a week.
> The more we grouse the more we may,
> It makes no difference to our pay.[19]

There were obscene parodies too, but they were written about so coyly that a polite public could not take offence. At Ladysmith the defenders sang "choruses about the extraordinary feats of extraordinary but scarcely sober heroes, or about the charms of ladies whose universally proclaimed popularity must have endangered their modesty".[20] Perhaps Sir Winston Churchill knew those choruses for "many of his favourite songs dated back to his days as a correspondent in the Boer War. 'They were rather naughty soldiers' songs' . . ."[21] Old soldiers are surprisingly reticent when it comes to discussing obscene songs, but English soldiers admit that Irish soldiers sang, to the air of *The bard of Armagh* (also called

I*

The streets of Laredo) how *The Dublin whores were the pride of them all,*[22] and the same tune was the vehicle for a suggestive lament which began :

> Now at the corner these two girls were standing
> One turned to the other and these words did say.
> Here comes the young soldier whose money we squandered,
> Here comes the young soldier cut down in his prime.[23]

One of the South African veterans interviewed was Major G. Tylden of the 1st Battalion, Imperial Yeomanry, whose fondness for music and remarkable memory have made it possible to write with unusual depth about the music of a particular unit. The wealth of material stemming from one battalion — which had no reason to be more musical than any other — is yet another testament to the vast amount of music there was in the war, and the researcher is left regretting that soldiers comparable to Major Tylden could not be found for twenty or thirty different units.

Several Yeomanry songs originated in the music hall but were adopted because they were appropriate. One of these was *I was there a-watching them*, sung in the style and accent of a cockney policeman.

> I was there a-watching them,
> I was there a-watching them,
> Straight I say, the fun was nice,
> I saw him kiss the lady in the same place twice.
> Oh good gracious, it was a pantomime!
> The rest of the evidence I ain't a-going to tell,
> But I was there a-watching all the time.

A second verse was sung more warily if there were any Guardsmen about, since it could be interpreted under the wrong circumstances, as an invitation to "belts", containing as it did one provocative couplet :

> Down in the kitchen I saw my dear,
> Perched on the knee of a Grenadier.

An even better song for riding, written about 1880 and possibly used in earlier African campaigns, was a "coon song" traditionally sung only when the battalion came off rearguard and if they had engaged the enemy.

51
Razors in the air

WORDS B. Maxwell
MUSIC B. Maxwell

Come, my love, and go with me,
Ah, my love, I'll meet you.
Take you down to Tennessee,
Meet you by and by.
Wipe your eyes and don't you cry.
Come my love, I'll meet you.
I'll be back to stop that sigh,
Meet you by and by.

    Hoe de corn,
    Hoe de corn, Moses.
    Hoe de corn,
    Moses, hoe de corn.
    Get away from dat window,
    My love and my dove.
    Get away from dat window
    Don't you hear?
    Oh my, yes!
    Come some other night,
    For dar's going to be a fight,
    Dar'll be razors a-flying in de air.

Don't you hear de niggers now?
Ah, my love I'll meet you,
Oh, der's going to be a row,
Meet you by and by.
All dem nigs is cut to death,
Ah, my love, I greet you!
I'm the only nig who's left
Meet you by and by.

  Hoe de corn, etc.

Ole man he has gone to rest,
Oh, my love, I greet you.
Dress yourself up in your best,
Meet you by and by.
To de parson we will run
O, my love, I greet you.
Soon he'll make us darkeys one,
Meet you by and by.

  Hoe de corn, etc.

Another music-hall song relished by the Yeomanry was this practical but peremptory proposal.

Darling Mabel, now I'm able
To provide a happy home.
Since they've raised my screw, love,
I've enough for two, love.
Do not tarry, say you'll marry,
Answer yes or no.
I conclude with love and kisses.
Yours for ever, Joe.

The 1st Battalion, Imperial Yeomanry, served with the 16th Brigade under Major-General Barrington Campbell, whose great popularity was acknowledged to the air *Come landlord, fill the flowing bowl*.

> There was a man, a fat man,
> So fat he scarce could amble.
> He loved his men, his men loved him,
> He loved his men, his men loved him,
> They called him Old Barr Campbell.

Positive echoes from earlier campaigns included in the Yeomanry's repertoire were *The tarpaulin jacket* and *The elephant battery*.

Just as World War One is fixed in popular mythology as "the trench war" so South Africa (because of Mafeking and Ladysmith and to lesser degree Kimberley) is "the siege war". In the first two towns music played an important part in sustaining morale. At Mafeking Colonel R. S. S. Baden-Powell not only organized concerts but was probably the first British commanding officer to entertain his troops since Wolfe recited Grey's *Elegy*. "B-P" had considerable talent and is said to have" brought the house down with his musical sketches".[24] In the trenches the Cape coloured boys played concertinas oblivious to danger,[25] and their lack of concern spread — perhaps without too much difficulty — to the Irish defenders. On St. Patrick's Day "a concertina broke out into riotous discord in our trench and the fellows danced and sang and otherwise made noises", all of which sounds suicidal in the presence of the renowned Boer marksmen. But not everyone in the trench was celebrating, because when the Boers with uncharacteristic rashness looked over their parapet two of them were promptly shot.[26] If this seems unchivalrous it needs to be remembered that the Boers themselves had an unenviable reputation for being "slim", or crafty. Their cunning (or naïvety) extended to grotesque limits, and they had been known to hoist a white flag over a knocked-out gun until it was serviced and ready to fire again.

At Ladysmith, which unlike Mafeking was defended by regular troops, "the tum tum of the banjo and the drone of the accordion were heard on all sides".[27] On St. Andrew's day the pipers of the Gordons skirled merrily[28] and the Natal volunteers gave concerts in the open air and at Christmas organised a burlesque cavalry band.[29]

All over South Africa concerts and sing-songs were organised whenever it was feasible and sometimes when it was seemingly not. Major Corbyn of the Royal Artillery was a great organizer of impromptu concerts, building stages from wagons, and magically acquiring pianos even in the middle of the veldt.[30] Bennet Burleigh, THE DAILY TELEGRAPH correspondent who had covered the Sudan campaign, was a "camp fire" organiser[31] and two Welsh brothers called Richards from the Durban Light Infantry were also famous for their concerts.[32] At Blickfontein camp fire sing-songs were regularly organized by Colonial troops on the grand scale. A huge fatigue party would bring in several wagon-loads of wood for an enormous bonfire around which senior officers and hundreds of men would assemble to sing.[32]

Singing on the march was encouraged, although apparently neither fifes and drums nor regimental bands were heard on the road. One soldier explained how "our officers endeavoured to keep us awake by suggesting our having a song or a row or a violent discussion on early morning marches."[34] Another recalled how as "many a time we marched along in blinding rain . . . thinking perhaps of luxury and friends at home . . . (some-one) would commence to whistle or sing a popular ditty until gradually every soul in the column joined in chorus".[35] One of the Rhodesia Sharpshooters gives the impression that they sang from dawn to dusk and longer, for he comments with unreasonable surprise that "it was peculiar that in the morning the songs were of the cheeriest description while at night they were of the saddest."[36] Singing was probably easier for mounted men and the Imperial Yeomanry and Rimington's Scouts, who favoured *Coming through the rye*,[37] were great singers.

Dust and fatigue could bring singing to a halt. The Reverend E. P. Lowry, a Wesleyan chaplain with the Guards Brigade, once advised some gloomy marchers "to try the effect on their pedestrian powers of a lively song", and playfully suggested—

Cheer, boys, cheer,
No more of idle sorrow,
Cheer, boys, cheer,
There'll be another march tomorrow.[38]

The marchers replied, with no playfulness whatsoever, that "it was impossible to sing on three quarters of a pound of uncooked flour in place of a day's rations". These unfortunates had apparently been given the raw material of "dampers" but no time to cook, and their plight was perhaps not uncommon, for the Oxfordshire company, Imperial Yeomanry, had a song about this sort of situation, to the tune of the *Soldiers' chorus* from *Faust*.

Yeomen live on nothing but lumps of dough,
Bloody great lumps,
Bloody great lumps,
Hi—diddle—hi.[39]

In his book, WITH THE GUARDS BRIGADE, Reverend Lowry gives the impression of being a likeable but ingenuous soul. He was told, and presumably believed, that "sometimes amid actual battle scenes our lads caught up and encouraged themselves by chanting some more or less appropriate music hall ditty. One battalion when sending a specially large consignment of whizzing bullets across the Boer lines did so to the accompanying tune of—

You have to have 'em,
Whether you will or no.

Another fighting group when especially hard pressed began to sing *Let 'em all come*."[40] But men with whom this claim was discussed dismissed it as nonsense saying that British regulars would not have dreamed of taking such liberties with the Boer crackshots and their Mauser rifles.

One of the Reverend Lowry's most remarkable statements was that "seldom if ever has an army contained so many who themselves were praying men"[41] and he supports this with an observation about the camp at Bloemfontein. "Here as at Modder River secular song was nowhere while sacred song became all and in all".[42] He also said that "absolutely the only concert or public meeting held in Bloemfontein while the Guards were in the neighbourhood was in connection with the Army Temperance Society, Lord Roberts attending".[43] These are surprising remarks, although there is evidence that soldiers would sing hymns even without the encouragement of a clergyman. "It being the sabbath a few of us at sunset went aside on the veldt from the distractions of the camp . . . Returning to camp we commenced singing *Lead kindly light* . . . Others quickly joined our ranks until we had a good muster around us and the lusty voices of the sturdy Derby and Lancashire lads sounded far over the camp".[44] *Onward, Christian soldiers* was sung on the march[45] as well as at church parades, and according to the Reverend Lowry a soldier in the Waterval prison camp near Pretoria composed a hymn which is no worse than many patriotic hymns that found their way into hymn books.[46]

Lord, a nation humbly kneeling,
For her soldiers cries to Thee.
Strong in faith and hope, appealing
That triumphant they may be.
    Waking, sleeping,
     'Neath Thy keeping,
Lead our troops to victory.

Of our sins we make confession,
Wealth and arrogance and pride,
But our hosts against oppression,
March with freedom's flowing tide.
    Father, speed them,
     Keep them, lead them.
God of armies, be their guide.

And if Victory should crown us,
May we take it as from Thee.
As Thy nation deign to own us
Merciful and strong and free.
    Endless praising,
     To Thee raising,
Ever Thine, may England be.

A conflicting view of the British soldier was offered by a war correspondent. "Barring a very small minority, principally Irishmen, there is no place for religion in Tommy's intellectual kit. It has just degenerated into being an old magazine from which he draws his swear words – a sort of bandolier of blasphemy".[47] The true verdict might be that while the army was not as religious as Lowry believed – the practising Christians naturally congregating around the padres, blocking their view of the distant pagan hordes – among 200,000 British volunteers there was bound to be a good proportion of church-goers and hymn-singers. It was a less impious host than Wellington's, but not an army of saints.

Every type of song was sung in South Africa, but the sentimental variety predominated. "Mr. Atkins inclines towards mournful sentiment and such songs as *Break the news to mother* were always great favourites".[48] Others highly rated included *Queen of the earth, Comrades, Two little girls in blue, Annie Roonie, Bluebell, my bluebell, Home sweet home, Mother, come back from the echoing shore, The anchor's weighed,* and of course *Dolly Gray.* Unlike the American Civil War, South Africa inspired little sentimental music in which the soldier himself was the hero, although there were some songs of this sort. *The lad in the Scotch Brigade,* which looked back to Egypt and the Sudan was a favourite with Private J. W. Paice and his comrades of the Royal Sussex Regiment.[49]

On the banks of the Clyde stood a lad and a lassie,
The lad's name was Geordie, the lassie's was Jean,
She flung her arms round him and cried do not leave me,
For Geordie was going to fight for his Queen.
She gave him a lock of bright auburn tresses,
She kissed him and pressed him once more to her heart
Till his eyes spoke the words which his lips could not utter,
But the last word is spoken—they kiss and they part.

    Over the burning plains of Egypt,
    Under the burning sun,
    He thought of the stories he'd have to tell
    His love, when the fight was won.
    He treasured with care that dear lock of hair,
    For his own darling Jeannie he prayed
    But his prayer was in vain, for she'll ne'er see again
    Her lad in the Scotch Brigade.

Though an ocean divided the lad from the lassie
The Geordie was forced far over the foam.
His roof was the sky, his bed was the desert
But his heart with his Jeannie was always at home.
The morning that dawned on the famed day of battle,
Found Geordie enacting a true hero's part
Till an enemy's bullet brought with it its billet,
And buried that dear lock of hair in his heart.

    Over the burning plains, etc.

On the banks of the Clyde dwells a heart-broken mother
They told her of how the great victory was won.
But the glory of England to her was no comfort
For glory to her meant the loss of her son.
But Jeannie is with her to comfort and shield her
Together they weep and together they pray,
And Jeannie her daughter will be while she lives
For the sake of the laddie who died far away.

    Over the burning plains, etc.

There was also this lament sung by Private Patrick Carrol of the Royal Irish Rifles.

He was only a private soldier, one of the rank and file,
But he fought for the honour of England, like a son of Erin's isle,
And he left his grey-haired mother, and also his good old dad,
In a neat little cot in old Ireland. How they cried for their only lad.

    He thought of his dear old mother, he longed for his good old dad,
    He knew if he fell at Ladysmith the cot would be lonely and sad.
    For the shot and shell were flying, he fought in the bravest style,
    And he died like a true Irish soldier. He was a son of old Erin's isle.

The night before the battle his sleep was far from sound,
He thought of his home in old Ireland, as he lay on the cold, cold ground,
When the day of strife was dawning he knelt upon his knees,
And prayed for the ones he would ne'er see again, in that village far over the seas.

    He thought of his dear old mother, etc.

> Beside his sword they found him, all covered with wounds was he,
> And tightly grasping a picture of the ones he would never more see.
> With the Union Jack wrapped around him, the flag he had died to save,
> Near the spot where he bravely fell fighting, he was laid in a soldier's grave.[50]

Less dignified than the preceding songs was this cloying bit of nonsense.[51]

> The Boers have got my daddy,
> My soldier dad.
> I don't like to hear my mummy cry,
> I don't like to hear my mummy sigh.
> And I'm going on the big ship,
> To cross the raging main.
> I'm going to fight the Boers I am,
> And bring my daddy home again.

As the Scots Guards left Southampton on October 21, 1899, they sang a more than normally soulful loth-to-depart.[52]

> For old times sake,
> Don't let your enmity live.
> For old times sake,
> Say you'll forget and forgive.
> Life is too short for quarrel,
> Hearts are too precious to break.
> Shake hands and let us be friends,
> For old times sake.

Patriotic songs included *The Yeomen of England*, and best known of all, the self-confident *Soldiers of the Queen*. An American war correspondent who found the war less colourful than he had hoped — "great armies without uniform marching drearily without music" — still found pageantry through this song. "After all my other memories of Bloemfontein have passed away I think I shall continue to hear . . . the almost chant-like singing of the *Soldiers of the Queen* by the Lancers as they headed the column marching up Monument Avenue".[53]

5 2
Soldiers of the Queen

WORDS L. Stuart
MUSIC L. Stuart

CHORUS

Britons always loyally declaim, about the way we rule the waves.
Every Briton's song is just the same, when singing of our soldiers brave
All the world has heard it, wonders why we sing, and some have learned the reason why.
We're not forgetting it, we're not letting it
Fade away or gradually die; fade away or gradually die.
So when we say that England's master, remember who has made her so.

  It's the soldiers of the Queen, my lads,
  Who've been, my lads, who've seen, my lads,
  In the fight for England's glory, lads,
  Of its world wide glory let us sing.
  And when we say we've always won,
  And when they ask us how it's done,
  We'll proudly point to every one
  Of England's soldiers of the Queen.

War clouds gather over every land, our treaties threatened east and west.
Nations that we've shaken by the hand, our honoured pledges try to test.
They may have thought us sleeping, thought us unprepared, because we have our party wars.
But Britons all unite, when they're called to fight
The battle for old England's cause; the battle for old England's cause.
So when we say that England's master, remember who has made her so.
It's the soldiers of the Queen, etc.

When we're roused we buckle on our swords, we've done with diplomatic lingo.
We do deeds to follow our words, we show we're something more than jingo
The sons of merry England answered duty's call, and military duties do,
And though new at the game, they show them all the same,
An Englishman can be a soldier too; an Englishman can be a soldier too.
So when we say that England's master, remember who has made her so.
It's the soldiers of the Queen, etc.

The American was also enthusiastic about the way in which the national anthem was sung. "I think if this national anthem could be heard more often the enemies of Great Britain would be drawn more closely to that grand old country."[54]

There is no doubt that in 1899–1902 *God save the Queen* had an appeal that has never been equalled; even in World War Two it would be difficult to find anyone writing of a concert that "the event of the evening was *The Queen*"[55] (or as it was then, *The King*). *The Red, white and blue* to the air *Columbia, the pride of the ocean* was frequently sung, and when Pretoria was captured it was part of a special show for the benefit of the city's many American residents.[56] The Volunteer Company of the Norfolk Regiment saluted the Stars and Stripes waving over one building with *Yankee Doodle*, which was one of their own regular favourites.[57]

Two popular regimental songs by professionals, which the soldiers accepted, were *Fighting with the Seventh Royal Fusiliers* and the now virtually forgotten *Bravo, Dublin Fusiliers*. The first of these was written before the war and although it is fictitious melodrama of the worst kind it is said to have attracted a flood of recruits.

Dark was the hour, but gaily song and story ran,
Through the British camp some forty years ago.
We were waiting the word to fight near Inkerman,
Burning to avenge past insults.
Camped were we beside a friendly stream,
Victory our theme, little did we dream,
We'd be victims of a Russian scheme
To trap each brave defender.
But one morn there came a fearful cry,
"River now is dry!" "Cossacks," said a spy,
"Have dammed the stream, and left us here to die
Of thirst, or else like curs surrender."

Oh, fighting with the Seventh Royal Fusiliers,
Famous Fusiliers, gallant Fusiliers.
Through deadly Russian shot and Cossack spears
We carved our way to glory, oh glory!

Three days passed, not a drain of water came in sight.
Then up spoke our Colonel, "Boys, who'll volunteer to
Make his way through the Russian lines at dead o' night,
Cut the dam and flood this streamlet?".
Fred, my dearest brother answered "I.
I will have a try, comrades all good-bye."
Spade in hand he went to do or die,
Nor were our prayers unheeded.
Hours we waited, breathlessly, until
Came a tiny rill, growing bigger still,
Then in volume rushed a-down the hill,
"Hurrah, hurrah, the lad's succeeded!"
    Oh, fighting with the Seventh Royal Fusiliers, etc.

But as the water came tumbling there,
Flooding the stream through the morning air,
Musket shots rang out and told
An awful sequel to my story.
For when the fighting was o'er we found,
Dead our young hero upon the ground.
Though he fell his name shall proudly swell
The scroll of British glory.
    Oh, fighting with the Seventh Royal Fusiliers, etc.

Bravo, Dublin Fusiliers[58] celebrated the Royal Dublin Fusiliers' role at the Battle of Talana or Dundee, and although there is no denying their bravery the song was typical of the extravagant effusions written at the start of many wars. But even the song writer did not dare conceal that this was a Pyrrhic victory costing over 500 casualties.

53
Bravo, Dublin Fusiliers

WORDS G. D. Wheeler
MUSIC G. D. Wheeler

Some dare to say that I-rish-men should re-fuse to fight for Brit-ain's crown; Some dare sug-gest that they should pre-pare to turn and strike the Eng-lish down. What cow-ar-dly trai-tors to

try and in-cite our sol-diers to be-come mut-in-eers!

Those ag- it - at - ors have had their re-ply from the gall-ant Dub-lin Fu - si -

CHORUS

liers Bra-vo! Dub-lin Fu-si-liers! You're no cra-ven mut-in-

eers, You brave - ly storm'd and won the Glen -coe Heights;

Put four thous-and craf-ty Boers to flight, 'Twas a grand and glor-ious sight, Bra-vo! Dub-lin Fu - si - liers!

Some dare to say that Irishmen should refuse to fight for Britain's crown.
Some dare to suggest that they should prepare to turn and strike the English down.
What cowardly traitors, to try and incite our soldiers to become mutineers!
Those agitators have had their reply from the gallant Dublin Fusiliers.
    Bravo, Dublin Fusiliers!   You're no craven mutineers!
    You bravely stormed and won the Glencoe Heights,
    Put four thousand crafty Boers to flight
    'Twas a grand and glorious sight.   Bravo, Dublin Fusiliers!

Boers have derided men of our race, insulted Britain's dear old flag.
Boasted Majuba—said we were curs, called our flag 'the old white rag'.
Sanguine of victory and anxious to fight they came to Glencoe Hill to attack.
They'll cease to boast of Majuba—they've seen the colour of the Union Jack.
    Bravo, Dublin Fusiliers!, etc.

Brave General Symons led our attack amidst the deadly shot and shell.
Foremost and first were brave Irish boys, and many gallant soldiers fell.
Dear was the price—for that victory we paid with many, many British lives,
'Tis but our duty if help we provide for those heroes' children and their wives.
    Bravo, Dublin Fusiliers!, etc.

The soldiers also sang about a general whose ineptitude is still remembered despite greater bungles in two World Wars — and the incredible thing is that they sang of him affectionately. The subject of their song was Sir Redvers Buller who was appointed commander-in-chief in South Africa at the beginning of the war, and from whom much was expected. He was brave — a V.C. — and with experience of Africa gained in the Zulu War when he had led irregular cavalry. But when it came to the test his three efforts to relieve Ladysmith were disasters which differed only in their magnitude. His antics on the Tugela River earned him the nickname of the Tugela Ferryman, and for his costly setbacks he became Sir Reverse Buller (Redvers being pronounced 'Reevers'). But even in 1900 when wounds were still raw it could be written that "the soldiers still had confidence in him" and – staggering observation – "his failures could hardly be designated defeats". Survivors of the war endorsed this view, and recalled how when he was replaced by Lord Roberts *Cheer up, Buller* was sung with great feeling.[59]

54
Cheer up, Buller

WORDS F. V. St. Clair
MUSIC F. V. St. Clair

In for- mer days the Bri - tish race was proud of her - oes true; The more you toil'd for Eng-land then, the more she hon-oured you. To - day a fa - mous sol-dier who has serv'd us long and

well, is told to go—For what? we ask! For what we can-not
tell. But Cheer up, Bul-ler my lad Don't say
die!____ We'll know the rea - son why;____ To slight you some would
try.____ You've done your best for Eng - land—And Eng-land won't for-

get!___ Cheer up, Buller my lad, You're not dead yet.

In former days the British race
Was proud of heroes true.
The more you toiled for England *then*,
The more she honoured you.
Today a famous soldier who
Has served us long and well
Is told to go—For what? we ask.
For what we cannot tell.

> Cheer up, Buller, my lad,
> Don't say die.
> We'll know the reason why,
> To slight you some would try.
> You've done your best for England,
> And England won't forget.
> Cheer up, Buller, my lad,
> You're not dead yet.

For forty years he proved himself
A soldier and a man.
The fame of Buller was, and is,
And shall be in the van.
When future generations read
About our heroes true,
They will admit that Buller had
The hardest work to do.

Cheer up, Buller, etc.

Let us remember all his past,
Just think what he has done.
Must we condemn the hero who
The Cross of Valour won?
Although he may have made mistakes,
On Honour's scroll we shall,
Find Buller's name—and written 'neath,
"This soldier saved Natal!"

Cheer up, Buller, etc.

Tommy also had no hesitation in singing praises about himself.

> You can take him from the city or the plough,
> And dress him till he doesn't seem the same.
> But with a uniform and shilling, his heart is always willing.
> You can call him Tommy Atkins by name.
> > Oh Tommy Atkins, you're a good and hearty hand
> > You're a credit to your calling,
> > And to your native land.
> > May your heart be ever faithful,
> > And your love be ever true,
> > God bless you Tommy Atkins,
> > That's your country's prayer for you.[60]

The popularity of Rudyard Kipling's work among the troops has been contested. Field-Marshal Sir Evelyn Wood is supposed to have doubted Kipling's popularity because his songs showed the rank and file in "an unnatural and unworthy aspect",[61] while a civilian who had been in South Africa with the army said that "the soldiers spoke of *The absent minded beggar* and did not like it".[62] On the other hand many soldiers were pleased to carry handkerchiefs showing Queen Victoria, Lord Roberts, a map of South Africa, and words and music of the song, which they would hardly have done if they found it obnoxious. Every Chelsea Pensioner who fought in South Africa includes *The absent minded beggar* among his memories. And although this is no proof of Kipling's popularity among the rank and file, it was nevertheless his *Recessional* that was sung by 10,000 men before the Parliament House in Pretoria when the city had been captured.

> God of our fathers, known of old,
> Lord of our far-flung battle line,
> Beneath whose awful hand we hold,
> Dominion over palm and pine—
> Lord God of hosts, be with us yet,
> Lest we forget—lest we forget.[63]

The Scots pipes were often heard in South Africa. "If (a Scot) goes to the river with a bathing party, a swaggering perspiring piper plays him down and back,"[64] wrote a marvelling American war correspondent. After the Black Week Battle of Magersfontein, where the Highland Brigade was terribly mauled, the pipers wailed *The flowers of the forest* and *Lochaber no more* as its commander, Major General Wauchope, was buried with many of the men he had led.[65] The Boer marksmen limited a piper's chance of survival but even at the slaughter of Magersfontein a piper of the Argyll and Sutherland Highlanders was heard playing *Johnny Cope*.[66]

After the Battle of Doornkop in which the Gordon Highlanders lost nine officers and eighty-eight men they could still find solace in the music of the pipes. A Canadian described how "when they came to our lines they braced up and swung past to the skirl of the pipes with the same old debonair swagger that does for church parades in Edinburgh".[67] The Scots and Canadians struck up a close friendship, all the warmer for a spice of rivalry. Approaching Paardeberg after a hard day's march the Gordon pipes broke into *The white cockade*, to drag something extra out of the tired troops in the column, and particularly the 2nd Battalion of the Royal Canadian Regiment who were famed as fast marchers.[68]

Pipers did not play only in difficult times. When the capital of the Orange Free State, Bloemfontein, fell the 100 pipers of the Highland Brigade gave an impressive display of music and countermarching.[69]

Although few sailors got ashore in the South African War those who did made their mark as usual. The big guns that the khaki-clad "bluejackets" rushed up from Durban to Ladysmith before the town was invested literally saved it. True to their traditions the sailors were irreverent comedians. Their guns were named after girls, (Lady Anne and so on), an armoured train became Hairy Mary, and an enemy unit with a big Italian contingent was the Ice-cream Brigade. As in the Crimea and the Indian Mutiny sailors excelled in comic songs. "Our bluejackets were the boys who provided the lighter vein of amusement", reported a war correspondent with the forces trying to relieve Ladysmith,[70] while inside the town it was observed that "as usual the sailors had the best of it in comic songs".[71]

Books about the war make few comments about bands. The Gloucestershire Regiment had a band in Ladysmith,[72] and the Derbyshire Regiment played the City Imperial Volunteers into Edenburg camp,[73] as well as being present at the entry into Pretoria.[74] Drums and fifes heralded Christmas Day 1899 in Buller's camp at Chievely in Natal,[75] and drums and fifes sounded "the march which they all know and love so well" as the Guards Brigade entered Kroonstad in the Orange Free State.[76] But it seems that the main use to which the army put its bands, apart from concerts, was to impress the stolid Boers. The band of the Somerset Light Infantry played in the town square of Heidelberg[77] and at Lichtenburg the 5th Battalion, Imperial Yeomanry presented selections from *The circus girl* and *The geisha*.[78]

In fact it would have been polite on these occasions to play religious music for the Boers were a devout people and their love of hymns was often cause for comment. A City Imperial Volunteer wrote. "Every night in camp you may hear deep-throated choruses swelling up from the prisoners' laager. The first night I heard it I was puzzled to know what they were singing . . . It was not till the third night that I recognized the tune of *Oh God our help*, but chanted so slowly as to be difficult to catch, with long luxurious rests on the high notes and mighty booming crescendos".[79]

The same journalist who considered most Tommies irreligious remarked how "the Boers sang hymns without any drawl or nasal intonation, straight out from the chests".[80] On that occasion they were singing Dutch hymns but he also heard them sing "Let God arise and let his enemies be scattered . . . like Cromwell's soldiers at Dunbar".[81] A Royal Engineer who guarded a train-load of Boer prisoners recalled them giving a doleful rendering of the air, *Jesus loves me, this I know*.[82]

The Boers were not inevitably stern and dour. When Field Cornet Pienaar and his commando occupied Elandslaagte in October 1899 they were desperately anxious to show that they were not, in their own words, "barbarians" and a concert was organized. Although "the Boers of the old school, the Transvaal Podsnaps, gathered to intone doleful psalms . . . the younger generation crowded the hotel canteen, drinking and joining the prisoners in a sing-song". The varied programme included the Dutch *Wij leven vrij* and *Wilhelmus van Nassau*, the Boers' *Volkslied*, *God save the Queen*, *Rule Britannia*, *God bless the Prince of Wales*, *All's well*, and *Sweet and low*. An Englishman named Ganthorpe played the accordion and obliged with a comic rendering of *They all take after me*.[83]

The Boers also had topical war songs. *Prinsloo's March* celebrated the invasion of Natal, Buller's several defeats, modern weapons like Maxim guns, lyddite shells, and pom-poms, and ended with the exhortation, "Stry, broeders, vir die land" – "fight for the land, brothers".[84] *Sarie Marais* was sung with versions that changed daily to record current events, and *Tafelbai* (*Table Bay*) was also very popular.

From Table Bay to the far Transvaal
Stands one united people with a common speech.
A speech for our protection, a speech we must protect,
And now it is famous—in north, south, east and west.[85]

1. J. B. Lloyd, *One Thousand Miles with the C.I.V.* (1901), p.25.
2. H. J. Bryant, *The Autobiography of a Military Raincoat* (1907), p.26.
3. E. P. Lowry, *With the Guards Brigade* (1902), pp.158–161.
4. Sgt. A.Cattrall (Hampshire Regiment and 18th Hussars). Interview, 1969.
5. Jourdain, p.114.
6. Lowry, p.24.
7. Sgt. W. H. Smart (Royal Horse Artillery). Interview, 1954.
8. Cattrall (interview).
9. Letter from Mrs. B. Groves, 1969.
10. Letter from Pte. J. Deakin (Rifle Brigade), 1969.
11. C. Rose-Innes, *With Paget's Horse to the Front* (1901), p.97; Smart (interview).
12. Rose-Innes, p.97.
12.A Letter from Trooper W. D. Dodd, 55th Imperial Yeomanry, 1969.
13. Cattrall (interview).
14. G. Tylden (interview).
15. *Ibid*
16. Lloyd, p.25.
17. Cattrall (interview).

18. C.S.M. R. Ewald (Royal Engineers). Interview, 1969.
19. Cattrall (interview).
20. J. Stuart, *Pictures of War* (1901), p.193.
21. W. Frischauer, *Onassis* (1968), p.235.
22. Interviews at Royal Hospital, Chelsea, 1969.
23. Ewald (interview).
24. F. D. Baillie, *Mafeking: A Diary of the Siege* (1900), p.225.
25. *Ibid*, p.177.
26. J. E. Neilly, *Besieged with B.-P.* (1900), p.211.
27. D. Macdonald, *How We Kept the Flag Flying* (1900), p.76.
28. *Ibid*, p.109.
29. *Ibid*, p.153.
30. F. M. Crum, *With the Mounted Infantry in South Africa* (1903), p.137; Smart (interview).
31. G. C. Musgrave, *In South Africa with Buller* (1900), p.273.
32. J. O'Connell, *Campaigning with the Durban Light Infantry* (1900), p.52.
33. Rose-Innes, p.97.
34. T. C. Wetton, *With Rundle's Eighth Division in South Africa* (1904), p.71.
35. A Mounted Black (pseud), *Campaigning in South Africa 1900–1901* (undated), p.59.
36. R. Stevenson, *Through Rhodesia with the Sharpshooters* (1901), p.117.
37. L. M. Phillipps, *With Rimington* (1901), p.60.
38. Lowry, p.216.
39. Tylden (interview).
40. Lowry, pp.28–30.
41. *Ibid*, p.97.
42. *Ibid*, p.28.
43. *Ibid*, p.30.
44. Wetton, p.104.
45. Stevenson, p.117.
46. Lowry, p.150.
46. G. Lynch, *The Impressions of a War Correspondent* (1903), p.64.
48. Rose-Innes, p.97.
49. Letter from Mrs. T. F. Tribe, 1969.
50. Letter from Mrs. A. Carroll, 1969.
51. Corporal A. Westwood (Royal Dublin Fusiliers). Interview, 1969; Deakin (letter).
52. Lowry, p.14.

53. F. W. Unger, *With 'Bobs' and Kruger* (1901), p.197.
54. *Ibid*, p.97.
55. H. W. Nevinson, *Ladysmith: The Diary of a Siege* (1900), p.142.
56. Bryant, p.139.
57. *Ibid*, p.139.
58. Westwood (interview).
59. Interviews at Royal Hospital, Chelsea, 1954.
60. Cattrall (interview).
61. Sir G. J. H. Evatt, *Our Songless Army* (1906), p.6.
62. J. Barnes, *The Great War Trek* (1901), p.100.
63. C. Stone, *War Songs* (1906), p.iv.
64. Barnes, p.101.
65. *Ibid*, p.101.
66. *Ibid*, p.53.
67. W. Hart-McCarg, *From Quebec to Pretoria with the Royal Canadian Regiment* (1902), p.215.
68. H. V. Mackinnon, *War Sketches* (1900), p.58.
69. B. Moeller, *Two Years at the Front with the Mounted Infantry* (1903), p.29.
70. B. Burleigh, *The Natal Campaign* (1900), p.225.
71. Nevinson, p.142.
72. G. W. Steevens, *From Capetown to Ladysmith* (1900), p.24.
73. Lloyd, p.112.
74. Hart-McCarg, p.222.
75. Burleigh, p.225.
76. H. F. Mackern, *Sidelights on the March* (1901) p.74.
77. T. F. Dewar, *With the Scottish Yeomanry* (1901), p.58.
78. K. B. Spurgin, *On Active Service with the Northumberland and Durham Yeomen* (1902), p.198.
79. E. Childers, *In the Ranks of the C.I.V.* (1900), p.191.
80. Lynch, p.65.
81. *Ibid*, p.67.
82. Ewald (interview).
83. H. Johnson, *With Our Soldiers at the Front* (1900), p.41; Macdonald, p.24; Musgrave, p.105.
84. Wetton, p.459.
85. Tylden (interview).

K

Conclusion

SONGS AND MUSIC OF THE REDCOATS, it is hoped, has demonstrated the rich tradition of British war music – a far richer tradition than Sir John Fortescue supposed. On the other hand it would be foolish to pretend that the British soldier sang as readily or as well as the German soldier. The Germans have also retained more of their old traditional marches, and these are often – in a musical sense – better than most British marches. So far as war music is concerned the Germans are our superiors in all respects, and the French might well claim to be at least our equals. Nor have we fought a war that compares with the American Civil War for the number of excellent songs that came from it – *The battle hymn of the Republic, Dixie, The bonnie blue flag, Sherman will march to the sea, Stonewall Jackson's way,* and *Lorena* among them (although some of these were new words to traditional tunes).

Nevertheless, the redcoats – regardless of their background – were not unmusical. They sang traditional words, improvised their own, and enjoyed the music of bands and of less ambitious instrumental combinations. It is apparent that while some nations might have sung with their greatest sincerity in trying conditions, the British – certainly the English it seemed – were at their most musical in convivial surroundings. No other army, for example, had a custom to compare with the playing of *The roast beef of old England* when the officers went to dine. The air was written in 1736 and although the first mention of the ceremony dates from 1813[1] it undoubtedly existed much earlier.

55
The roast beef of old England

WORDS C. Leveridge
MUSIC C. Leveridge

The band was also expected to entertain the company with music
after each of the many toasts that were part of a formal dinner – in war
even more than in peace. When the Connaught Rangers gave a dinner

to the brigade staff on March 17, 1813, an appropriate tune followed each bumper — *St. Patrick's Day, God save the King, The prince and old England for ever, The Duke of York's March, Rule Britannia, The downfall of Paris, Britons, strike home, See, the conquering hero comes, The British Grenadiers,* and *The Battle of Salamanca.*[2] Many toasts had their traditional tunes in response; "The Ladies" would be followed by *Kiss my lady,* and when glasses were raised for "The East India Company" (whose nabobs came home worth their weight in gold, if they survived to come home at all) the band played *Money in both pockets.*[3]

56
Money in both pockets

MUSIC   Traditional
SOURCE   W. Brown MS

After these formalities the band continued "by way of drowning the cries of the wounded bottles",[4] but as drink destroyed whatever inhibitions the company may have originally possessed, vocal music displaced the band. The same officer who was fascinated by the music of Germans,

Spaniards and Portuguese in the Peninsula has left a lively picture of yet another tribe – young officers in their mess. After dinner a typical subaltern designated as Buckskin decides it is time for song to "make the evening" and Ensign Luby obliges with *The glasses sparkle on the board* "so completely out of tune that nobody knows what to make of it; the conclusion is loudly applauded". The rowdy Buckskin then responds with the time-honoured salute for a solo.

> A very good song and very well sung,
> Jolly companions every one,
> We only live to enjoy,
> We only live to enjoy.

The entire well-soused company provides a chorus before Buckskin resumes his somewhat disjointed solo.

> How happy's the soldier who lives on his pay,
> And spends half a crown out of sixpence a day.
>
> We are the boys for mirth and glee,
> We are the boys for jollity,
> And so we fell a-drinking,
> And so we fell a-drinking,
> Drinking, drinking,
> So we fell a-drinking.
>
> We shan't go home till morning,
> We shan't go home till morning,
> We shan't go home till morning,
> Till daylight doth appear.

By now a fine party hysteria has been whipped up, with everyone howling cries from the hunting-field (just as they did in battle) – "Yoix! Hark forward! Gone away!"[5]

These young rowdies, many of whom came from public schools, brought public school customs with them; anyone who could not sing a solo was forced to drink a mug of salt water, as was the procedure at Tom Brown's Rugby. But even the non-singers could avoid this unpalatable penalty with simple chant, and it was suggested that the non-singers thus rendered a service by keeping ditties of this sort alive. In the 1840's a Lieutenant-Colonel Wilkie looked back to what he called "the days of drinking and singing" and recalled such a refrain, which was "sung to a tune easily acquired and repeated ad infinitum".

> At the siege of Belleisle,
> I was there all the while,
> All the while,
> At the siege of Belleisle.[6]

Solo efforts linked by choruses are still part of stag celebrations.

> That was a jolly good rhyme,
> Sing us another one,
> Just like the other one, ·
> Do!

In the years between this contemporary chorus and Ensign Buckskin's song, there existed these words sung by the Rifle Brigade in the Sudan.

> Jolly good song, jolly well sung,
> Jolly companions every one.
> If you can beat it you're welcome to try,
> Always remember the singer is dry.
> Soup![7]

Although the officers did not have to be awash with liquor before singing, lubrication undoubtedly helped. At a dinner-dance in Simla during the 1840's the warriors bade farewell to their ladies at midnight and returned to the banqueting room "to drink and sing until dawn". This carousal is not as wild as the one featuring Buckskin and Luby, but is gay enough. "The harmony is still kept up, interspersed with recitations however. One tells of bloody wars, and another sings of battles fought on the field of love. One sings of home and another speaks of exile", and "a hero" delights the company with his idyllic tale of military joys.

> How merry, how merry we soldiers be,
> Gay and frolicsome, bold and free.
> Ever in love and ready for fun,
> Suitors where'er there's a lass to be won.
> We kiss and we sport and we nectar quaff,
> And at trouble and care we do but laugh.
> How merry, how merry we soldiers be,
> Hurrah, a soldier's life for me![8]

If officers sang in their cups – and out of them – so did the rank and file, who also depended on music while they marched. References to singing on the road have been quoted from the 19th century but the need was recognized earlier. In 1789 Captain Innes Munro saw fit to record the death of a mere corporal, John Mackay of the 73rd Regiment, simply because Mackay was the son of Robert Donn [sic], "the famous Highland bard", and had "frequently revived the drooping spirits of his countrymen upon the march by singing in a pleasant manner the humorous and lively productions of his father".[9]

The British Army, throughout the 18th and 19th centuries, was a singing army – but in its own fashion, and on its own terms. Few songs have survived as collectors' items, fewer still in contemporary favour, because – as with many marches – they were subjected to unfair criticism and disparagement. "The standards of both officers' and soldiers' songs seemed to improve slowly as the drinking habits of the army as a whole declined," wrote Colonel De Watteville in 1954,[10] and Colonel Wilkie's nostalgic reference in 1840 to "the days of drinking and singing" is obviously a glance at a departed age. In 1857 J. H. Stocqueler claimed that "the modern songs of the soldiery are of a far superior character to those roared out through the barrack room thirty or forty years since".[11] In what way they were superior Stocqueler does not explain, but he added – not as one who is describing anything inferior or paltry. "Yet are the old ditties not quite forgotten . . . They are preserved like old silver watches, dim miniatures and other family relics, to be exhibited from time to time and admired for their quaintness, simplicity, and oddity". If he was talking of *Sahagun, Barrosa*, and their like, although those songs may not have been musical or literary gems, their sincerity and pleasing melodies make them no less aesthetically satisfying than "refined" songs written for and sung (briefly) by soldiers – *Go where glory waits thee*,[12] or *There's a land that bears a well-known name*.[13]

As the 19th century progressed and officers became more distant from the men they led the very fact that rankers sang a song branded it as unacceptable. As these songs fell into disuse, "martial songs" were written to take their place, but these failed to strike the redcoats' fancy, and thus no permanent traditions were built. In 1843 someone who took Tom Sabre as his *nom de plume* published THE SWORD AND THE LYRE – a collection of 177 verses to well-known tunes. Some of the songs were about particular regiments and battles, and the collection is by no means bad, yet not a single line that Sabre wrote has been found in military memoirs of the 19th century. Two ludicrously bad volumes by Nugent Taillefer – BRITISH CAVALRY SONGS (1866) and RONDEAUX OF THE BRITISH VOLUNTEERS (1878) also fell on stony ground.

Although the redcoats would not be force-fed with specially written songs there were periodic attempts to introduce them to existing songs of the theoretically "right" sort. In 1898 Charles Williams, thinking how "desirable it would be to have a book of songs something on the lines of the SOLDATENLIEDERBUCH of the Prussian Army but adapted to our more popular institutions and the Voluntary Service" compiled SOLDIERS SONGS which was dedicated to Field-Marshal Viscount Wolseley. Unhappily

Williams had discovered that the soldiers' choice – despite the improvements that were supposed to have taken place since the "days of drinking and singing" – did not coincide with his own. With Victorian nicety he notes : "Very many of the songs I had in mind were of a nature that implied reference to religion or politics past or present, or had some such inherent defect as, in my judgement, barred them from these pages, in which I have striven to meet the taste of the better class of soldier." His selection included *Pro patria mori, Cherry ripe, While history's muse the memorial was keeping, The angel's whisper,* and *My mother bids me bind my hair,* and although these may seem bizarre it must be remembered that the army had in fact marched to *Ben Bolt* and *Kiss me, mother,* and was as well notoriously fond of slush. To this extent, Williams was only meeting a demand, and he should not be criticized for his choice, but his deliberate suppression of traditional songs did a sad disservice to posterity.

After Williams' attempt at practical education came Surgeon-General G. J. H. Evatt's OUR SONGLESS ARMY (1906). His happy view was that organized singing developed the lungs, inspired camaraderie, was excellent for morale, and a pleasant way of passing leisure hours. But organization of singing, Evatt contended, was lacking and needed, and he sought to impose his theories on an army that was temperamentally unsuited to them. Nevertheless, at least one of his ideas was sound. "No territorial organization of the Army is complete that does not secure that the county regiment, be where it may, shall sing the county songs which for generations have cheered the forefathers of the men of the battalions".[14] Rather less sound was his demand that "only the best – nay, the very best songs, should be put before the soldier to practise or sing. A very grave responsibility weighs on those who fall short of this . . . standard. Any individual, however high the status, who allows in institute or theatre or canteen or by the camp fire, any fall from the standard of the best sins greatly against the soul of the nation . . . Nothing common, poor or mean should be sung under or around the national flag".[15] A totally unrealistic supposition which presumed that the traditional songs which pleased the men would also please the arbiters of taste and standards, and Williams had already shown that this happy unanimity was unlikely. Soldiers would as soon march to *Blaydon races, The Lincolnshire poacher,* or *Garryowen* as to anything that has ever

K*

been written, for they are fine swinging tunes, yet their heroes are Tyneside roughs, an idle apprentice who sounds as if he were bound for Botany Bay, and a mob of Irish hooligans. High moral tone was conspicuously lacking in the songs that "cheered the forefathers of the men of the battalions". One of Evatt's collaborators summed it up in a pompous nutshell. "A man born low is not at all likely in making unconsciously his choice to fix upon the higher class of music ; early lilting melodies 'catch on' not altogether because they are lilting and easy but rather because they are wedded to some stupid doggerel".[16] In other words, soldiers being what they were, they refused to wear a musical straight-jacket fashioned in the drawing-room.

One of the few "authorities" to say anything of value in OUR SONGLESS ARMY was Cecil Sharp who was doing so much to rediscover and popularize folk songs. "The music you select . . . must not only be good music . . . but it must also be 'catchy' and as easily assimilated as that which the soldier now sings. Otherwise the songs that you teach will make no headway in their competition with the street songs". Sharp thought that folk songs stood a better chance of being accepted than 'national' or 'patriotic' songs. "The Admiralty commissioned Dibdin a century or more ago to write songs for the people. How many of these are sung nowadays by those for whom they were written?"[17]

Anyone with a modicum of common-sense would have been able to predict that OUR SONGLESS ARMY would achieve nothing. Evatt might have profited by the experience of his Army contemporary Mackenzie Rogan, who had formed a singing class in Calcutta, where as many as 250 men happily trilled *Sailing, Our Jack's come home,* and *The men of Harlech.* But as soon as their choirmaster tried to introduce part-singing the class dwindled. "The men told me candidly that they did not understand it, and only wanted to sing songs that they knew and liked. . . The British soldier will sing what he knows and likes but I do not think any power on earth will induce him to alter his tastes".[18]

These tastes could seem odd. Colonel De Watteville tells a story (which may be apocryphal but is nevertheless typical) about an artillery battery in search of a song. "After four days discussion in barrack room and canteen the sergeant-major arrived to state that the troops had formally expressed the strongest views on the matter. As a battery song they wished to adopt a music hall ditty which began, 'When we are married we'll have sausages for tea, sausages for tea'".[19]

Although this might seem odd, there is nothing extraordinary in it, nor does it give anyone the right to suggest that soldiers with such tastes needed either practical or moral education. The soldier needs "stirring" songs less than anyone else. Such songs provide the civilian with a vicarious outlet for physical involvement in war, but the soldier, conversely, has committed himself to face the ultimate danger and needs no substitutes. For him music can be part of war – but it can also be a relief from the starker realities of the conflict. The soldier has no intense need to assault the enemy by word of mouth – for he has more lethal weapons. Where his songs are "war songs" in the literal sense – bellicose and breathing fire – they owe their appeal less to the ardour they express than to the circumstances of their composition. The redcoat certainly seemed to prefer songs of this kind written by his own comrades than by outsiders.

The British soldier is not alone in his liking for improbable songs. He shares this taste with Germans, whose temperament and military traditions are far removed from his own. In World War Two Major G. Jellicoe's booklet on songs in the series ARMY HISTORY AND TRADITION THROUGH CURRENT AFFAIRS suggested that the English soldier shuns the kind of song preferred by the German, "professing pride and faith in himself, his regiment, his profession, his country and his cause". But this was to misunderstand German soldier songs. Undoubtedly the Germans have some jingoist songs of the type described, but even under the Nazi regime, when Dr. Goebbels and his ministry encouraged chauvinism, these songs remained in the minority. Most ballads in the 1939–1945 song books are about true loves waiting in the valley, the old home town, and the pleasure of striding across the wind-swept heath. Without their music the words are treacly, unsoldierly, uninspired, and uninspiring; it was only the manner of their singing which imbued them with the rousing quality that made them "soldier songs".

However idiosyncratic the taste of the British soldier is supposed to have been, it is easy to see how in a different climate of opinion a fair number of his songs would have survived. Broadly speaking, the redcoats sang three types of song; regimental ballads, ordinary popular songs, and – in the 19th century – sentimental songs. "The soldier takes especial delight in songs of the sentimental pattern ; and even when for a brief period he forsakes the region of sentiment it is not to indulge in the outrageously comic but to give vent to such sturdy Bacchanalian outpourings as *The good Rhine wine*, *Old John Barleycorn*, and *Simon the cellarer*. But these are only interludes. *The soldier's tear, The white squall, There came a tale to England, Ben Bolt, Shells of the ocean* and other melodies of a lugubrious type are the special favourites of the barrack room".[20] The popular songs were, of course, ephemeral, but the regimental songs and the traditional songs of conviviality would have persisted if they had not been consistently criticized and disparaged, for the rank and file were attached to every kind of traditional music. In the 1860's when the 14th Hussars were stationed in Dublin they encountered an old soldier named Heffernan who had blown the charge at Talavera for the 14th Light Dragoons. These Hussars were rough fellows – the breed who rejected the work of Tom Sabre and Nugent Taillefer – but their sergeant recalled : "I never saw men so strangely moved".[21]

Nothing else can profitably be said, on the evidence available, about British war music in the past, but although the rule in this book has been to limit hypothesis, a brief glimpse into the future will not be out of place.

SONGS AND MUSIC OF THE REDCOATS has tried to rediscover lost Army music and to draw attention to some that was in danger of being forgotten. Is it too fanciful to suggest that there is a place for this music in the modern Army? The Army is now being transformed – units disbanded and amalgamated – and if the old *esprit de corps* is to be maintained it would seem advisable to preserve every possible past tradition. Even in the nuclear age our Army will not become merely an agglomeration of technicians without need for ceremonial. There has never been a fighting force in history that has not gloried in affectation and idiosyncracy, and derived a practical strength from traditions which were often expressed through ceremony. Thus music should be an unequalled way of reminding today's soldiers that they are the lineal descendants not only of Tommy Atkins but also of Tom Lobster – the feared and famed redcoat.

If this eloquent future for music provokes wry smiles it is only because there has been, all too often, an unjustifiable neglect of musical tradition. Any regiment would receive with delight the news that a Victoria Cross won by one of its members and thought lost had been rediscovered. But most regiments would remain more or less indifferent to the discovery of a tune played or sung at some historical moment in their past. The medal would be publicised and, literally, honoured; the march, at very best, consigned to the archives.

And yet it could be claimed that music has infinitely more value in every way than a medal. A medal is a bit of metal of no great intrinsic merit; it is the deed for which the medal was awarded that should provide inspiration. If the story of the deed is well known the sight of the medal is unlikely to add anything. Music, on the other hand, is constantly evocative. It has the power to stimulate the imagination, and to link the men who hear it in the 20th century with those who knew it a century or more ago. Besides uniting the present and the past it provides a cohesive force that welds individuals into a single body. None of this reasoning is intended to decry the concept of military awards, which are a just and desirable recognition of bravery, but only to suggest that a historic tune should be recognized as no less honourable and worthy of preservation.

Whether the Army that is now developing will want to find a use for historic music remains to be seen, and inevitably the question arises – how would the process begin? Traditionalists and those who believe that history repeats itself might derive comfort from the revolution in military music affected by the Crown Prince of Prussia in 1888. "While reviewing his brigade, as one of the Foot Guards marched past its band played the march from Verdi's *Aida*. The Crown Prince stopped it and commanded the band to play the *Dessauer March*. Following this episode came an order that 'hereafter regimental commanders will see that their bands play during reviews and parades only such marches as have long been familiar to the Prussian Army and to which Prussian soldiers have been accustomed to march to victory'."[22]

Nothing so autocratic could be expected in Britain, but in the Royal Military School of Music the country has a more democratic institution to effect a change. The School may not be a policy-making body but its status and achievements must have given it great influence in Army circles on everything pertaining to music. At a different level, the School's educational function enables it to remind Army musicians of historic vocal and instrumental music and to encourage them to popularize this when they return to their units from Kneller Hall courses. As every commanding officer is directly interested in promoting *esprit de corps* it is to be expected that he would welcome the activity of a bandmaster who restores traditional music for use on appropriate occasions.

Such a trend would accelerate, for if some regiments played, as a matter of course, music which was attractive in its own right and also had notable associations – *The English March*, *The Marquis of Granby*, *Love farewell* – others would surely follow. Band programmes would be poorer if marches like *Sambre et Meuse*, *Anchors away* and *Old Panama* were dropped – the idea is unthinkable – but it is equally unjust that traditional British war music should be excluded.

In the years following the Crimean War, and as the British Army changed, the Royal Military School of Music altered the entire aspect of its music. Now, as the Army develops again, another musical renascence would be timely. Old music for a new Army.

1. Daniel, p.125.
2. *Ibid*, p.125.
3. J. Blakiston, *Twelve Years Military Adventure in Three Quarters of the Globe* (1829), p.44.
4. *Ibid*, p.46.
5. *Officer of the Line*, II, pp.74–75.
6. *USM* (1840), Part II, p.204.
7. Steevens, *With Kitchener to Khartum*, p.214.
8. One in the Service (pseud.), *Sketches of Naval and Military Adventure* (1849), p.230.
9. Munro, p.266.
10. H. De Watteville, *The British Soldier* (1954), p.224.
11. Stocqueler, p.268.
12. *USM* (1832), Part I, p.170.
13. Mole, p.131.
14. Evatt, p.3.
15. *Ibid*, p.3.
16. *Ibid*, p.17.
17. *Ibid*, p.19.
18. Rogan, p.107.
19. de Watteville, p.219.
20. A. Forbes, *Camps, Quarters, and Casual Places* (1896), p.115.
21. Mole, p.100.
22. *The British Bandsman* (July, 1888), p.178.

Acknowledgements

IN writing SONGS AND MUSIC OF THE REDCOATS I have benefited from the help of many people in Britain and abroad; without them this would have been a slim and sorry book.

I am indebted to Colonel C. A. Morris CBE, Lt.-Col. C. H. Jaeger OBE, and Mr. R. W. Sanders of the Royal Military School of Music, to Major-General Sir Nigel Tapp KBE CB DSO, and Major S. H. Andrew of the Royal Hospital, Chelsea, and to Mr. B. Mollo and Mrs. E. A. Steele of the National Army Museum. The staff of the Ministry of Defence Library (Central and Army), and of the British Museum Reading Room have also given invaluable help.

My adviser of longest standing is Dr. Donal O'Sullivan of Trinity College, Dublin, who has been a mine of information. I was fortunate in having the help of Major H. Barker MBE of the Queen's Own Highlanders, Mr. C. W. Black, Glasgow City Librarian, Major G. A. N. Boyne of Royal Irish Rangers, Dr. M. W. Dewar of Banbridge, Co. Down, Lt.-Col. J. E. E. Fry of the Duke of Cornwall's Light Infantry, Professor G. A. Hayes-McCoy of University College, Galway, Lt.-Col. I. Jarman MBE of the South Wales Borderers, Professor James Kinsley of Nottingham University, Major J. R. Laing MBE DCM of the 15th/19th The King's Royal Hussars, Mr. A. Y. McPeake and Mr. J. J. O'Hara of the Connaught Rangers, Mr. D. Marks, Mr. John Prebble, Dr. Nessa Robb of Bangor, Co. Down, Captain T. L. Sharpe MBE of the Coldstream Guards, Major R. W. J. Smith MBE and Colonel F. Walden DL of the Middlesex Regiment, and Mr. J. W. Vitty of the Linen Hall Library, Belfast. Many of my informants — mostly veterans of the South African War and their relatives — are named in the footnotes.

I am grateful for permission to quote received from Major G. J. Flint-Shipman TD, editor of the JOURNAL OF THE SOCIETY FOR ARMY HISTORICAL RESEARCH, from Lt.-Col. J. Granville in respect of the OXFORDSHIRE LIGHT INFANTRY CHRONICLE, from Colonel F. W. S. Jourdain in respect of RANGING MEMORIES by Lt.-Col. H. F. N. Jourdain, and from Lt.-Col. A. G. D. Palmer MC in respect of the RIFLE BRIGADE CHRONICLE.

Boosey and Hawkes Ltd. permitted me to use their arrangements of *Paddy's resource* and *One and all. Soldiers of the Queen* is reproduced by permission of Leslie Stuart Enterprises Ltd., and *Cheer up, Buller, Fighting with the Seventh Fusiliers* and *Bravo, Dublin Fusiliers* by permission of Francis, Day and Hunter Ltd. *Ye're o'er long o' coming* is reproduced by kind permission of the Regimental Council, Queen's Own Highlanders (Seaforth and Camerons) from STANDARD SETTINGS OF PIPE MUSIC, Queen's Own Highlanders.

Outside the British Isles, I am indebted for advice to Harvard College Library, to Colonel J. R. Harper OBE TD of Montreal, to Mr. W. Lichtenwanger of the Music Division, Library of Congress, Washington DC, and to Oberstleutnant Fritz Masuhr, Musikinspizient der Bundeswehr. I acknowledge with gratitude the co-operation of the New York Historical Society and the Sutro Library, San Francisco, which made available copies of the MS books of John Greenwood and William Brown.

Many friends have encouraged me in this work, but I must single out Brian and Yvonne Cox for practical assistance when the book was in its gestatory period. My sincere thanks are due to Miss C. M. Broughton who arranged the music, and to Mrs. Jill Truman who helped prepare the MS.

Musical Notes

The arrangements have generally been based on the versions of tunes which were in use at the time when they are mentioned in the text of the book. For example, no attempt was made to find the earliest version of *The souters o' Selkirk*, because that song only becomes important, so far as this book is concerned, in 1804; accordingly the most appropriate version was the one in the contemporary SCOTS MUSICAL MUSEUM. Similarly, *The Rogues March* is not the well-known tune found in Chappell's POPULAR MUSIC OF THE OLDEN TIME — a two-volume work published in the 1850s, when the ceremony with which *The Rogues March* was most intimately connected — drumming out — may have been obsolete. The version preferred is from ENTIRE NEW AND COMPLEAT INSTRUCTIONS FOR THE FIFE, published in the 1790s when drumming out was still very much in fashion.

Because SONGS AND MUSIC OF THE REDCOATS has been written for the folk music enthusiast as well as the military historian the musical arrangements were made with due regard for amateur singers and pianists. This means that they are easy to perform, but they are also accurate, and would be immediately recognisable by the old redcoats.

Most of the numbers have been quite simply presented, with the top line of the piano arrangement following faithfully and without embellishment the vocal melody of the song. In all these cases the words are set out in full below the music. A few items were judged not to lend themselves to this treatment. In some instances the original character of the piece would have been lost by full harmonisation. In other cases the vocal line is given with separate piano accompaniment, for the sake of more effective performance.

Unless otherwise indicated, musical examples were found in collections of sheet music at the British Museum.

Bibliography

Anonymous, *Adventures of a Young Rifleman in the French and English Armies* (1826).
—— ("A Mounted Black"), *Campaigning in South Africa, 1900–1901* (1901).
—— *The Diary of a British Soldier* (date unknown).
—— *Memoirs of the Late War* (1831).
—— *Memoirs of the Life of John, Earl of Craufurd* (1769).
—— ("Officer of the Line"), *Military Sketch Book* (1827).
—— ("Officer"), *Personal Narrative of Adventures in the Peninsula During the War in 1812–1813* (1827).
—— *Reminiscences of School and Army Life, 1839 to 1859* (1875).
—— ("One in the Service"), *Sketches of Naval and Military Adventure* (1849).
—— *The Soldier's Companion* (1824).
—— *A Subaltern in America* (1833).
—— *Vicissitudes in the Life of a Scottish Soldier* (1827)
Alexander, A., *The Life of Alexander Alexander* (1830).
Alexander, W. G., *Recollections of a Highland Subaltern in 1857, 1858 and 1859* (1898).
Anburey, T., *Travels through the Interior Parts of America* (1789).
Ancell, S., *A Circumstantial Journal of the Siege of Gibraltar* (1783).
Atteridge, A. E., *Towards Khartoum* (1897).
Baillie, F. D., *Mafeking. A Diary of the Siege* (1900).
Bancroft, N. W., *The Bengal Artillery of the Olden Time* (1885).
Barnes, J., *The Great War Trek* (1901).
Barrett, C. R. B., *History of the XIII Hussars* (1911).
Bates, E. T., *The Life and Memoirs of Mr. Ephraim Tristram Bates* (1756).
Bell, G. C., *Rough Notes by an Old Soldier* (1867).
Bellairs, Lady B., *The Transvaal War, 1880–1881* (1885).
Bennett, Sir E. N., *The Downfall of the Dervishes* (1898).
Bishop, M., *The Life and Adventures of Mathew Bishop* (1744).
Blackader, J., *Select Passages from the Diary and Letters of the Late John Blackader* (1806).
Blakeney, R., *A Boy in the Peninsular War* (1899).
Blakiston, J., *Twelve Years' Military Adventure in Three Quarters of the Globe* (1829).
Bostock, J. A., *Letters from India and the Crimea* (1896).
Bostonian Society Proceedings (January, 1949).
Bryant, H. J., *The Autobiography of a Military Raincoat* (1907).
Burleigh, B., *Desert Warfare* (1884).
—— *Khartoum Campaign 1898* (1899).
—— *The Natal Campaign* (1900).
Burnet, G., *The History of my Own Times* (1832).
Burnett, E. C., *Letters of Members of the Continental Congress* (1921–1936).
Burney, C., *A General History of Music* (1789).
Burton, R., *Admirable Curiosities, Rarities, and Wonders in England, Scotland and Ireland* (1684).
Butler, L. W. G., *The Annals of the K.R.R.C.* (1913).
Butler, R., *Narrative of the Life and Travels of Serjeant Butler* (1854).
Buzzard, T., *With the Turkish Army in the Crimea and Asia Minor* (1915).
Calladine, G., *The Diary of Colour-Sergeant G. Calladine* (1922).
Carr, Sir J., *Caledonian Sketches* (1809).
Chambers, R., *History of the Rebellion of 1745–1746* (1869).
Chappell, W., *Popular Music of the Olden Time* (1859).
Chastellux, F. J. de, *Travels in North America, Translated by an English Gentleman* (1787).
Childers, R. E., *In the Ranks of the C.I.V.* (1900).
Clerk, A., *Memoir of Colonel John Cameron* (1858).

Cobbold, R., *Mary Anne Wellington* (1846).
Colborne, J., *With Hicks Pasha in the Soudan* (1884).
Cooper, J. S., *Rough Notes of Seven Campaigns* (1869).
Coopland, R. M., *A Lady's Escape from Gwalior* (1859).
Cornish-Bowden, J. H. T., *Notes on the History of the Duke of Cornwall's Light Infantry. No. I* (1913).
Cosson, E. A. de, *Days and Nights of Service at Suakin* (1886).
Costello, E., *The Adventures of a Soldier* (1841).
Cowell-Stepney, Sir J. S., *Leaves from the Diary of an Officer of the Guards* (1854).
Crane, B. P., *The Ninth Lancers in Afghanistan 1879–1880* (1883).
Creagh, J., *Sparks from Camp Fires* (1901).
Cruikshank, G., *A Pop-gun Fired off by George Cruikshank in Defence of the British Volunteers of 1803* (1866).
Crum, F. M., *With the Mounted Infantry in South Africa* (1903).
Dalyell, Sir J. G., *Musical Memoirs of Scotland* (1849).
Daniel, J. E., *Journal of an Officer in the Commissariat Department of the Army* (1820).
Danvers, R. W., *Letters from India and China* (1898).
De La Colonie, M., *The Chronicle of an Old Campaigner* (1904).
Deane, J. M., *A Journal of the Campaign in 1708* (1846).
Denny, W. H., *Military Journal of Major Ebenezer Denny* (1860).
Dewar, T. F., *With the Scottish Yeomanry* (1901).
Digby, W., *Some Account of the American War* (1887).
Donkin, R., *Military Collections and Remarks* (1777).
Doveton, F. B., *Reminiscences of the Burmese War in 1824-5-6* (1852).
Drake, F. S., *Life and Correspondence of H. Knox* (1873).
Drinkwater, J., *A History of the Late Siege of Gibraltar* (1785).
Du Val, C., *With a Show through Southern Africa and Personal Reminiscences of the Transvaal War* (1884).
Duberly, F. I., *Journal Kept During the Russian War* (1855).
Dudley, D., *Extracts from the Diary of D.D.* (1876).
Elliot, Sir G., *Life and Letters* (1874).
Evatt, Sir G. H. J., *Our Songless Army* (1906).
Ewart, J. A., *The Story of a Soldier's Life* (1881).
Farmer, J., *Scarlet and Blue* (1896).
Faughnan, T., *Stirring Incidents in the Life of a Soldier* (1885).
Ferguson, J., *The Scots Brigade in the Service of the United Netherlands 1572-1782* (1899–1901).
Forbes, A., *Camps, Quarters and Casual Places* (1896).
Forbes, R., *Jacobite Memoirs of the Rebellion of 1745* (1834).
Forbes-Mitchell, W., *Reminiscences of the Great Mutiny 1857–1859* (1893).
Fortescue, Sir J. W., *History of the British Army* (1899).
—— *The Last Post* (1934).
Fraser, A. D., *Some Reminiscences and the Bagpipe* (1907).
Fraser, G., *Memoirs in the Life and Travels of G.F.* (1808).
Frazer, Sir A. S., *Letters* (1859).
Freeman, E. A., *The History of the Norman Conquest of England* (1869).
Garden, A., *Anecdotes of the Revolutionary War* (1822).
—— *Anecdotes of the American Revolution* (1828).
Germon, R. C., *A Diary Kept by Mrs. R. C. Germon at Lucknow* (1870).
Gordon, W., *The History of . . . the United States of America* (1788).
Gordon-Brown, A., *The Narrative of Private Buck Adams* (1941).
Gleichen, Count A. E. W., *With the Camel Corps up the Nile* (1888).
Gleig, G. R., *The Subaltern* (1825).
Gowing, T., *A Soldier's Experience* (1883).
Graham, D., *An Impartial History . . . of the Late Rebellion* (1774).
Grattan, W., *Adventures of the Connaught Rangers, from 1808 to 1814* (1847).
Greathed, W. H., *Letters Written During the Siege of Delhi* (1858).

Greenwood, J., *Narrative of the Late Victorious Campaign in Affghanistan* (1844).
Griffiths, C. J., *A Narrative of the Siege of Delhi* (1910).
—— *The Antiquities of Scotland* (1789).
Grose, F., *Military Antiquities* (1786).
Grove's Dictionary of Music (1954).
Gwyn, J., *Military Memoirs of the Great Civil War* (1822).
Hamley, Sir E. B., *The Story of the Campaign of Sebastopol* (1855).
Harley, J., *The Veteran* (1838).
Harrison, Sir G., *Seventy-one Years of a Guardsman's Life* (1916).
Harrison, Sir R., *Recollections of a Life in the British Army During the Latter Half of the 19th Century* (1908).
Hart-MacCarg, W., *From Quebec to Pretoria with the Royal Canadian Regiment* (1902).
Hawkins, Sir J., *A General History of the Science and Practice of Music* (1853).
Henegan, Sir R. D., *Seven Years Campaigning in the Peninsula and the Netherlands from 1808 to 1815* (1846).
Hodgson, J., *Memoirs* (1806).
Hope, J., *The Military Memoirs of an Infantry Officer* (1833).
Hume, J. R., *Reminiscences of the Crimean Campaign with the 55th Regiment* (1894).
Hutchinson, H. D., *The Campaign in Tirah, 1897–1898* (1898).
Jameson, R., *Historical Records of the 79th Regiment of Foot* (1863).
Johnson, H., *With Our Soldiers at the Front* (1900).
Jones, G., *The Battle of Waterloo* (1817).
Jourdain, H. F. N., *Ranging Memories* (1934).
Jowett, W., *Diary* (1856).
Kapp, F., *The Life of Frederick William Von Steuben* (1859).
Kelly, B. W., *The Conqueror of Culloden* (1903).
Kelly, Sir R. D., *An Officer's Letters to His Wife During the Crimean War* (1902).
Kelly, T., *From the Fleet in the Fifties* (1902).
Kincaid, Sir J., *Adventures in the Rifle Brigade . . . from 1809 to 1815* (1830).
—— *Random Shots from a Rifleman* (1835).
King, W. R., *Campaigning in Kaffirland* (1853).
Kinglake, A. W., *The Invasion of the Crimea* (1863).
Lamb, R., *Memoir of His Own Life* (1811).
Larpent, F. S., *The Private Journal of F. S. Larpent* (1853).
Laurie, W. F. B., *The Second Burmese War* (1853).
Lawrence, A. A., *Storm Over Savannah* (1853).
Leeke, W., *The History of Lord Seaton's Regiment (The 52nd Light Infantry) at Waterloo* (1866).
Lennox, Lord W. P., *Three Years with the Duke* (1853).
L'Estrange, Sir G. B., *Recollections of Sir G. B. L'Estrange* (1874).
Lewin, H. R., *The Life of a Soldier* (1834).
Lloyd, J. B., *One Thousand Miles with the C.I.V.* (1900).
Logan, W. H., *A Pedlar's Pack of Ballads and Songs* (1869).
Lowry, E. P., *With the Guards Brigade* (1902).
Lynch, C., *Impressions of a War Correspondent* (1902).
Lysons, Sir D., *The Crimean War from First to Last* (1895).
Macaulay, Lord T. B., *The History of England from the Accession of James II* (1914).
MacBride, M., *With Napoleon at Waterloo* (1911).
MacDonald, A., *Too Late for Gordon and Khartoum* (1887).
MacDonald, D., *How We Kept the Flag Flying: The Story of the Siege of Ladysmith* (1900).
MacKern, H. F., *Side-Lights on the March* (1901).
Mackesy, P., *The War for America, 1775–1783* (1964).
MacKinnon, H. V., *War Sketches* (1900).
MacMullen, J. M., *Camp and Barrack Room* (1845).
MacPherson, A. J., *Rambling Reminiscences of the Punjab Campaign* (1889).
Majendie, Sir V. D., *Up Among the Pandies* (1859).
Malcolm, C. A., *The Piper in Peace and War* (1927).

Malcolm, J., *Reminiscences of a Campaign in the Pyrenees and the South of France in 1814* (1826).

Malcolm, T., *Barracks and Battlefields in India* (1891).

Male, A. H., *Scenes through the Battle Smoke* (1891).

Marchant, J., *The History of the Present Rebellion* (1746).

Markham, F., *Five Decades of Epistles of Warre* (1622).

Maxwell, E. H., *With the Connaught Rangers* (1883).

Maxwell, W. H., *Peninsular Sketches* (1845).

Metcalfe, H., *The Chronicle of Private Henry Metcalfe* (1953).

Mitchell, A., *Recollections of One of the Light Brigade* (1885).

Moeller, B., *Two Years at the Front with the Mounted Infantry* (1903).

Mole, E., *A King's Hussar* (1893).

Monro, R., *Monro, His Expedition* (1637).

Montague, W. E., *Campaigning in South Africa* (1880).

Moore, F., *Songs and Ballads of the American Revolution* (1856).

Morley, S., *Memoirs of a Serjeant of the 5th Regiment of Foot* (1842).

Morris, T., *Recollections of Military Service in 1813, 1814 and 1815* (1845).

Moultrie, W., *Memoirs of the American Revolution* (1802).

Mountain, A. S. H., *Memoirs and Letters of the Late Colonel A. S. H. Mountain* (1857).

Munro, I., *A Narrative of the Military Operations on the Coromandel Coast* (1789).

Munro, W., *Records of Service and Campaigning in Many Lands* (1887).

Murray, Sir H., *Memoir and Correspondence of the Late Captain Arthur Stormont Murray* (1859).

Musgrave, G. C., *In South Africa with Buller* (1900).

Napier, W., *Life of Sir C. Napier* (1857).

Neale, A., *Letters from Portugal and Spain* (1809).

Neilly, J. E., *Besieged with B.-P.* (1900).

Nevins, A., and Commager, H. S., *America. The Story of a Free People* (1954).

Nevinson, H. W., *Ladysmith. The Diary of a Siege* (1900).

Norman, F. M., *At School and Sea* (1899).

O'Callaghan, J., *History of the Irish Brigades in the Service of France* (1870).

O'Connell, J., *Transvaal War, 1899–1900* (1900).

O'Donnell, H., *Historical Records of the 14th West Yorkshire Regiment* (1893).

Oldmixon, J., *The History of England During the Reigns of the Royal House of Stuart* (1730).

Ordericus Vitalis, *The Ecclesiastical History of England and Normandy* (1854).

Ormerod, G., *Tracts Relating to Military Proceedings in Lancashire During the Great Civil War* (1844).

Owen, A., *Recollections of a Veteran of the Days of the Great Indian Mutiny of 1857* (1916).

Paget, Lord G., *The Light Cavalry Brigade in the Crimea* (1881).

Pargellis, S. M., *Military Affairs in Northern America, 1748–1765* (1936).

Parry, D. H., *The Death-or-Glory Boys* (1899).

Parry, S. H. J., *An Old Soldier's Memories* (1897).

—— *The Adventures of Captain John Patterson . . . from 1807 to 1821* (1837).

Patterson, J., *Camp and Quarters* (1840).

Peard, G. S., *Narrative of a Campaign in the Crimea* (1855).

Pearl, C., *Bawdy Burns* (1958).

Pemberton, W. B., *Battles of the Crimean War* (1968).

Phillipps, L. M., *With Rimington* (1901).

Pococke, T., *Journal of a Soldier of the 71st Regiment* (1828).

Prebble, J., *Culloden* (1967).

Rees, L. E. R., *A Personal Narrative of the Siege of Lucknow* (1858).

Reid, D. A., *Memories of the Crimean War* (1911).

Robinson, F., *Diary of the Crimean War* (1856).

Rogan, J. M., *Fifty Years of Army Music* (1926).

Rose-Innes, C., *With Paget's Horse to the Front* (1901).

Ruggles, J., *Recollections of a Lucknow Veteran, 1845–1876* (1906).

Russell, H., *Cheer, Boys, Cheer!* (1895).

Russell, Sir W. H., *The War* (1856).

Ryder, J., *Four Years Service in India* (1853).

St. Clair, T. S., *A Residence in the West Indies and America with a Narrative of the Expedition to . . . Walcheren* (1834).

Scobie, I. M., *Pipers and Pipe Music in a Highland Regiment* (1924).

—— *The Antiquary* (1816).

Scott, Sir W., *Letters* (1932–1937).

Seaton, Sir T., *From Cadet to Colonel* (1866).

Shadwell, T., *The Volunteers* (1693).

Shipp, J., *Memoirs of the Extraordinary Military Career of John Shipp* (1829)

Sibbet, R. M., *Orangeism in Ireland and Throughout the Empire* (1914).

Slingsby, Sir H., *Diary* (1836).

Smith, J. G., *The English Army in France* (1831).

Smythies, R. H. R., *Historical Records of the 40th (2nd Somersetshire) Regiment* (1894)

Spurgin, K. B., *On Active Service with the Northumberland and Durham Yeomen* (1902).

Stanley, H. M., *Coomassie and Magdala* (1874).

Steevens, G. W., *From Capetown to Ladysmith* (1900).

—— *With Kitchener to Khartum* (1898).

Steevens, N., *The Crimean Campaign with the Connaught Rangers* (1878).

Stevenson, R., *Through Rhodesia with the Sharpshooters* (1901).

Stewart, D., *Sketches of . . . the Highlanders of Scotland* (1822).

Stewart, Sir N. R., *My Service Days* (1908).

Stocqueler, J. H., *The British Soldier* (1857).

Stone, C. R., *War Songs* (1908).

Stone, W. L., *Ballads and Poems Relating to the Burgoyne Campaign* (1893).

—— *Letters of Brunswick and Hessian Officers During the American Revolution* (1891).

—— *Memoirs and Letters and Journals of Major General Von Riedesel* (1868).

Stothert, W., *A Narrative of the Principal Events in the Campaigns . . . in Spain and Portugal* (1812).

Stuart, J., *Pictures of War* (1901).

Surtees, W., *Twenty-five Years in the Rifle Brigade* (1833).

Swett, S., *History of the Bunker Hill Battle* (1827).

Symonds, R., *Diary of the Marches Kept by the Royal Army During the Great Civil War* (1859).

Taylor, G. C., *Journal of Adventures with the British Army* (1856).

Taylor, W., *Scenes and Adventures in Afghanistan* (1842).

Thacher, J., *A Military Journal During the American Revolutionary War* (1823).

Thomsett, R. G., *Kohat, Kuram and Khost. Experiences and Adventures in the late Afghan War* (1884).

—— *With the Peshawar Column* (1899).

Trant, T. A., *Two Years in Ava* (1827).

Trenchard, F., *The Young Dragoon* (1870).

Turner, Sir J., *Pallas Armata* (1683).

Uhlendorf, B. A., *The Siege of Charleston* (1938).

Unger, F. W., *With "Bobs" and Kruger* (1901).

Vicars, J., *Jehovah Jireh* (1646).

Von Riedesel, F. C. L., *Letters and Memoirs Relating to the War of American Independence* (1827).

Walker, Sir E., *Historical Discourses Upon Several Occasions* (1705).

Ward, H., *Five Years in Kaffirland* (1848).

—— *Recollections of an Old Soldier* (1849).

Ward, Ned, *The London Spy* (1955).

Watkins, O. S., *With Kitchener's Army* (1898).

Watteville, H. de, *The British Soldier* (1954).

Welsh, J., *Military Reminiscences* (1830).

Wetton, T. C., *With Rundle's Eighth Division in South Africa* (1904).

Wheeler, W., *The Letters of Private Wheeler, 1809–1828* (1951).

Wilberforce, R. G., *An Unrecorded Chapter of the Indian Mutiny* (1895).
Wood, Sir H. E., *The Crimea in 1854 and 1894* (1895).
Woodberry, G., *Journal* (1896).
Woon, H. V., *Twenty-five Years Soldiering in South Africa* (1909).
Wright, H. C. S., *Soudan '96* (1897).
Principal periodicals used:—
    Journal of the Society for Army Historical Research.
    Notes and Queries.
    United Service Magazine.

Index